THE CHAMBERLAINS

THE CHAMBERLAINS

D. H. Elletson

JOHN MURRAY
FIFTY ALBEMARLE STREET LONDON

© D. H. Elletson 1966

Printed in Great Britain by
Cox & Wyman Ltd., London, Fakenham
and Reading

To the City of Birmingham
which the Chamberlain family have
loved and served
I dedicate this book

Look here, upon this picture, and on this,
The counterfeit presentment of two brothers.

WILLIAM SHAKESPEARE: *Hamlet*

Act III. Scene 4.

Contents

Contents

Illustrations

THE FAMILY TREE

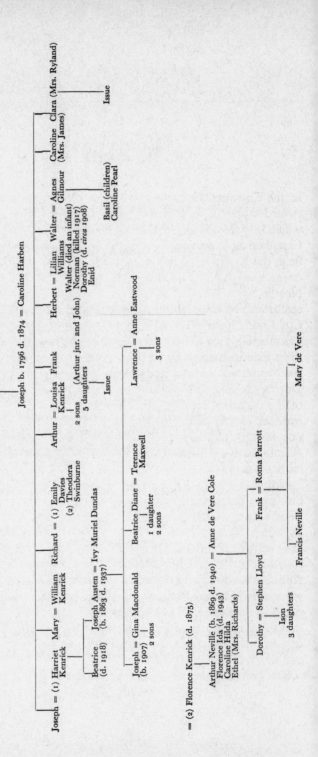

Daniel Chamberlain
Maltster, Lacock, Wilts (d. 1757)

Foreword

In the Chamberlain story, the history of a great family is inter-twined with that of a great city and a great nation in a manner which is quite unique. With only two short intervals, there was a Chamberlain in every Cabinet from 1880 to 1940. In the municipal field, the record is no less remarkable. In the forty-odd years be-tween 1872 and 1914, three Chamberlains, Joseph, Richard and Neville, were Mayors of Birmingham and two others, Arthur senior and Norman, were important members of the Birmingham City Council and did work of great value on it. If we look on the Chamberlains (as we should in this context) as part of a larger en-tity which included their relations – the Kenricks, the Martineaus, the Nettlefolds and the Beals, the record is more remarkable still. During the first three decades of the nineteenth and the first half of the twentieth century, there was hardly a year in which some member of 'the clique', as this larger entity was once called, did not occupy a position of great importance and influence in Birmingham's municipal affairs – and the tradition is still being carried on.

Nor was it only in the fields of politics and local government that the Chamberlain family have made so great an imprint on Birmingham. In the industrial field, their contribution was highly significant. It is not, perhaps, commonly recognized how much of their early development some of Birmingham's greatest businesses owe to the Chamberlain family – Guest, Keen and Nettlefold, Kynochs (now part of Imperial Chemical Industries), Tube In-vestments, Avery's Ltd and the Birmingham Small Arms Com-pany, to mention only a few. The two outstanding businessmen in the family were probably the two Arthurs and the story of their careers and achievements as industrialists is, by itself, a fascinating one and well worth recording.

The contribution which the Chamberlain family made to the

advancement of Birmingham and the welfare of its citizens was very great; the contribution which Birmingham made to the greatness of the Chamberlains was equally great or even greater. 'Without Birmingham,' Austen once said, 'I am nothing.' Certainly so far as their political careers are concerned, this remark could be applied with equal force to his father and his brother. Under present conditions such a career as that of Joseph Chamberlain would, of course, be impossible anyway. But even to his own day and age it could not have taken place, had he not enjoyed the undeviating loyalty and support of large masses of his fellow-citizens.

In writing about a family, three of whose members occupied for so long such a prominent position on the national stage, it is inevitable that one should devote a considerable amount of space to the political events with which they were concerned. But it is for what they were, just as much as for what they did, that the Chamberlains deserve to be remembered and we are concerned here not only with their political acts and business dealings but also with their human characteristics – to show them not only as statesmen and businessmen but also as husbands and fathers.

It is from this letter standpoint in particular that I have been fortunate in having had access to the important and considerable collection of Chamberlain papers at Birmingham University. These include most of the private papers of Joseph and Austen as well as the long series of highly interesting and informative letters written by Joseph's third wife to her mother, giving intimate pictures of her life in Birmingham, in London, and on the French Riviera, and also the papers of Lady Chamberlain (Austen's widow). To make selections from such a vast mass of material has not been easy. It must be emphasized that the letters which seem most important to biographers writing during the lifetime or shortly after the death of their subjects are not necessarily those which will seem so to the historian and biographer of a later date. It has been my aim to give prominence to those letters which seem to throw light on the habits, way of life, beliefs, characters and personalities of the Chamberlains rather than to those which relate only to political issues which, however vital they may have been considered at the time, are now largely, and perhaps inevitably, forgotten.

I have not had access to all the private papers of Neville Chamberlain, which are not yet included in the collection at the University, though it is understood that, one day, they may be so included. If and when this happens, this collection will be one of the most important of its kind in the world. Meanwhile the treatment of Neville has had to be more restricted than it would have been had all his papers been available for public examination. There is a further and even more important fact which militates against a full and final assessment of Neville. This is the so called 'fifty-year rule' which so severely handicaps historians and biographers of British statesmen. As Sir Keith Feiling wrote in his excellent biography of Neville,* 'Of the official sources from which final history will in great part be drawn, none is yet available: neither the archives of the British Government, its allies and its foes, nor the correspondence of contemporary statesmen.' This is still very largely the position.

Throughout the Chamberlain story there runs one golden thread. This is the spirit of sympathy with and the desire to serve their fellow-men, particularly the less fortunate of them, and of pride in and affection for the great city which was to the older of them the city of their adoption and to the younger that of their birth. 'My life is bound up in Birmingham,' said Joseph Chamberlain. 'All its institutions, its prosperity, its politics have been my care and my principal thought for the whole course of my public life. I know its people; your faces, if not your names are familiar to me. As I walk through the streets, I seem to gather instinctively the minds of the people. And I say that to me there is no position to which I can attain, there is no triumph which can come to me, there is no success which I can possibly hope for that would in any degree compensate for the loss of the respect – ay, and of the affection – that has hitherto been shown me.'†

* *The Life of Neville Chamberlain* by Keith Feiling (Macmillan, 1946).

† In the course of the celebrations of his seventieth birthday – *The Right Hon. Joseph Chamberlain: The Man and the Statesman* by N. Murrell Marris (Hutchinson, 1900).

Acknowledgements

I am grateful to Her Majesty the Queen for graciously permitting me to publish two letters, one from His late Majesty King George V and the other from His late Majesty King George VI to Austen and Neville Chamberlain respectively.

My next word of thanks must be to the members of the Chamberlain family who have helped and encouraged me throughout and to whom I am indebted for much kindness and hospitality. I would mention especially in this connection the late Frank Chamberlain and Mrs. Stephen Lloyd (son and daughter respectively of Neville), Mrs. Maxwell (daughter of Austen), Mrs. Helen and Mr. Arthur Chamberlain (widow and son respectively of Arthur junior), Mrs. Frank Chamberlain, Mrs. Farmer (granddaughter of Walter) and finally and most especially Mrs. Enid Chamberlain (daughter of Herbert and sister of Norman) who kindly placed at my disposal a number of important and hitherto unpublished letters from Austen and Neville as well as other important documents relating to the family history. I must also thank Mrs. Stephen Lloyd, the late Mr. Frank Chamberlain and Mrs. Maxwell for the permission which they have given me to make quotations from letters written by their respective fathers and by their grandfather.

Next, I must thank the Librarian of Birmingham University for permission to make quotations from copyright material contained in 'The Chamberlain Collection' and to him and his staff my thanks are also due for unfailing kindness, courtesy and help in the course of my researches.

I wish to thank Lords Birkenhead and Derby for permission to quote from letters written by their father and grandfather respectively and Lady Halifax for permission to quote from her late husband's diary. I also wish to express my thanks to the Beaverbrook Foundation for permission to make quotations from *The*

Acknowledgements

Decline and Fall of Lloyd George by Lord Beaverbrook and from *The War Memoirs of David Lloyd George,* to Messrs. Cassell and Co. for permission to make use of copyright material contained in *Down the Years* and *Politics from the Inside – An Epistolary Chronicle from 1906 to 1914* by Sir Austen Chamberlain and in *The Eden Memoirs* by the Earl of Avon, and Messrs. Macmillan and Messrs. Hart Davis for a similar permission in regard to *The Life of Neville Chamberlain* by Keith Feiling and *Old Men Forget* by Lord Norwich. The *Birmingham Post* has proved an invaluable source of information and I am most grateful to the Editor for permission to make quotations therefrom.

I have derived great benefit from reading and have made use of the books, newspapers, periodicals and other publications particulars of which are given in the Notes at the end of this volume and I wish to thank the authors, publishers, editors and owners of the copyright thereof for the help they have been to me. I also wish to thank the staffs of Imperial Metal Industries (Kynoch) Ltd., and of the Birmingham Central Reference Library, the British Museum, the London Library, the Oldham, Lancashire County, Blackpool, Thornton Cleveleys and Knott End Libraries for constant kindness and help.

Finally, my thanks are due to Miss Janet Turnbull for typing the original manuscript and to Mrs. Osyth Leeston and Sir John Murray for much useful criticism and for many helpful suggestions.

The Chamberlains Come
to Birmingham

About the year 1730, a certain William Chamberlain left the pleasant village of Lacock in North Wiltshire to seek his fortune in the
city of London. For several generations his ancestors had been
maltsters in Lacock, but he was not the first Chamberlain to mi-
grate to London. A generation earlier, an uncle of his had done
the same thing and this relation was now established in the capital
as a confectioner. To him William was for a time apprenticed, but
not unfortunately with very satisfactory results. William annoyed
his uncle by his indulgence in pranks and practical jokes – he is
said to have broken the sweet bottles when trying to balance a
broom on his nose – and soon he was forced to look round for
alternative employment. In May 1733, he became apprenticed to a
master shoemaker. His new occupation suited him much better and
in it in due course he prospered. He started his own business and
this descended from father to son for the next two generations and
provided William, his sons and grandsons with a decent though
not extravagant livelihood. In time they became leading members
of the Cordwainers Company and the business prospered to such
an extent that by the end of the eighteenth century the capital invested in it amounted to the considerable sum (for those days)
of £11,800. The income, however, was not commensurately
great. It seldom exceeded £600 and often fell short of that figure
and in at least one year there was a serious loss. During the
early part of the nineteenth century, however, the business
increased both in size and profitability and more than once the
income exceeded £1,800, rising in one exceptionally good year
to £2,656.(1)

This resulted in the Chamberlains becoming solid and substantial business people, able to achieve a considerable degree of

comfort in their standard of life. For nearly one hundred years after William Chamberlain started in business as a shoemaker, the family lived over their shop at number 36 Milk Street, Cheapside. Here two generations of Chamberlains attended diligently to business and to the affairs of the Cordwainers Company, in which ancient guild no less than six members of the family, at different times, occupied the position of Master. But more important than their civic activities were those which centred on their religion. The Chamberlains were and would remain convinced and devoted Unitarians but, in order to avoid being banned from a very wide field of civic activity under the Test Acts, they practised 'occasional conformity', partaking of the sacrament from time to time at St. Lawrence's Jury, near the Guildhall, of which both William Chamberlain and his second son Joseph were churchwardens. But, though they worshipped with their lips at St. Lawrence's, the church at which they worshipped with their hearts, and which absorbed more fully their philanthropic and social activities, was the old Unitarian Chapel in Little Carter's Lane, Doctors' Commons, at which for more than one hundred and twenty-five years there was always one of the family in the congregation, and assiduous not only in attending the services but in acts of charity and in all that pertained to the common weal of this small but closely knit community. Writing during the third decade of the nineteenth century, a contemporary observer records that 'the Carter's Lane people are few but united – and one family in particular, the Chamberlains, have shown me as much kindness as ever I received in my life. The congregation is composed for the most part of the higher sort of tradesmen, plain honest and sincere.'(2) And from the same source, an amusing description is forthcoming of the then head of the family, the first Joseph Chamberlain. 'The old gentleman is very friendly and I am sometimes disposed to think him sensible but he gives pudding before meat at dinner which staggers me a good deal.''(3)

In the year 1834 William's grandson, the second Joseph, married Caroline Harben. She was one of eight children and her ancestry, like that of her husband, was middle class, the original Harben, like the original Chamberlain, having been a maltster. But there was, perhaps, rather more dash and colour about the Harbens than about the Chamberlains. In the Harben family story, land speculation on a considerable scale, a large country mansion and bankruptcy had each found a place – all things completely foreign to the Chamberlain character. Caroline had taste and a love of beauty and art. It was the opinion of Sir Austen Chamberlain that it was from her that her children derived their intellect and culture.(4)

On getting married, the second Joseph decided not to live at Milk Street as his father and grandfather had. He himself bought and settled down in a large, semi-detached, late Georgian house in Camberwell, on the south side of the river. This had recently become a fashionable suburb for successful City business men. Though their villas were already springing up fast, the predominant note was still rural, Camberwell being well wooded and having a large village green, noted for its summer fairs; and market gardens abounded in the area. It was more than four miles from the heart of the City, but a walk over the high ground behind where the Chamberlains lived soon gave magnificent views of some of London's leading buildings, including St. Paul's Cathedral, standing out in all its majesty, with the wide sweep of the Thames from Chelsea eastwards, and, in the far distance, on clear days, the heights of Highgate and Hampstead could be distinctly seen.

Browning and Ruskin both spent a considerable part of their youth in the district and the description of it given by the former in *Preaterita* is well known. Ruskin wrote of looking out of his house and seeing 'the Norwood Hills on one side and the winter sunrise over them . . . the valley of the Thames on the other, with Windsor telescopically clear in the distance, conspicuous always in fine weather to open vision against the summer sunset'. He added that 'the glory of Herne Hill', which was within a mile of the Chamberlains' house, was that 'after walking along its ridge southward from London through a mile of chestnut, lilac and apple trees hanging over the wooden palings on each side – suddenly the trees stopped on the left and out one came on the top of a field sloping down to the south into Dulwich valley with its open field, animate with cow and buttercup and below the beautiful meadows and high avenues of Dulwich.'(5)

The Chamberlains' house was situated near the top of a hill. It is still standing and is now number 188 Camberwell Grove, having been built on land adjoining what was originally the private drive of a certain Dr. Lettsom, a well-known local character who had bought part of the manor of Camberwell in the eighteenth century. The house had a railed plot in front, a large entrance porch at the side and a large garden behind. It was here, on July 8th, 1836, that the first of the second Joseph's children was born. This was Joseph the third, the future statesman.

He did not go to school until he was eight years old and it was his mother who taught him to read and write. His first introduction to formal education was at a school kept by two sisters whose name was Pace. Here, for an annual fee of eight guineas, the Misses Pace gave their young pupils a grounding in 'distinct speaking', English, history, Latin, French, and drill. The description which Miss Charlotte Pace gave later of Joseph Chamberlain as a schoolboy was that 'he didn't care much for games; he was not so much solitary as solid, industrious and intelligent, but rather too anxious about his lessons, conscientious and very solemn as a rule'.(6)

In the year 1846, the Chamberlains left Camberwell, moving to number 25 Highbury Place, Islington, where Joseph's parents remained for nearly twenty years. A delightful picture has come down to us showing the kind of people the Chamberlains were and the kind of life they lived during this period. It takes the form of a letter to her daughter from Mrs. Bailey, the sister of Mrs. Joseph Chamberlain the second (*née* Harben, mother of the statesman), and it describes a party given by the Chamberlains in honour of Dr. Martineau the Unitarian divine. The Chamberlains and Martineaus later became connected by marriage.

'I arrived at Highbury(7) about twenty minutes to six and was ushered into the drawing room by a very quiet, pleasant looking waiter,' Mrs. Bailey wrote. Then she gave a list of the guests, ten in number, and went on to describe the meal.

'Two covers on the table. Asparagus soup – very good . . . then the noble piece of salmon was displayed. . . . There was a profusion of hot lobster sauce and cool cucumber – that was removed and in next to no time the table was covered again, boiled chickens at top, covered with white sauce and prettily ornamented with something green – a pretty little forequarter of

4

bottom-tongue and stewed beef, asparagus, cauliflower, mushrooms and mashed brown potatoes. . . . Champagne and Hock in course. . . Third course – Guinea fowl . . . some kind of hot pudding, jellies, creams and a peculiar dish – it looked like a sea or lake of custard, surrounded by a range of snow-covered mountains, the peaks tinged by the rosy hues of the rising sun – – then cream and other cheeses were handed round, then all vanished and the dessert made its appearance. . . . As to the conversational part of the entertainment it was very pleasant. . . . I took Mr. Martineau upon myself . . . and plunged into Comte's philosophy.' At about a quarter past eight, after dinner had been over for some time, the main body of guests (about sixteen people) arrived. The letter continues: 'The dining-room had been cleared and thrown open in a wonderfully short time and the rooms looked very pretty and well lighted . . . supper was served . . . at a quarter past ten. . . .'(8).

The move to Islington meant that a new school had to be found for Joseph. From ten to fourteen, he attended an establishment at number 36 Canterbury Square, kept by the Rev. Arthur Johnson, whom he later described as 'one of the handsomest men I have ever seen, an excellent teacher and one to whom I owe much', and as 'a man of remarkable power and influence'. In 1850, he went to University College school in Gower Street, then the foremost school for Nonconformist children in the country. He stayed there for rather over two years, arriving when he was fourteen and leaving at sixteen. He appears to have been a clever and industrious pupil but he did not mix a great deal with the other boys but seemed to keep himself to himself as far as he could. He was not at all keen on games, for which there were, in fact, scant facilities. All this does not mean that he was a prig but he was serious minded and looked on school as the place to which he went to get that knowledge which he would turn to good account in the world later. One of the mistresses at the school declared later that 'he always wanted to take the lead in anything that was going on'. At the end of his first year, he won prizes in both French and mathematics.

In 1852, when young Joseph was sixteen, his father decided that it was time for him to leave school and make a start at earning his living. He went into the family business at Milk Street. But this certainly did not mark the end of his education. On the contrary he continued with his French, reaching such a proficiency in that language that soon he could read French novels with ease, and the keen interest in science which he had at first acquired at Gower Street was further developed by assiduous attendance at lectures in chemistry and electricity at the Polytechnic. In his home surroundings, however, the lighter side of life was never omitted, amateur theatricals and dancing being amongst his greatest delights. Both then and later, he always went to a dance if he could.

When he was eighteen, a dramatic change occurred in the young man's life. His uncle, John Sutton Nettlefold, was a screw manufacturer in Birmingham but most of his screws were made by hand. The whole process was rudimentary. Recently, however, an American, whose name was Sloane, had brought over a patent for the automatic manufacture of screws, using steam power and giving to the completed product a pointed end and a much more finished appearance generally. Sloane's patent, though expensive to install initially, would, in the end, greatly reduce the cost and Nettlefold realized that if he did not acquire it someone else would and that this might well result in his being driven out of business. The total cost of the patent rights and the necessary factory and equipment was likely to be around £30,000 and this amount, at the time, he could not raise. In this dilemma he went to his brother-in-law, Joseph Chamberlain senior, who, after considerable heart-searching and after a visit to the proposed site in Birmingham, agreed to supply a substantial part of the capital. It was much more than he could afford to lose, however, and he felt it was essential that either he himself or one of his sons should be on the spot and in constant touch with the business, and so it was that his eldest son Joseph found himself setting out for Birmingham, the place with which he was to be so closely identified for the remainder of his life.

In the year 1854, when Joseph Chamberlain first came to Birmingham, the Industrial Revolution had been in full swing for upwards of seventy years. It had affected different towns in different ways. There were, for example, marked points of contrast between Birmingham and its two great northern counterparts – Manchester and Liverpool. Birmingham, from early times the home of metal trades and hardware generally, was a city of a thousand trades, but no one of these was carried out on a very big scale. The typical Birmingham businessman of that era worked at the bench himself and employed anything from two or three to a dozen workmen. The great industrial magnates with huge factories employing hundreds of workmen were almost non-existent in the Midlands city. This had important consequences on its social and political life. In Manchester, where vast fortunes had been accumulated in the textile industry within a generation or two, the wealthy business families had tended to become less and less intimately connected with the life of the city, and to spread out into the countryside where they had acquired great country mansions, taking up shooting, farming and other country pursuits, and becoming part of the landed gentry. Indeed, some of them lived on a far more lavish scale in the country than did any of the older families. The difference between the two was well portrayed by Richard Cobden in a letter to John Bright which has often been quoted:

'The social and political state of that town (Birmingham) is far more healthy than that of Manchester and it arises from the fact that the industry of the hardware district is carried on by small manufacturers, employing a few men and boys each, sometimes only an apprentice or two, whilst the great capitalists in Manchester form an aristocracy. . . . There is a freer intercourse between all classes than in the Lancashire town where a great and impassable gulf separates the workmen from the employer.'(9)

His father and uncle both decided that young Joseph must start from the lowest rung of the ladder and learn the commercial side of the business from the bottom, but there was never any idea of making him a skilled technician and though, when he first arrived, and for several months thereafter, he was treated exactly the same as any newly arrived clerk, it was generally recognized that it would not be long before he was 'one of the bosses'. But he was soon on excellent terms with his fellow-clerks and with the workpeople generally, and indeed he was very much more popular in Broad Street, Birmingham, the headquarters of the firm, than he had ever been at University College School. He took to business easily and naturally and threw himself into it with enthusiasm.

None of the Chamberlain sons stayed at school after they were sixteen. On going to Oxford for the first time with John Morley, Joseph exclaimed, 'Ah, what would I not give to have been to this place.' In actual fact, however, it is doubtful whether either he or any of his brothers lost as much through this omission as they were apt to imagine. For each of them had in a remarkable degree the power of self-education. They all read widely and travelled extensively and nothing that they read or saw was ever lost on them. Joseph so improved on the foundation in the French language which had been laid for him at University College School that he could both speak the language fluently and read widely and easily in French literature. And his brother Richard, building on a similar foundation, became in time an expert mathematician and, when Mayor of Birmingham, would astonish his colleagues on the Council by the ease with which he could make difficult computations with his slide-rule.(10)

Instead of going to the University, each of the three older boys went straight into the family business on leaving school. Here they learnt, or started to learn, the business of shoemaking; an important result of this was that they worked cheek by jowl with their workpeople, listened to their talk and acquired from the beginning the ability to appreciate the working-class point of view and a keen interest in the lives of their workmen. This sympathy with and desire to improve the lot of those less fortunate than themselves has always been a strong Chamberlain characteristic. There was ample scope for its exercise when later the family moved to Birmingham.

They soon found that thousands of their fellow human beings were living in conditions of extreme wretchedness. It had not always been so. During the eighteenth century the cottages occupied by the artisans of Birmingham and its surrounding villages were noted for their attractive gardens. Furthermore, many, if not most, workmen had their own allotments on which they grew fresh vegetables. Their lives were hard and primitive but the scents and sounds of the country were still theirs. The advent of steam power, followed by mass production and a rapid rise in land values, changed all this. Around what is now the heart of the city, workmen's dwellings were rushed up with no regard to town planning or public health. The only considerations were speed and cheapness of erection. Nearly all the houses were built back to back and most of them looked out on to dark and foetid courts in which filth and garbage of all kinds accumulated.(11) There was no sewerage scheme at all worthy of the name, the collection and removal of refuse being totally unprovided for by any public organization and much of it finding its way into the few streams which were the only source of the town's water supply. In these circumstances, the prevalence of preventible disease is hardly surprising.

When the third Joseph first came to Birmingham he went into rooms in Edgbaston, walking every day to the head office of the firm in Broad Street. This led him through some of the worst housing conditions in the town and what he saw struck him most forcibly and unfavourably. For what he, and later his father and brothers, noticed most particularly was that many of the unfortunate inhabitants of these quarters were men not fundamentally different from themselves. Often, pausing on his way to and from work to talk to them, Joseph could see that they were decent, honest, hard-working folk and that it was in no sense their own fault they they should be situated as they were. There but for the grace of God and the fact that he had hit on a prosperous business went Joseph himself. As, with his keen intelligence, generous impulses and sympathetic outlook Joseph Chamberlain, in his early days as a businessman in Birmingham, penetrated into some of the foul quarters in which his fellow-creatures were condemned to live, deep, searching questions which had lurked for a long time in his subconsciousness, started to come to the surface. Furthermore, there were others who were asking the same questions and whose influence helped him to provide the answers both as to the cause of all this misery and as to their appropriate remedy.

Amongst the most important of these others, whose influence was so powerful, was the great tribune of the people, John Bright, whose political connection with Birmingham dated from 1858, the first of his great speeches in the Town Hall having been made in October of that year. Joseph Chamberlain heard every one of those speeches and it was an unforgettable experience. For there he got a glimpse of the great power which public speaking gave in those days, the immense sway which the born orator could achieve over large masses of his fellow-countrymen. Long before Bright rose to deliver his address, the building was invariably packed. Men whose faces were black with the grime of the factory and the mine poured into the place to listen to him and so great was the demand for room that the seats had to be taken out and men were so closely crowded together that it was only with difficulty they they could lift their arms. Bright was amongst the foremost in arousing in the people of Birmingham a sense of their mission. He reminded them of what their fathers had done in the agitation which had preceded the first Reform Bill of 1832. 'Shall we then, I ask you, even for a moment, be hopeless of our great cause?' he asked in the first of these great speeches. Then he went on:

'I feel almost ashamed even to argue it to such a meeting as this. I call to mind where I am and who are those whom I see before me. Am I not in the town of Birmingham – England's central capital; and do not these eyes look upon the sons of those who, not thirty years ago, shook the fabric of privilege to its base? Not a few of the strong men of that time are now white with age. They approach the confines of their mortal day. Its evening is cheered with the remembrance of that great contest, and they rejoice in the freedom they have won. Shall their sons be less noble than they? Shall the fire which they kindled be extinguished within you? I see your answer in every face. You are resolved that the legacy which they bequeathed to you you will hand down in an accumulated wealth of freedom to your children. As for me, my voice is feeble. I feel now sensibly and painfully that I am not what I was. I speak with diminished fire: I act with a lessened force; but as I am, my countrymen and my constituents, I will, if you will let me, be found in your ranks in the impending struggle.'

And again, in a later speech:

'I want our country to be populous, to be powerful and to be happy. But this can only be done – it never has been done in any country – but by just laws, justly administered. I plead only for what I believe to be just. I wish to do wrong to no man. For twenty-five years I have stood before audiences – great meetings of my fellow-countrymen – pleading only for justice. During that time, as you know, I have endured measureless insult and have passed through hurricanes of abuse. I need not tell you that my clients have not been generally the rich and the great but rather the poor and the lowly. They cannot give me place and dignities and wealth; but honourable service in their cause yields me that which is of far higher and more lasting value – the consciousness that I have laboured to expound and uphold laws which, though they were not given amid the thunders of Sinai, are not less the commandments of God and not less intended to promote and secure the happiness of men.'(13)

Bright held that the chief of the miseries which afflicted the 'poor and the lowly' was the inordinate power and influence of the aristocracy and the established church. Swathed in luxury, from childhood onwards, relieved of the necessity for any form of uncongenial exertion, living lives which were remote from those of their fellow human beings, fawned on and flattered at every turn, the average hereditary peer was, in Bright's view, the last person who should be given the wide power which he then possessed to affect the lives and destinies of his fellow-men. And he delighted his Birmingham audience by referring to 'another kind of Peer, that creature of – what shall I say? – of monstrous nay, even of adulterous birth – the spiritual Peer'.(14)

Nowhere did the seed sown by John Bright fall on more fertile ground than in the heart and mind of Joseph Chamberlain. Born into and steeped as he had been all his life in the very dissidence of dissent, hatred of the House of Lords and the established Church was part of his very nature and Bright's oratory fanned the flames which smouldered within him. It was this which made him amongst the foremost fighters on the Nonconformist side in the great battle over education. This question had, from a very early stage in his Birmingham life, stirred the consciences and excited the imaginations of himself and his family. The state of affairs was certainly deplorable. It was calculated that of the children between the ages of three and twelve only half at the outside received any kind of education, while 10 per cent went to work, and the remaining 40 per cent grew up in ignorance and idleness. It was largely to rectify this state of affairs that, in the year 1867, the Birmingham Education League was formed. This body, to which

Joseph Chamberlain senior and junior each contributed £1,000, included among its objectives a nation-wide campaign to make education (1) Universal (2) Compulsory (3) Nondenominational and (4) Free. Around this programme there raged for nearly a decade one of the bitterest storms which has ever convulsed British politics, a storm which threatened to tear the Liberal Party asunder, and out of that storm Joseph Chamberlain emerged as the champion of the Nonconformist conscience and a major figure in national politics.

In the year 1870, W. E. Forster introduced the first Education Bill into the House of Commons. This provided for school boards to be constituted with power to set up State schools which were to be complementary to but were not to replace the existing denominational schools, of which latter the great majority were church schools. The school boards were empowered but not obliged to compel attendance, they had the right to provide as they thought fit for religious instruction, subject to a conscience clause enabling pupils (or their parents on their behalf) to withdraw and finally, while fees were to be payable by all who could afford them, the boards were empowered, by Clause 25, to pay the fees of any pupil, whether at a purely state or a denominational school, who could not afford them. The whole Bill was repugnant to that extreme section of the Nonconformists to which the Chamberlains adhered; they felt that they had been betrayed by the leaders of the Liberal Party, of which down the years they had been loyal supporters and to which they had contributed so freely in time and money. None of their objectives were accomplished by the Bill which rendered education neither free, universal, undenominational nor compulsory. Clause 25 they regarded as particularly obnoxious and it was around this clause that the bitterest part of the controversy raged. The Nonconformist conscience was deeply disturbed at the prospect of being forced to contribute, through the rates, to the doctrines of the established Church in schools which that Church controlled. Joseph Chamberlain was, from the start, in the forefront of this battle; in him the Nonconformists found a singularly able and powerful advocate of their cause. His words travelled far and wide not only throughout Birmingham but throughout the land. One example out of many may be given of his eloquence on this subject.

'The impossibility of salvation for unbaptized persons, the worship of saints and the miraculous conception, the odiousness of dissent generally or the most systematic atheism may all be taught in the national schools at the same time and at the common cost and, as the composition of the Boards changes from time to time, it may be possible in districts in which opinions are nicely balanced that in the same schools in the same twelve months the children may be taught the sins and heresy of Protestant England and the abominations of the Scarlet Lady and the City of the Seven Hills.

'Now for all these anomalies and absurdities, pernicious as they must be to the cause of education and the spread of true religion, there is only one remedy and one specific. Let the State keep to its proper work and fit its children to take their places as citizens of a great Empire and let it leave their religious training and all that concerns their education for the Kingdom which is not of this world to the care of the churches and the responsibility of parents. . . . To my mind nothing but the most wanton indifference to religion could justify a proposal to subsidize all forms of religion at once on condition that the one we favour has its share of the plunder. The present system of denominational schools has notoriously failed to secure a religious tone and religious life amongst the people where it has had full sway. We have the remedy in our hands. Let us determine to make our opinions felt at the next election and to support no candidate who will not do us equal justice.'

It was his work for the Education League which first brought Joseph Chamberlain into prominence as a public man and was responsible for his election to the Birmingham Council and the Birmingham School Board – his first steps up the political ladder. Neither of these was achieved without considerable opposition and, from the beginning, Joseph Chamberlain was a controversial figure, invariably attracting attention not only by his political views but by the strength of his personality and the unusualness of his characteristics. While still quite a young man he smoked long, black cigars and 'amazed hostesses by the effrontery with which he talked pure, undiluted politics at social functions'.(16) He appeared at a political meeting in 'a large, sealskin top-coat', which, according to a local journalist 'made people gasp. Any man daring to dress thus,' added this commentator, 'must be a Caesar or a Napoleon.' And he was already starting to develop that fierce Radicalism tinged with Republicanism which was caricatured by the remark fictitiously put into his mouth. 'Now then, my lads, let's all be equal and I'll be your King.'(17)

Meanwhile, various important changes had taken place in his own circumstances and in those of the family as a whole.

2

Tragedy

In Birmingham in the middle of the nineteenth century, there was a highly intellectual group of leading Unitarian families who, besides giving themselves largely to good works, lived graciously and well and also entertained liberally. The Nettlefolds were promnent members of this group and it was through them that Joseph Chamberlain, soon after he arrived in Birmingham, was introduced to some of the others – the Kenricks, the Oslers, the Rylands and the Russells. Soon they invited him to their houses and made him feel thoroughly at home. There was a great deal about him at that time which commended itself to the younger and older members of these families alike. He was good-looking, intelligent and hard-working and was evidently likely to acquire a fair store of this world's goods, for largely owing to his efforts, the screw business was starting to do very well. He was still extremely keen on and good at amateur theatricals and never missed a dance if he could help it. And he had started to travel and could regale the local society with stories of his adventures amongst the mountains and glaciers of Savoy and Switzerland. It is not surprising that he was soon popular with these other families. It is also perhaps not greatly to be wondered at that it was not long before he fell in love and found that his affections were returned.

The young lady's name was Harriet Kenrick and her parents – the Archibald Kenricks – were well-to-do people, with a prosperous business, who lived at Berrow Court. He had first met the Kenricks shortly after he came to Birmingham for they were leading members of the Unitarian congregation at the church which he attended. But it was probably not until nearly six years later, when he was twenty-four, that he and Harriet fell in love. Then in the summer of 1860 he went again to Switzerland, but this time the weather was awful. He insisted on climbing the Breithorn in appalling conditions, for at that time he was greatly addicted to mountaineering, walking and swimming and other forms of physical exercise, but never to organized games, though later he came to the conclusion that it was a mistake to make a fetish of exercise, over-expenditure in which prevented men from making the best use of their brains; indeed he is reputed to have said later on in life that 'getting out of bed in the morning was enough exercise for anyone'. To return to the Breithorn expedition, he fell ill as a result of it and was in bed for a week. It seems likely that he thought a great deal during that time about Harriet for it was shortly after his return to England that he proposed and was accepted. They were engaged for rather over nine months, the marriage taking place at the New Meeting House in July 1861 and, at the time, they were both twenty-five.

They spent their honeymoon in Cornwall and there, in wonderful summer weather and in a part of the country where bright and vivid colours abounded, they found how much the beauties of nature meant to them both. There followed over two years of unalloyed happiness. They were well suited to one another and between them there existed from the start a deep spiritual affinity. Harriet proved to be a most delightful companion, a capable housekeeper, wise and cheerful and always ready and anxious to do anything she could to help other people. Her husband wrote of her later: 'She had the most keen and yet the most innocent capacity for all earthly enjoyment. The beauties of nature, music and art, the society of friends and acquaintances – all these she appreciated to the utmost. She was glad of worldly prosperity and of the comforts and pleasures that money can give, but she used them as not abusing them and had so strong a sense of purity and devotion that I do not believe any earthly prosperity could have spoiled or altered her.'

Early in 1862, their first child was born – a daughter, Beatrice. In the following year, the rest of the Chamberlain family had moved to Birmingham. The business in Milk Street was sold and Joseph senior rented a fine old house with a beautiful garden called Moor Green Hall. He also acquired an interest in another business, Smith and Chamberlain, brassfounders. Every day, in fine weather, he walked across the fields to Moseley where he took an omnibus or was picked up by a trap which carried him to his office. In cold weather, his wife wrapped him up in a warm scarf before he set out and, in the course of his walk, he would often come across children making their way to school and would stop and question them about their lessons, rewarding those who gave the right answer with stray pennies.(1) For him and for his sons education was always a leading interest. Arthur and Richard both went into Smith and Chamberlain and carried it on after their father's death.

When the Chamberlain family first went there, the district surrounding Moor Green Hall was almost entirely rural. Clara, one of Joseph's sisters who moved into Birmingham with the rest of them, wrote enthusiastically about the countryside around her new home, mentioning 'the daffodil fields which stretch from Northfield to the Lickey' and 'Weatheroak and Earlswood which abound in spring time in primroses and violets', and of visiting 'in the summer all the neighbouring lawns for wild roses'(2). At the gatherings of the leading Unitarians – social, political and religious – Joseph's brothers and sisters were soon to be found along with himself.

But Joseph's happiness was not allowed to last long. On October 16th, 1863, another baby was born – this time a son, Joseph Austen, destined in time to become a famous statesman with whom we shall be much concerned in these pages. There had been no complications over the pregnancy and, at first, there did not seem to be any cause for anxiety. Then, suddenly, two days after the birth, Harriet's condition rapidly deteriorated, and, after a further twenty-four hours of agonizing suspense for Joseph, the doctors were able to hold out little hope. On the Tuesday, she got much worse.

'Well, I have had a very happy life,' she said, 'and I am perfectly happy whichever way it is.'

The next day she entered a delirium and shortly after midnight she died. Joseph now realized the extent to which everything that he was and everything that he had and hoped and lived for had centred on Harriet. In a moment of intense anguish after the funeral, he wrote: 'There seemed to be such immense happiness in store for us in the future that I know there was only one blow which could possibly have dispersed them all and taken every interest in life away for a time. . . . As I write all this and think that I am never to know and feel her love or delight in her ways here again it seems almost impossible to live.'(3)

Practical considerations had to be faced and the most important of these was the children's future. The Kenricks immediately came to the rescue and Joseph and his children moved to Berrow Court, of which he had already become very fond, rejoicing in its orchids among which he liked to spend as much of his spare time as possible.

It was only in intense application to business and to those public activities which will be described in greater detail later that Joseph found alleviation from his great sorrow. Every morning he arrived at the office in Broad Street punctually at nine o'clock and he never left before six. He travelled widely on the firm's business, pushing its products for all he was worth. When he was at home, his evenings were taken up with the Edgbaston Debating Society and the Working Men's Institute with its Glee Club, its Penny Readings and its own Debating Club. He was the life and soul of this latter institution which he had done a great deal to originate. In thus identifying himself with the needs of his work-people, in making himself one of them and in constantly giving everything that he had in him to promote their happiness and well being, Joseph Chamberlain found the cure for his own sorrow.

Time healed the wounds caused by Harriet's death and soon he was his old self again. And in the passage of time his gaiety returned and he once more found himself in love – Florence Kenrick was Harriet's cousin and, though a few years younger, had many of her attributes. Joseph made up his mind that she was necessary to his happiness. 'We were married on June 8th, 1868, nearly five years after Harriet's death,' he wrote, 'that great and terrible loss, constantly in my mind up to my second marriage, left me with always a sense of insecurity and a dread of possibilities which were too full of pain to dwell upon continually.'(4)

In the year 1865, there came to Joseph Chamberlain a fresh interest and a new connection, he became a Director of Lloyd's Bank. The Lloyds were a quaker family, descended from Welsh Kings, who for hundreds of years had owned land at Dolobran near Welshpool. In the seventeenth century, they had been cruelly persecuted, imprisoned and despoiled but this period of adversity had brought out all their fine qualities and they, like many dissenters, had been brought to Birmingham by the Five Mile Act, going in for the iron trade and for banking in both of which they prospered. It was a high compliment that the Lloyds paid to

Joseph Chamberlain when they invited him on to the board of their bank for they had always been Conservatives. A certain Sampson Lloyd made more than one attempt to enter Parliament as representative of Birmingham but he was unsuccessful and his political opponents later celebrated the discomfiture of the unfortunate Sampson by means of a 'funeral card' couched in the following terms:

Sacred to the memory of
SAMPSON S. LLOYD and SEBASTIAN EVANS, LL.D
who departed their political life on Tuesday,
November 17th, 1868, having fallen victims to
that dreaded disease Public Opinion, accelerated
by the action of the 'Vote as you're told Committee'.
They were interred at the hustings, Town Hall,
November 18th, amid the woeful lamentations
of their chapfallen supporters.(6)

Chamberlain remained a Director of Lloyd's Bank until the year 1877, when he resigned shortly after entering Parliament. The connection between the Chamberlain and Lloyd families was further strengthened later, when Mr. (now Alderman) Stephen Lloyd married the daughter of Neville Chamberlain.

Meanwhile, the bonds between the Chamberlain and Kenrick families were drawing ever tighter. In due course, Joseph's sister Mary married William Kenrick and his brother Arthur married Louisa Kenrick. As time went on a whole troop of little cousins would grow up to enjoy children's parties and dances and picnics in the various Chamberlain and Kenrick homes in and around Edgbaston. As for Joseph his keen zest for life, his fun and gaiety had now all returned. Florence entered into all his interests and accompanied him when he went to address public meetings as he was now doing with increasing frequency, studied botany so as to be able to share his passion for gardening and particularly the growing of orchids and helped him with the articles which he was now contributing to various periodicals.

'The articles . . . in the *Fortnightly Review* were submitted to her criticism first and it was with her approval and at her desire that the first of these articles were sent to the press,' he wrote, adding that 'she gave up much time to the arrangement of reports and extracts and speeches which might be useful in my work and which she took pleasure in indexing and arranging for ready reference. But she was never very strong, and had a delicate and spiritual look which sometimes made me anxious, but her spirit was indomitable and she did not know what idleness was.'

For the time being, however, no shadow crossed his path. The firm of Chamberlain and Nettlefold was prospering exceedingly. They were now producing nearly three-quarters of all the screws coming from Birmingham. Joseph's drive and energy were tremendous and the great success which the firm achieved was in no small sense due to him, though he was not made a partner until 1869, the year after his second marriage. As time went on, more and more of the smaller firms were absorbed into or amalgamated with his own. He was later to be accused of unscrupulousness in this connection but these charges were entirely without foundation; the terms arranged were invariably sensible and, indeed, generous and the other parties generally did well out of them. Indeed the conclusive answer to the charge that the Chamberlain family acted unscrupulously in buying up other firms is to be found in the fact that, shortly after this, they themselves sold out. In the year 1874, the Nettlefolds acquired the entire Chamberlain interest in the business for the sum of about £600,000. Of this Joseph himself got about £120,000. In possession of an extremely comfortable fortune, he could now devote himself entirely to public affairs.

But the following year, fate dealt him another shattering blow. At the beginning of 1875, he was a very happy man. Now that the ties and cares of business had fallen away, he was able to concentrate more on his home and family – the greatest sources of happiness of all. He now had six children – Beatrice and Austen by the first marriage and Neville, Ida, Hilda and Ethel by the second. Neville was born on March 18th, 1869. Florence was just as fond of Harriet's children as she was of her own and an equally good mother to them all and that meant being a very good mother indeed. She was now expecting another child which was due to be born in February. Joseph was then Mayor of Birmingham, in which capacity Florence had been an enormous help to him, entering the social side of the position with great charm and enthusiasm, and becoming a Lady Mayoress of great popularity and distinction. Late on the night of February 13th, the child was born; there did not then seem to be any cause for anxiety. Indeed as late as four-thirty on the following afternoon the doctor came down and said that all was well. But, at five o'clock, Florence fainted and died within a few minutes. The child also died shortly after as also did Mrs. Chamberlain senior, Joseph's mother.

Not only did Joseph Chamberlain's whole world seem to crash in ruins about him but he could find little consolation in the hope or expectation of any future world. In spite of his deep sense of and indeed enthusiasm for his own church, Joseph, like his two distinguished sons, Austen and Neville, was, and remained through life, what he himself once called a 'reverent agnostic'. His grief amounted almost to despair. Something of the agony of spirit through which he passed can be gathered from a letter which he wrote to two men who were then amongst his most intimate friends. To Jesse Collings he wrote:

'Drive on – we shall come to the journey's end in time and perhaps then we shall know where we have been going and whose business we have been doing all the time.'(8)

And to John Morley:

' . . . Does not the presence of this great grief . . . impress you with the cruelty of this life as you and I are compelled to see it? It is a hideous business, and our conception of its end and meaning is thoroughly unsatisfactory. We may be right – I fear we are – and I refuse to try and buy comfort by forcing myself into insincere conviction – but still I thoroughly abhor the result at which I have arrived, and I think it a grievous misfortune to have been born into such a destiny.'(9)

Of Florence herself, Joseph wrote shortly after her death in a letter intended to be read by her children:

'I have had in my wife a friend and counsellor, intensely interested in the objects for which I have striven, heartily rejoicing in my success and full of loving sympathy in occasional failure and disappointment. And looking back I see how the path has been smoothed for me by her unselfish affection and how much strength I have gained from the just confidence I have reposed in the judgement and devotion she has displayed in the part reserved for her. It is easy to give time and thought and labour to public work while the mind is relieved from any anxiety about home duties and all the responsibilities of life are shared by a real helpmate and companion. . . . And the result of this complete similarity and identity of interest has naturally been to knit us both together so that I can now say that there is no thought or action of my later years which my wife has not shared with me, and no place or ambition or desire formed for the future which has not been shadowed by her death.' (10)

The children were looked after by two of Joseph's sisters in turn – first by Caroline and then, when she married, by Clara. For Joseph himself there seemed nothing left but work – 'to work double tides – to work constantly and not to think'. This was the only way, he considered, to save himself from going mad and time would give him a certain interest in his work, though it could not bring back 'the subtle pleasure due to the sense of untiring sympathy and intelligent companionship.'(11) The work was the government of a large town, whose affairs its citizens had committed to his care – and to this we must now turn.

3
An Outstanding Mayoralty

Joseph Chamberlain was elected to the Birmingham Council as the representative for the St. Paul's Ward in 1869. Four years later, he became the Mayor and it was his work in this capacity which made him one of the best known men in the country and which paved the way to an outstanding political career. In all this he was greatly assisted by certain extraneous circumstances and by good luck, as nearly all men are who rise to great heights from relatively obscure beginnings. The recognition of this latter fact need not in any way belittle the enormous value of the work he did and the credit to which he is undoubtedly entitled for it, but we need not go to the other extreme and assume that whereas, before, the town was governed by a small group of parsimonious oligarchs meeting at 'The Old Woodman' in Easy Row the whole scene was completely transformed by the emergence into the municipal arena of Joseph Chamberlain.(1)

The truth is that a strong civic sense had always existed in Birmingham and this, as well as the town's rapid growth in size and wealth, was due, curiously enough, to the fact that, throughout the eighteenth and the first three decades of the nineteenth centuries, there had been attracted into the town a large number of dissenters, who, by the Five Mile Act, were not allowed to live within five miles of a Corporation. These men – particularly those who were Unitarians and Quakers – were often of great ability, thrifty, industrious and imbued with a strong sense of their duty towards their neighbours. It was largely owing to them that the Birmingham Street Commissioners came into being and they, though handicapped by lack of funds and very limited powers, did excellent work, so that, in 1829, an official visitor from Manchester declared that 'the streets of Birmingham have an air of cleanliness and comfort to which Manchester is a complete stranger'. And, after its incorporation as a Municipal Borough by the Act of 1835,

Birmingham included amongst its councillors men such as William Schofield, Philip Henry Muntz, Robert Martineau, Joseph and Charles Sturge and George Dixon, whose civic sense was as strong as that of any other councillors of any other town or city in that or any other age.(2)

During the 'hungry forties', however, and the decade which followed them, trade had not been at all good and this had given rise to a cry for economy in municipal affairs. The 'economy group' on the council got the upper hand and the members of this group met sometimes at an inn called 'The Old Woodman' in Easy Row, where Old Joseph Allday, their leader, would roar forth condemnation of municipal extravagance. (3)

Two factors, in particular, contributed, together with his own innate ability and intense industry, to Joseph Chamberlain's success as a municipal reformer and gave him advantages which the earlier city fathers whose names have been mentioned did not enjoy. The first of these was the great improvement in trade which occurred during the seventh decade of the nineteenth century. The late sixties and early seventies were indeed boom years and Disraeli referred to this period as a 'convulsion of prosperity'. This made much more money available for public purposes. The second factor was that Chamberlain happened to enter the Council in a climate which was particularly favourable to municipal reform and this in turn was due to the efforts in arousing public opinion of a small, very vocal, very able and very enthusiastic group of nonconformist clergymen. Perhaps the best known of this group was the redoubtable Dr. R. W. Dale, the incumbent of Carter's Lane Chapel and the very embodiment of the Nonconformist church militant. There has probably never been a time when Nonconformist ministers wielded the political power that they exercised then and Dr. Dale was in the forefront not only of every local battle but of the great national battles as well. He did not confine himself to Birmingham but travelled far and wide, addressing great meetings all over the country, attending Parliamentary committees and interviewing the foremost statesmen in the land from Gladstone downwards. His name was one to conjure with and his appearance at a Liberal meeting was calculated almost to bring the roof off.(4)

The spirit in which Dale and his kindred spirits (including the

Chamberlains) approached municipal matters can be judged from the following letter which Dale wrote to his wife while in Switzerland:

> 'At this moment when I raise my eyes, the Lake of Lucerne with its guardian mountains is before me – the noblest scenery, as some think, in all Europe; but I declare that there is nothing in this magnificent view which makes me feel half the thrill I have sometimes felt when I have looked down on the smoky streets of Birmingham from the railway, as I have returned to my work among you after a holiday. The thought of having to do, more or less directly, with all that mass of human thought and action, which is covered with the ceaseless smoke which hangs over us, – the thought that you and I together may, with God's help, save multitudes – sends the blood through one's veins with an exultation and glow which the most magnificent aspects of the material universe cannot create.'(5)

Dale and other ministers like him inculcated into an important group of Birmingham businessmen the need for municipal reform, emphasizing how important it was that they should play their full part in local affairs. 'In a country like this,' he once said 'where the public business of the state is the private duty of every citizen, those who decline to use their political power are guilty of treachery both to God and man.' And he had great influence on business men for his was a very practical brand of religion and since his arrival in Birmingham he had made a close study of the business life of the town – its factories, shops and offices. Ignorance and indifference to these matters were, in his view, not the handmaid but the enemy of true religion and one of his most popular and widely quoted sayings was, 'The eleventh commandment is that thou shalt keep a balance sheet'. It was largely as a result of his influence that a group of Birmingham businessmen, of whom Chamberlain was one, banded together to reform the town. Dale himself described the sequel:

> 'Towards the end of the sixties, a few Birmingham men made the discovery that perhaps a strong and able Town Council might do almost as much to improve the conditions of life in the town as Parliament itself. The Council became invested with

a new attractiveness and dignity . . . the speakers, instead of discussing small questions of administration and economy, dwelt with glowing enthusiasm on what a great and growing town like Birmingham might do for its people. They spoke of sweeping away streets in which it was not possible to live a healthy and decent life; of making the town cleaner, sweeter and brighter; of providing gardens and parks, and music; of erecting baths and free libraries, an art gallery and a museum; they insisted that great monopolies like the gas and water supply should be in the hands of the corporation; that good water should be supplied without stint and at the lowest possible prices; that the profits of the gas supply should relieve the pressure of the rates. Sometimes an adventurous orator would excite his audience by dwelling on the glories of Florence and of the other cities of Italy in the Middle Ages, and suggest that Birmingham too might become the home of a noble literature and art.'(6)

Joseph Chamberlain was, from the start, an enthusiastic member of this group. Dr. Dale, whose influence on him was undoubtedly very great, declared later:

'Mr. Dawson was the prophet of the new movement but Mr. Dawson had not the kind of faculty necessary for putting faith into practice. . . . This was largely done by Mr. Joseph Chamberlain, who began to show proof of those great powers which have since been recognized by the nation. . . . Mr. Chamberlain gave himself to the work with a contagious enthusiasm. . . . He used his social influence to add strength to the movement. He appealed in private to men who cared nothing for public life and he showed how much they might do for the town if they would go into the council: he insisted that what they were able to do it was their duty to do. He dreamt dreams and saw visions of what Birmingham might become, and resolved that he, for his part, would do his utmost to fulfil them.'

Chamberlain never failed to acknowledge the inspiration he had derived from Dale. Years later, when he first became a member of Parliament, he declared publicly:

'I have seen a statement that I go to Parliament as the representative of Dr. Dale. Well, if that be so, there is not a representative in the House of Commons who will have a better, wiser or nobler constituency. But you will at least remember this – that if Dr. Dale has any influence over the fifty thousand electors of Birmingham, he owes it to his devotion to their highest interest and to his eloquent and outspoken advocacy of all that is good and great.'(8)

Chamberlain was recommended to the electors of St. Paul's Ward by the committee which chose him as their candidate as 'a large ratepayer, a man of thorough business habits, enlarged views and marked ability, belonging indeed to precisely the class of burgesses most desirable to the Council'. He soon showed that he had all these attributes in full measure and, in the year 1873, after only four years as a councillor, he became the Mayor. 'Birmingham,' he declared shortly afterwards, 'is not my native town – I wish it were; but it is the town of my adoption and predelection. I have lived here about twenty years and I think it the finest, the most intelligent, the most patriotic town on the face of the universe, and I am prepared to maintain the same opinion before any audience in or out of Birmingham. At the same time, my favourite town, I admit it with grief and sorrow, is not perfect. . .'

Then he went on to speak of some of the evils, such as bad sanitation and housing conditions, which cried out for remedy, ending by saying that so long as any of these blots remained 'on the fair fame of our town, all its well-wishers are bound to put their shoulders to the wheel and try to remove them, and so, by God's help, we will; and by the assistance of my colleagues in the council I hope that in twelve months the town will not know itself'.(9)

Most of the first year was taken up with the municipalization of the town's gas supplies. Here the main objective was to secure that a monopoly should be a source of profit to the ratepayers rather than to private enterprise. Chamberlain's plans were bold but simple and this was the first time that the town got the full benefit of his shrewdness and business ability on a large scale. His proposals involved buying out the existing owners of the gas works for a figure which would raise the town's debt from £500,000 to £2,000,000 but he claimed that, after paying all interest charges and allowing for a sinking fund there would be a clear profit for the town of at least £25,000 per annum and this without increasing the price of gas.(10) He carried the Council with him but some of the ratepayers arranged a meeting to recruit opposition to the scheme. Chamberlain addressed this meeting and, when challenged, he said that if the Council would allow him to take over the project himself, he would undertake to pay them £20,000 per annum for the next fourteen years, and that, at the end of that time, the debt would have been paid off, the council would own the entire gas undertaking and he himself would, without any rise in the price, be left with a 'snug little fortune' of about £200,000. The audience was deeply impressed. They realized that Chamberlain knew how to make a good bargain and so he carried the day. In actual fact, after the first few years, the Council's profits, after paying all charges, were running at a substantial rate and at the same time the price of gas per unit was actually reduced.

In dealing with the town's water supplies, he acted on a different principle. Here he considered that the transcendent consideration should be the health of the people. The Corporation should certainly take over the existing water works, but they should not seek to make a profit but rather to secure a better and cheaper supply for the benefit of all the people. The body which was supposed to be responsible for this at the time was called the Birmingham Water Works Company but, with the expansion of the town, this company was unable to provide more than a fraction of the total need. In the year 1869, more than fifteen thousand people were dependent on open wells for their water. These were in a disgraceful condition, being largely contaminated by sewage. 'What do you think of the inhabitants being compelled to drink water which is as bad as sewage before clarification?' asked Chamberlain, and he went on to assert that some of the poorer people were actually compelled to steal water from the Company's taps, so devoid were they of any other means of obtaining this vital commodity. Furthermore, as he pointed out, it was precisely in those areas where this was happening that disease was most prevalent and the death rate highest. The battle to secure the water works was a long and bitter one but, in the end, thanks largely to Chamberlain, the Corporation was victorious and the Bill giving the necessary powers received the Royal Assent in August 1875, the works being actually transferred on January 1st, 1876. They were thereafter substantially extended and the supply of water increased. Also during Chamberlain's mayoralty, a Health Committee was set up to deal with the clearing away of sewage and waste matter, the abating of nuisances, the inspection of properties and foodstuffs, the promotion of cleanliness generally and the maintenance of facilities for securing disinfection and combating infectious diseases. As a result of these and other measures taken during the time that Chamberlain was the Mayor, the death rate, which had been 3·2 per cent above the national average, fell progressively during the years that followed.(11)

But his greatest achievement during these years was the Improvement Scheme. It was here that the imaginativeness which Dr. Dale had referred to was first brought to practical effect for this was one of the boldest and most imaginative schemes evolved by any municipal corporation during the nineteenth century. It was to affect some ninety-three acres of land, over most of which slum conditions prevailed, including, according to the report of the Medical Officer of Health, 'narrow streets, houses without back doors or windows, situated both in and out of courts, confined yards, courts opening at one end only, and this small and narrow; the impossibility in many cases of providing proper privy accommodation; housing and shopping so dilapidated as to be in imminent danger of falling, and incapable of proper repair'.(12) The whole area was to be demolished and rebuilt. The town was to be replanned on modern lines with great wide streets, suggestive of the Paris 'boulevards' along which Chamberlain himself had often walked and of which he was so great an admirer.

In introducing his 'Improvement Scheme' Chamberlain referred to the conditions in which some of the poorer sections of the people were living. 'We want to make the people healthier and better,' he said. Then he continued:

'I want to make them happier also. Let us consider for a moment the forlorn and desolate lives the best of these people must live, in courts like those described. It made my heart bleed when I heard the descriptions of Mr. White and others of the dreariness – the intense dreariness – and the lack of everything which would add interest or pleasure to the life which obtains among that class . . . I know for a fact that there are people there almost as ignorant of what is going on around them as if they lived in a lonely and savage island. . . . Some would even lose themselves in New Street. There are people who do not know that there is an existence on the other side of the Town Hall; people who are as ignorant of all that goes to make the pleasure, the interest, the activity, and the merit of our lives, as if they were savages in Ceylon, instead of being Englishmen and Englishwomen in the nineteenth century enjoying all the blessings of civilization. . . .

'We bring up a population in the dank, dark, dreary, filthy courts and alleys such as are to be found throughout the area we have selected; we surround them with noxious influences of every kind, and place them under conditions in which the observance of even ordinary decency is impossible. And what is the result? What can we expect from that kind of thing? I think Mr. White said the other day that to some extent the position of the people was their own fault, and I heard a cheer when that statement was made. But I am sure Mr. White only meant that to be true in a very limited sense.

'Their fault!

'Yes it is legally their fault, and when they steal we send them to gaol, and when they commit murder we hang them. But if the members of this Council had been placed under similar conditions – if from infancy we had grown up in the same way – does any one of us believe that we should have run no risk of gaol or the hangman? For my part I have not sufficient confidence in my own inherent goodness to believe that anything can make headway against such frightful conditions as those I have described. The fact is, it is no more the fault of these people that they are vicious and intemperate than it is their fault that they are stunted, deformed, debilitated, and diseased. The one is due to the physical atmosphere – the moral atmosphere as necessarily and surely produces the other.'(13)

Of the ninety-three acres, the freehold in some forty or fifty was to be acquired by the Corporation. It was here that Chamberlain's great shrewdness, drive and business ability came most fully into prominence in the service of the town of his adoption which, down the years, has reaped a rich reward from them. The total cost of the freehold acquisitions was likely to be in the region of £1,300,000. Streets and roads would take up about eight acres and would cost some £34,000 to build. Chamberlain considered that the necessary funds could be borrowed by the Corporation at 3½ per cent and that sites could be let to builders on leases of seventy-five years, thus securing for the benefit of the town reversions of immense value, which would, in his own words 'make this the richest borough in the kingdom sixty or seventy years hence', and finally he was of the opinion that as a result of all the improvements there would be a threefold increase in rateable value. Taking all this into account, he calculated that the average net cost of the scheme would be £12,000 a year. 'Is that too heavy a burden for the town of Birmingham to contemplate for such an improvement as that proposed?' he asked. 'I believe the town and above all the next generation will have cause to bless the Town Council of Birmingham if it carries the scheme before it, and exercises what I venture to call a sagacious audacity.'(14)

Once more the proposals were hotly contested both at Government Inquiries and before Parliamentary Committees. So great was Chamberlain's knowledge of the subject, and so considerable his powers of persuasion, that his fellow councillors felt that it was unnecessary to brief Counsel so long as the Mayor was available to appear on behalf of the Corporation. Thus, on most of the hearings he appeared himself, triumphing with ease over the learned Counsel arrayed against him. In this way he saved his fellow-ratepayers a considerable amount in legal fees though, in doing so, he may not have made himself very popular with the Bar.

In his fight for slum clearance and the improvement of the town, Chamberlain derived essential help from an unexpected quarter. The Conservatives were then in power and, in the year 1875, Disraeli's Government produced the Artisans' Dwellings Act, which the Home Secretary, Cross, actually referred to Chamberlain for his approval before it became law. This Act gave local authorities the power to acquire compulsorily and then to demolish and rebuild insanitary areas within their boundaries. Without this, the Improvements Scheme in Birmingham would have been impossible and Chamberlain was duly appreciative. Parliament, in passing this Act, had recognized something greater than property, he said. And Mr. Sclater Booth, the President of the Local Government Board in the same administration, went out of his way to be helpful, as the following extract from one of Chamberlain's letters to John Morley shows: 'I have been to London and had a private interview with Sclater Booth who has promised to throw over the Commission of inquiry and give me all I want. Hooray for the Tories!'(15)

All Chamberlain's calculations proved to be well founded and the Improvement Scheme was a great success. In particular has he been proved to be a true prophet in regard to the financial benefit to the Corporation. The properties must have multiplied in value a least a hundred-fold. Nor must mention be omitted of the part played by the other members of the Chamberlain family in all this. Before the end of Joseph's mayoralty, both his parents had died, but two of his brothers, Arthur and Richard, had entered the Council. Both gave Joseph the most active support throughout and carried on with the good work after Joseph had ceased to be the Mayor. Arthur was Chairman of the Licensing Committee and Richard continued the Improvement Scheme and was responsible for the extension of that scheme to provide for working-class houses. In the year 1880, Richard was elected Mayor.(16)

It was while Joseph Chamberlain was the Mayor that his second wife died. He did not, at first, feel that he could continue with his municipal work and wrote offering to resign on the ground that 'besides the ordinary work of the Council and the committees, which perhaps I might still hope to perform, the Mayor of Birmingham is called upon to perform many other social and public duties, the fulfilment of which has been a source of happiness and satisfaction in the past, but is quite beyond my power in the future'. But the Council refused to accept his resignation and assured him that 'everything possible would be done to relieve the Mayor from those merely ceremonial duties which he justly feels that he cannot now discharge'.

While gas, water and the Improvement Scheme were the most important of Chamberlain's achievements on the Council there were other spheres in which he, his father and his brothers actively promoted the wellbeing of their fellow-citizens both before, during and after the time that Chamberlain became the Mayor. In 1875, he gave £1,000 'to be expended by the Free Libraries Committee in the purchase of objects of industrial art for permanent exhibition in the Art Gallery of this town', and in 1881 he presented two pictures valued at £1,800 to the Art Gallery. And, on leaving the Birmingham School Board to become a Member of Parliament, he gave them, as a parting present, £500 for the foundation of a scholarship at one of the schools on King Edward VI's foundation.

In the year 1874, Joseph Chamberlain stood as Liberal candidate for Sheffield in the General Election but was defeated. But, in 1876, Mr. George Dixon, one of the three Birmingham members, suddenly and rather unexpectedly resigned on the ground of his wife's ill-health. Only one name even received consideration as his successor, that of the Mayor. On June 17th, 1876, amidst scenes of wild enthusiasm, Joseph Chamberlain was returned unopposed as the junior Member of Parliament for Birmingham. He was now about to embark on what was to be one of the stormiest political careers of the nineteenth century, but, however fiercely the storms might rage, he would have behind and about him always the deep affection and gratitude of the overwhelming majority of his fellow-citizens. They never forgot all that he and his family had done for Birmingham. He might defy Gladstone, split the Liberal Party, be pointed to by Parnell as 'the man who killed Home Rule', join up with the Conservatives and then, declaring for Tariff Reform, split that Party also but Birmingham always remained true to him and this was the foundation and mainstay of his career and of Austen's and Neville's too.

4

The House of Commons and the 'Caucus'

Joseph Chamberlain's first speech to his Parliamentary constituents was made in the Bingley Hall, Birmingham, on June 28th, 1876. It was a hot summer night and the enormous crowd packed into the hall (estimated at about twenty thousand) must have found the heat suffocating. Nevertheless, they listened to him with rapt attention. Even Bright had seldom if ever received such an ovation when he rose to speak. Chamberlain said:

> 'No man could rise to address such an assembly as this without a feeling of grave responsibility and of some natural emotion and in my case these feelings are deepened by the sense of personal obligation under which I lie to this great constituency, which has ever shown me a generous consideraton and which has conferred on me the highest honour in its gift.'

Then he started to proclaim his beliefs on the great questions of the day. Amongst the most significant parts of this confession of his political faith was that which related to disestablishment.

> 'I have never been content to argue this question as if it were a squabble between dissenters and churchmen,' he said, 'nor have I ever attacked the religious work of the Church or the personal work of those who preach her doctrines; but I have maintained and I do maintain that it is an institution which divides the land into hostile camps upon all social, educational and political questions, and that it converts what ought to be a religious organ into the machine of a party opposed to progress. The fact is that union between Church and State is separation between Church and people.'

Then, turning to a wider field, he said that he wanted

> 'to secure better representation, to promote temperance, to

secure the prevalence of education and remove the great social discord and the great obstacles to political progress.'

He added:

'England is said to be the paradise of the rich, we have to take care that it does not become the purgatory of the poor.'

All this was in line with the programme which he had recently been enunciating up and down the country under the headings, 'Free Land, Free Labour, Free Schools and Free Church.'

When Chamberlain entered the House of Commons for the first time, the Conservatives had been in power for two years, Lord Beaconsfield being the Prime Minister. Gladstone had retired for the time being from the leadership of the Liberal Party, but this severance was destined to prove only temporary; he returned as Prime Minister in 1880. Chamberlain had referred to the leadership question both in speeches and in articles published in the *Fortnightly Review* from 1874 onwards. Referring to the resignation he wrote that 'the advanced Liberals will probably receive with comparative equanimity the announcement of Mr. Gladstone's resignation of the leadership of his Party'. And, in an article in the *Fortnightly* on 'The Next Phase of the Liberal Programme,' he wrote:

'The advanced Liberals . . . form an important element in the Liberal Party . . . without them it would be difficult to distinguish the Party of the moderate Tories who do not practise their principles from the Party of the moderate Liberals who have no principles to practise. . . . If it is really the desire of the country that nothing more should be done, the Conservatives are the proper people to carry out its wishes. . . . The Liberal Party will never regain power on terms like these. Much as Mr. Gladstone is honoured and respected it is not for his credit or for ours that we should take him back as we recover a stolen watch – on the condition that no questions are asked. . . . Anything would have been better than the course actually followed. At a moment's notice, the dissolution was resolved on, and Mr. Gladstone promulgated through the country the meanest public document that has ever in like circumstances proceeded from a statesman of the first rank.'

During his first four years in Parliament, Chamberlain's closest associate was Sir Charles Dilke; they were both extreme radicals and they had already met in the course of the struggle over Forster's Education Bill and they found themselves in general agreement over that and over most of the outstanding questions of the day. Dilke was not a scion of the aristocracy and was as opposed as Chamberlain to the domination of the Liberal Party by the great Whig families but he had inherited a baronetcy and had never been connected with trade and these facts, in the political atmosphere of that day, placed him in a different category from Chamberlain.

Dilke had a private income of several thousand a year and on this he could and did live on a considerable scale. He had a large house at number 76 Sloane Street and here he entertained lavishly. He was a brilliant man and a powerful speaker with great popular appeal and he had travelled widely and had many influential friends both in England and abroad. When Chamberlain, unmarried and having no London house, first became a Member of Parliament it was with Dilke that he stayed when the House was sitting. Dilke was the intimate friend and confidant of Gambetta and he had many other acquaintances and friends amongst the French. There were few other private houses in London where so much talent from all over Europe was to be found as at number 76 Sloane Street. At least twice a week there was a large dinner-party and the guests included men and women of European reputation – statesmen, men of letters, actors and actresses, and artists and lovers of art. Amongst those who went most frequently were Harcourt, Morley, Brookfield (the Queen's Chaplain), Sir Henry James, Browning, Riciotti and Moret (the Spanish Minister). Gladstone went there more than once and Cardinal Manning was a not infrequent visitor. Gambetta was invited whenever he was in London, as were also many other distinguished French men and women including the Comtesse Gilbert de Voisins (once the famous dancer Taglioni), and the French tragedian, Ristori, who became later the Marquise Capranica del Grillo. Sometimes, indeed, the conversation at dinner was conducted entirely in French and one of the features of these parties was the production of French comedies by M. Brasseur, the famous comedian.(2) It might be thought that a Birmingham screw manufacturer would have found himself out of his element at these brilliant gatherings. But it was not so. Chamberlain's wide reading, his knowledge of French (self-acquired but by now considerable), his quick wit and wide experience of so many sides of life enabled him fully to hold his own.

In due course, Chamberlain returned some of the lavish hospitality showered on him by Dilke, who paid a number of visits to Highbury. The two became close friends and, for a number of years after Chamberlain had secured his own establishment in London, they almost invariably left in the same cab when the House adjourned. Towards the end of his first Parliament, Chamberlain suggested to Dilke that they should form an 'offensive and defensive alliance' and that neither should accept office without the other. Dilke's reply to this was a trifle vague and the terms of the alliance were never precisely defined. Dilke's climb up the political ladder came to an abrupt termination a few years later when he was cited as co-respondent in a divorce suit in which another Member of Parliament, whose name was Crawford, alleged that Dilke had committed adultery with his (Crawford's) wife. It was suggested at the time by Chamberlain's enemies that he deliberately gave Dilke bad advice in order to ruin him and this suggestion has received wide publicity since, but those who have made it have never yet been able to produce a plausible motive. The most common innuendo, that Chamberlain was anxious to remove a possible rival to the future leadership of the Liberal Party, is completely refuted by the fact that, shortly afterwards, he resigned from Gladstone's Government and soon ceased, in effect, to be a Liberal. Chamberlain was certainly ruthless, impetuous and ambitious and perhaps apt at times to be a busybody but it is not true that he was actuated by mean and contemptible motives.

Indeed when he first entered the House of Commons, Chamberlain was not generally popular with the leaders of either Party. This is not altogether surprising when we consider not only his speeches but his general public behaviour. He lashed out in all directions and his sarcasms sometimes stuck in the mind of the victim for quite a long time. Hartington, for example, he referred to as 'the serious son of a respectable Duke'. He was equally disrespectful about Forster and Goschen. As for the opposite Party, soon after he became a Parliamentary candidate he described the

Conservative leader as 'a man who never told the truth except by accident; a man who went down to the House of Commons and flung at the British Parliament the first lie that entered his head'. Disraeli retorted characteristically by describing the attack as 'one of the coarsest and stupidest assaults I ever remember. No intellect or sarcasm or satire or even invective; coarse and commonplace abuse such as you might expect from the cad of an omnibus.' Chamberlain was forced to apologize and he gave as his excuse the fact that 'I have been greatly overworked lately' and that 'I was speaking without preparation under considerable mental strain and in face of somewhat irritating interruptions'.

Overwork was not, however, the chief cause of the mental strain. The fact is that he was still bitterly unhappy and suffered from fits of intense depression. Only about a fortnight after he became a Member of Parliament he wrote: 'I feel so terribly depressed that I catch myself continually wishing this wretched business of life were over once and for all. . . . It is a hard thing when one cannot find any hope in the future for, after all, it is hope which constitutes the real enjoyment of life.'(3) He had always been tinged with a certain intellectual arrogance and somewhat given to sarcasm, but these characteristics got far worse as the result of unhappiness caused by his second wife's death. He did not enter upon his new life in the House of Commons with any sense of fun, excitement or adventure as most men do, regarding it only as an exchange of means of getting away from the gnawing unhappiness and black depression which filled his inner being – and once elected, he was not at all sure that the exchange was a wise one. 'What a fool I am to be willing to go to Parliament, and give up the opportunity of influencing the only constructive legislation in the country for the sake of tacking M.P. to my name,' he wrote. 'Upon my word I think sometimes that both Birmingham and I will have cause to regret this step.'(4) And again, 'I have broken with my old life and have as yet no interest in, nor hope of, my future – everything reminds me of what might have been and recalls my present loneliness. I can neither look back nor forward with any satisfaction. . . . This life is a d—d bad business for me and I wish I were out of it.'(5) With this deep unhappiness and loneliness at the root of his being, he was unrelaxed and under constant strain compared with his more fortunate contemporaries in the

House and this explains to a considerable extent the almost dae-monic energy with which he applied himself to his new career and the impression he gave of hardness, ruthlessness and arro-gance. It is of interest in this connection to recall some of the descriptions given of him by outside observers – journalists and others – during his early years in Parliament. In an American newspaper, for example, there appeared the following from an acute observer of the English scene: 'He (Chamberlain) is the very opposite in appearance and manner of the professional dema-gogue . . . perhaps hardly quite free of what the House of Com-mons most abhors, a persuasion that he is a superior person. . . . Mr. Chamberlain is terse, polished and brilliant, and the House of Commons, which loves an epigram more than an argument, will get both from him when he is fairly roused and well in harness.'

And another eye witness, describing a few years later the im-pression which he got from listening to Chamberlain addressing a great public meeting, wrote: 'His face I thought disagreeable when I saw it for the first time close at hand, his mouth taking on a sneer more readily than a smile. The tones of biting sarcasm . . . gave force to the oration but they did not endear the man.'(6)

It is scarcely surprising, in these circumstances, that, during his first few years in Parliament, Chamberlain was not particularly popular in the House of Commons. By the Whigs in particular he was looked on with a mixture of apprehension and repugnance. Gladstone was forced to tolerate him but there was never any real affinity between the two men.

If, therefore, Chamberlain had had to rely entirely on the House of Commons, he would probably have made little headway, at least at first. His rapid rise was due almost entirely to his position in the country. Here he enjoyed a strength and a popularity in a vast industrial centre which few men have ever enjoyed. This position he was resolved to exploit and he was very successful in his methods of doing so. It is important to examine a little more closely the political situation in Birmingham and the way Chamberlain dealt with it. This involves a description of what became known as 'The Birmingham Caucus.'

Amongst the most important factors which led to the growth of 'the Caucus' were the Education Act of 1870, and the Represen-tation of the People Act of 1867. Under the former, school boards were elected by what was known as the 'cumulative vote' and, in Birmingham, the electors had as many as fifteen votes which they could either distribute amongst the different candidates or, if they so desired, they could give all fifteen votes to one man. In the first election, the Church Party was far better organized than the Nonconformists and, by skilful arrangement of their votes, they secured a majority on the school board though having a minority of the total votes cast. The 1867 Act, while giving Birmingham three members, restricted each voter to two votes. The Act had been brought in by the Conservatives and this particular provision was designed to secure that at least one of the three new members was a Conservative. The Liberals in Birmingham however, were convinced that, by skilful organization, they could acquire both a majority on the school board and all three Parliamentary seats. In this, they proved to be right.

Joseph Chamberlain did not actually create 'the Caucus' which was really an offshoot of the Education League and the Birmingham Liberal Association, which latter had been formed in 1856 before Chamberlain was even on the Town Council, under the aegis of a number of prominent Liberals, including William Harris and Dr. Dale. It was soon seen, however, that the results of the Acts of 1867 and 1870 were such that the Association would have to be remodelled and, in this, Chamberlain played a most important part. By reason both of his natural qualities and his business training, he was highly qualified to do so.

The most important objects of the reorganization were to secure firstly that all candidates for Parliament, for the local Councils and for the school boards were chosen as democratically as possible and secondly that every Liberal vote was given its maximum effect – both locally and nationally. The means that were adopted to achieve these ends were oddly suggestive of the American system and, indeed, Chamberlain was later accused of Americanizing English politics, but there is no evidence that anything that was done derived its inspiration from across the Atlantic. The general idea was that every Liberal voter was entitled to vote at the annual election of the committees for each ward. The committees so elected each chose a number of representatives who became known first as the Committee of Four Hundred then of Six Hundred and finally of Two Thousand, the membership being increased gradually to this number. There was a delegation of many important powers and functions from this large body to a Central Committee of about one hundred members and this latter in turn elected the members of the very important Management Committee which was responsible for the day-to-day administration of the Association's affairs.(7)

The results of this reorganization were everything that could be desired from the Liberal point of view. All their three candidates were returned at the Parliamentary Election of 1868, and the Nonconformists obtained a majority on the school board.

In the year 1873, a certain Francis Schnadhorst was appointed secretary of the Liberal Association. Formerly a draper in Birmingham, Schnadhorst had been for years an indefatigable worker on behalf of the Liberal Party. It was Dr. Dale who first spotted his talent as a political organizer and Schnadhorst owed his new appointment largely to Dale. Chamberlain also liked him – at least at first – and, for a time, the two worked well together. Chamberlain and Dale were the real brains behind the organization but they needed someone who would be responsible for daily administration. Schnadhorst seemed to be the ideal man. Conscientious and hard working to the last degree, he excelled in attention to detail.

Chamberlain was never ashamed of 'the Caucus' and he defended it stoutly against all its critics. He was particularly proud of its democratic basis and in November 1876 he told John Morley with evident satisfaction that 'three-quarters of the Committee of Six Hundred are working men'. Early the following year, two extremely important decisions were taken. The first was to close the old Education League, it being resolved 'to transfer its remaining work to the Liberal Associations of the country as part of the policy of the Liberal Party'. The second decision, which to some extent followed from the first, was that as the old Education League had been based on Birmingham, so the new organization which was to carry on its remaining work was also to be based there. What was involved here was nothing less than a federation of all the Liberal Associations throughout the country, based not on London but on Birmingham, and modelled on the existing organization which had worked so well. It was an extremely ambitious scheme and, once more, it was Chamberlain who supplied the brains and drive behind it. The plan having been decided on, his next move was a master stroke. He invited Gladstone to stay with him and address a great meeting of all the Liberal Associations which was to be held in Birmingham. Gladstone agreed and, with this to attract them, Chamberlain had no difficulty in persuading representatives of Liberal Associations from all over the country to attend.

Chamberlain took the chair at the conference of the Liberal Associations which was held in the afternoon and, in the evening, Gladstone addressed a great meeting in the Bingley Hall. It was the largest ever so far held in Birmingham, the number of people who thronged into the Hall and crowded into the galleries and on to the roof being estimated at the time as about thirty thousand. Even Bright had never commanded such a vast audience. No doubt flattered by this and by the colossal ovation which he received Gladstone gave his blessing to the new organization. He condemned 'the power of the purse' which, he said, had hitherto been far too prevalent in political organization and then added, 'It is in my opinion to the honour of Birmingham that she has held up the banner of a higher and nobler principle.' From Chamberlain's point of view nothing could have been better than this. The new 'National Liberal Federation', thus auspiciously inaugurated, soon established an office at Atlas Chambers, Paradise Row, Birmingham. Later, they moved to Colmore Row. Chamberlain was chosen as the president, and the inner committee included a number of his staunchest supporters including his redoubtable henchman Jesse Collings. Schnadhorst was appointed the secretary.

From the start, it was obvious that the new organization, if it succeeded, would, because of its broad, democratic basis, increase the Radical influence at the expense of the Whigs in the councils of the Liberal Party. This undoubtedly was the object of Chamberlain and his supporters from the start. 'The opponents of the "Caucus" are not to be convinced,' he wrote to Morley. 'They hate it for its virtues – because it puts aside and utterly confounds all that club management and Pall Mall selection which has been going on for so long and which has made of the Liberal Party the molluscous, boneless, nerveless thing it is. The "Caucus" is force, enthusiasm, zeal, activity, movement, popular will and the rule of the majority – the seven deadly sins in fact.'(8)

In one of his articles in *The Fortnightly Review*, however, he pointed out that, 'It cannot be too strongly insisted on that the Caucus does not make opinion, it only expresses it . . . It will not turn Conservatives into Liberals or secure for a Liberal minority a representation to which its numbers do not entitle it. . . . If the committees are not really representative . . . the Caucus will soon sink into deserved neglect and contempt . . . . All the machinery in the world will not rouse enthusiasm in England, unless there is a solid foundation of genuine and earnest feeling to work upon.' He added, however, significantly that, from time to time, 'Resolutions from the Central Committee would be sent to the local associations with a recommendation to call public meetings and take steps in support of the proposition. If they approve of the suggestion they will make the necessary arrangements to carry them out and will no doubt request their members to vote for the motion. But this can only be done if they agree with the recommendations of the Central Committee.'(9)

If Joseph Chamberlain did a great deal to make the new organization the success which it soon became, that body, in its turn, did much to forward his own political career. As more and more Liberal Associations entered the new scheme, so Chamberlain's importance was enhanced and the demand for him as a speaker throughout the country increased. He soon became a national figure and his popularity with the working classes, in particular, was great. Though at all times firmly radical, Chamberlain was careful not to offend the right wing of the Liberal Party more than he could help. Instead he directed all those powers of invective and acid satire of which he was rapidly becoming a past master towards the Conservatives. He delighted Liberals of every variety when, after Beaconsfield's triumphant return from Berlin, he declared that 'Peace with honour is really peace with humbug' and describing the Conservative Imperialism as 'not constructive but incendiary' went on to ask Liberals of every shade of opinion to unite and constitute themselves into a fire brigade, adding 'I do not stop to ask whether a man is a Whig or a Radical, but whether he is ready and willing to lend a hand at the pumps. Let us one and all determine to put out the fire.'

So it came about that when, the Liberals having won the election of 1880, Gladstone was called on to form his second

Government, Chamberlain had achieved a power and influence in the country and had a claim to office which the new Prime Minister could not wisely or safely ignore. Gladstone was still very far from having any affection for Chamberlain, but he was bound to recognize the danger of excluding him from the Government. So, at the end of April 1880, Chamberlain entered the Cabinet as President of the Board of Trade.

About the year 1880, Chamberlain acquired a large London house, number 40 Princes Gardens, which was near Hyde Park. This remained his London home for the rest of his life. He lived there in considerable style with a butler, two footmen and a large staff of indoor servants. Around the same time, he built himself a large country house near Birmingham. It was called Highbury and was near to Moor Green Hall, once his father's and now his brother Arthur's home. The position at the time was lovely. It stood on high ground which sloped down to a valley and a beautiful garden was soon designed as well as a number of orchid houses to provide for Joseph Chamberlain's favourite pastime. It was a large house, built of red brick and designed in the neo-Gothic style, and was, on the whole, typical of its period. Internally, it was ornate and rather hideous.

When Joseph Chamberlain first moved into his London house, it was his eldest daughter Beatrice who acted as his hostess. She was then little more than twenty years old but she acquitted herself well in helping her father to entertain not only his political associates and friends of many years' standing but also some of the new acquaintances whom Joseph was starting to make in the social world. Among these latter was Lady Jersey to whom Beatrice wrote appreciatively much later of the help Lady Jersey had given her 'when I . . . so very raw, was keeping house for Papa and came with him into this strange, unknown and uncharted world of London'. Lady Jersey had a very high opinion of Beatrice and wrote years afterwards that she became 'a very talented and distinguished woman' and that her death (in 1918) was a 'loss to many good causes'.(10)

Throughout her life both Beatrice's brothers were devoted to her and Neville was to write of her after she died: 'She was a wonderfully gifted woman of brilliant intellect and the highest moral character. She had the warmest heart and her love for children and genius for amusing them made her always a favourite. It is an awful gap in our family circle.'(11) And, later still, when he became Prime Minister, Neville would write, 'I wish our Bee could have lived to be aware of it for it would have meant an enormous lot to her.'(12)

5

Parnell, Ireland and the Peers

While at the Board of Trade, Chamberlain was responsible for some useful legislation – particularly in regard to bankruptcy and merchant shipping, but during this period, he by no means confined himself to the affairs of his Department. Between himself and his radical supporters on the one hand and Gladstone and the Whigs upon the other there was a truce but never any true partnership. Chamberlain's ideas for the future undoubtedly went far ahead of anything that Gladstone had in mind at that time.

In the spring of 1882, there arrived at Highbury a letter from one of the Irish members and this led to an important correspondence. William Henry O'Shea had recently been elected to the House of Commons as one of the two representatives for County Clare. He was the son of a rather shady Dublin solicitor who had made a large fortune by a combination of moneylending and land dealing. O'Shea senior was resolved that his son should have a very different future. He purchased a commission for him in the army and encouraged him to lead a life of luxury and fashion. He told him to become a smart officer adding to this, 'Do what the other men do and send the bill to me.' The result was what might have been expected. In spite of a very handsome allowance, young O'Shea was constantly getting into debt. After a year or two in the army he brought his father bills totalling £15,000 which the latter paid, though pointing out that further extravagance of this order would lead to disaster for the whole family. The young officer continued on his downward course with the exact result in the end which his father feared.(1) Meanwhile, young O'Shea had married Katherine Wood, the thirteenth child of an Essex clergyman, the Rev. Sir John Page Wood, and a niece of Lord Hatherley, a friend of Gladstone and for a time Lord Chancellor. Not long after the marriage, Captain O'Shea, as a result of intense

46

extravagance and gambling, went bankrupt, but his wife had an extremely wealthy aunt, Mrs. Benjamin Wood, who came to the rescue.

A few weeks after O'Shea had been elected to Parliament for the first time, the Irish Party met to choose a new leader. O'Shea voted for Parnell who was elected by a majority of five votes. Parnell and O'Shea had one thing and only one in common. They were neither of them typical of the other members of the party or of their constituents.

Charles Stuart Parnell was, on his father's side, of English ancestry while his mother had been the daughter of an American. The founder of the family fortune had been a draper in Congleton, Cheshire, who became mayor of that town. One of his sons purchased an estate in Ireland at a time when land in that country could be bought very cheaply and, by improving it, achieved the position of a solid and prosperous landowner. Charles Stuart Parnell, to whom the estate ultimately descended, had neither the characteristics nor the background that one would expect of one who became the idol of the Irish peasantry. His birth and upbringing had cast him in a mould that was everything that peasantry detested. He was a Protestant, a landowner, aloof, reserved and aristocratic by temperament and outlook if not by birth. Nor, till his late twenties, did he ever show the slightest interest in politics. His first entry into them is said to have been due to an unfortunate love affair. Jilted and thrown over and made to look small by a rather empty-headed American beauty his wounded pride made him determined to prove that he counted for something in the world.(2) On April 19th, 1875, he was elected member of Parliament for Meath. Within ten years he was the 'uncrowned King of Ireland' and well on the way to becoming the master of the House of Commons. Parnell was never a brilliant orator or even a particularly good speaker. He could not sway great audiences purely by the power of his rhetoric as Joseph Chamberlain could and did. Parnell owed his power to the skill and pertinacity with which he built up the movement in favour of Home Rule and identified himself with it. The twin foundation stones of his edifice were obstruction in the House of Commons and the Land League and 'boycotting' in Ireland. In the nineteenth century, England was loathed and hated by the Irish peasantry who longed to throw off its yoke. A long history of hardship and oppression, of unbelievable cruelty and selfishness on the part of a relatively small number of absentee and Protestant Landlords, of evictions, of emigrations, of bad harvests, of famine, injustice and starvation had led to this. In Southern Ireland at least the demand for independence from England was almost universal amongst the masses of the people and was, in many ways, entirely justified.(3)

It was Parnell's view that Home Rule could only be brought about by making conditions for the English intolerable both in the British Parliament and in Ireland until it was granted. Hence his policy of obstruction of Parliamentary business of which he became a past master. Similarly his plan for curbing the power of the landlords and putting an end to unjust evictions was the 'boycott' which meant making life unbearable for the minions of the landlords and for anyone who took a farm from which the previous tenant had been evicted. Parnell himself was clever enough to keep within the strict letter of the law but his followers were not always so scrupulous.

The years of oppression and misery had brought out a strong vein of cruelty in some of the Irish and there were horrible stories of the maiming of cattle, of the burning and mutilation of crops, farm buildings and dwelling-houses and of midnight murders. Ever and anon the dead body of some victim of Parnell's Land League or one of its offshoots was found lying by the roadside and no one in the district would give any clue as to the identity or whereabouts of the murderer.(4)

The maintenance of law and order by ordinary means soon became impossible. No Irish jury would convict anyone accused of an offence against someone known to be under the interdict of the Land League. Gladstone's answer was the policy which became known as 'Coercion'. He did not like it, nor did his Chief Secretary, Forster, and nor did Chamberlain but the two former felt that it was the only course open to them. Coercion meant, in effect, putting the whole country under martial law and giving the Government power to arrest and imprison without trial people suspected of subversive activities. Parnell denounced Coercion not only in the House of Commons but throughout Ireland and so strong was his language, that in the end, Gladstone, in exercise of the powers contained in the Coercion Acts, ordered the arrest of Parnell and his imprisonment in Kilmainham gaol. It was shortly before this that Parnell first met Mrs. O'Shea.

O'Shea had gone from bad to worse. Gambling and racing, he had got through most of his father's fortune and was now bankrupt. However, by reason of the large allowance given by her aunt to his wife he was still able to live quite comfortably. Mrs. O'Shea gave pleasant dinner-parties to Members of Parliament who were likely to be useful to her husband and she had more than once invited Parnell, whom she had never met, but he, though he had accepted several of her invitations, had never in fact appeared at any of her parties. Her curiosity was aroused and she was determined to meet him. So one evening she went down to the House of Commons and sent a message asking him to see her. At last he came out, looking worn and far from well.

At this time (the summer of 1880) Parnell was under great strain. He was leading a lonely and rather depressing life, most of it either in the House of Commons, in lodgings, in hotels or travelling to and from and in and around Ireland. Mrs. O'Shea too was lonely, for O'Shea had treated her abominably and it was only because of her aunt that the outward façade of marriage was kept up between them. During the few minutes that Charles Stewart Parnell and Katherine O'Shea were alone together outside the House of Commons they fell in love with one another. As Katherine leant out of her cab to say good-bye to him a rose fell from her bosom and Parnell picked it up and pressed it to his lips. He kept it for the remainder of his life.

Parnell went to one of Katherine's dinner parties and after that they began to see each other constantly, but they were stolen, furtive meetings, in hansom cabs and (when O'Shea was safely out of the way) in the little house on the edge of her park at Eltham which Mrs. Wood had made available to Mrs. O'Shea.

Joseph Chamberlain was anxious to play a leading part in solving the Irish problem, and as soon as O'Shea wrote to him, he was immediately interested; O'Shea's ambition was to act as the liaison between Parnell on the one hand and the Liberal Government on the other. Mrs. O'Shea was also in touch with Gladstone, who knew her because she was Lord Hatherley's niece. The result of the negotiations which followed was the Kilmainham Treaty under which Parnell agreed to give general support to the Liberal

Party and gave certain undertakings as to his future conduct and Gladstone gave corresponding undertakings on Coercion and on security of tenure including the vexed question of arrears.

Forster, the Chief Secretary, disagreed with the Kilmainham treaty and resigned in consequence. It was strongly rumoured that Chamberlain would be his successor but, instead, Lord Frederick Cavendish was appointed. Shortly after he reached Ireland, however, Cavendish was brutally murdered in Phoenix Park. Again there were rumours that the post would be given to Chamberlain, who, in spite of the danger, was more than willing to go. The unity of the Chamberlain family is shown by an interesting letter which his brother Arthur wrote to Joseph at this time:

> 'Dear Joe,
> I cannot believe that W. E. G. [Gladstone] would be so mean as to ask you to take *now* the appointment that he did not offer when it seemed your due.
>
> But if you should go over there, it is impossible that we should let you go alone. I hope and believe that there will be no danger for the new Secretary, but there must be a terrible strain, and if you think it your duty to accept the post, you must allow one of us to be with you, not to get in your way and follow you about, but to be handy when you have time to talk, so that you should have one of your own family to talk with.
>
> I am waiting now to see Dick and Herbert and Walter to settle who should go with you. I think I ought to be allowed to go and have agreed with Louey [his wife] so, but must consult with the others to obtain their agreement. In any event, one of us will come. . . .'(5)

But again, this particular post did not go to Chamberlain. Instead, G. O. Trevelyan was appointed.

The result of the Phoenix Park murders was the re-introduction by Gladstone's Government of Coercion in the form of the Crimes Act of 1882, and this in turn brought to an end, at least for the time being, the alliance with Parnell who, annoyed about Coercion and the suppression of his Land League, now started to flirt with the Conservatives. He was also at this time particularly interested in the extension of the franchise and here he had something in common with Chamberlain for it was clear that to both men, though in very different ways, that extension would bring greatly increased power.

Under the Conservative Act of 1867, the artisans in the towns had largely been enfranchised but the agricultural labourers had not. There were nearly two million of these latter who were in Chamberlain's words 'knocking at the portals of the Constitution' and he was resolved that they should be admitted. Another plank in his programme was that each vote should have equal value and this could only be achieved by a redistribution of seats and (in Chamberlain's view) by equal electoral districts. In the year 1884, the Government introduced a Bill designed to bring the agricultural labourers on to the register but the House of Lords held it up for a time on the ground that the extension of the franchise and the redistribution of seats should be accomplished at one and the same time. They were unwilling to commit the country to the former without knowing what was intended in regard to the latter.

Chamberlain was furious at this interference by the Upper House, and in speeches up and down the country he directed all the force of an oratorical armoury which by then was considerable to a tremendous indictment of the peers. It was not the first time that he had attacked them. The year before, when Lord Salisbury had the temerity to carry the war into the enemy's camp by denouncing the Caucus in Birmingham, Chamberlain had replied, 'Lord Salisbury constitutes himself the spokesman of a class – of the class to which he himself belongs – who toil not neither do they spin, whose fortunes as in his case have originated by grants made in times gone by for the services which courtiers rendered kings, and have since grown and increased while they have slept by levying an increased share on all that other men have done by toil and labour to add to the general wealth and prosperity of the country.' Now his denunciations became sharper still. To their great delight he told a mainly Radical audience that most of the peers owed their positions and fortunes to the deeds of illustrious ancestors whose talents unfortunately, however, had not been transmitted to their descendants. The peers, he declared amidst loud derisive laughter, were like potatoes – 'the best part was under ground'. In August 1884, before an enormous audience at the Bingley Hall, Birmingham, he declared:

'The House of Lords courts investigation into its past history. Investigation it shall have. It has protected every abuse and sheltered every privilege. . . . It has denied justice and delayed reform. It is irresponsible without independence, obstinate without courage, arbitrary without judgment and arrogant without knowledge. . . . The "Divine Right of Kings" – that was a dangerous delusion but the "Divine Right of peers" is a ridiculous figment. . . . We will never be the only race in the civilized world subservient to the insolent pretensions of an hereditary caste.'

And, in Wales, where his passionate admirers included a young solicitor, David Lloyd George, who, a few years later, would himself lacerate the peers with even stronger invective, Chamberlain spoke in the mocking, sarcastic strain of which by now he was a past master.

'I have no desire to see a dull uniformity of social life. I am rather thankful than otherwise to gentlemen who will take the trouble to wear robes and coronets and who will take up a certain state of splendour which is very pleasant to look upon. They are ancient monuments [*loud laughter*] and I should be sorry to deface them. But then, gentlemen, I don't admit that we can build upon these interesting ruins the foundations of our Government. I cannot allow that these antiquities should control the destinies of a free Empire.'

In time Chamberlain's remarks about the class 'which toils not neither does it spin' brought forth replies from the masters of invective on the Conservative side. Thus, commenting on the fact that Chamberlain had been entertained at a banquet by Lord Durham, Lord Randolph Churchill said:

'If by any means it is legitimate to stigmatize any individual as enjoying great riches for which he has neither toiled nor spun . . . such a case would be that of the Earl of Durham and yet it is under the patronage of the Earl of Durham and basking in the smiles of the Earl of Durham that this stern patriot, this rigid moralist, this unbending Censor, the Right Honourable Joseph Chamberlain flaunts his Radical and levelling doctrines.'(6)

And another Conservative member describing Chamberlain as one who lived in a palatial mansion, smoked big cigars and enjoyed an unearned income of between £10,000 and £20,000 a year inquired in what sense he himself toiled and spun.(7)

Chamberlain's ironical remarks, emanating as they did from a Birmingham screw manufacturer, were even more offensive to the aristocracy in that day and age than outright abuse. Even more serious was their effect on the Queen. She had never liked Chamberlain and suspected him, not without some reason, of Republicanism. Now she addressed a number of letters to Gladstone, remonstrating in the strongest terms against Chamberlain's speeches:

> 'The Queen will yield to no one in TRUE LIBERAL FEELING, but not to destructive, and she calls upon Mr. Gladstone to restrain, as he can, some of his wild colleagues and followers'.(8) 'The Queen must again call Mr. Gladstone's attention to Mr. Chamberlain's speeches. . . . His language if not disavowed justifies the worst apprehensions of the Opposition.'(9) 'It is, the Queen thinks, absolutely necessary for the honour of the Government that Mr. Gladstone should take a firm stand and separate his name from Mr. Chamberlain, with which it is often, wrongly no doubt, connected. Mr. Chamberlain must restrain his language or else not remain in the Cabinet. In any other Cabinet such freedom of language has not been tolerated.'(10)

For once, Gladstone agreed with Her Majesty. He replied that 'concurring in your Majesty's regret and disapprobation of the language used, Mr. Gladstone . . . at once adopted measures which he hopes will have a good result'.(11) He was about to enter upon negotiations with Lord Salisbury (with whom he got on quite well) for the settlement of the franchise issue, thus ending the deadlock between the two houses and he did not want these to be sabotaged by the tirades of a member of his own Government. The negotiations ultimately ended in an agreement on the basis of the admission of the agricultural labourers and a redistribution of seats which, however, left single member constituencies in all the counties, an arrangement greatly to the advantage of the Conservatives.

Chamberlain knew that an extension of the franchise was inevitable and he was determined to be the champion of the new voters. Early in 1885, therefore, he announced in a series of speeches the programme which became known as 'The Unauthorized Programme'. This was to include Free Primary Education, Local Government for the Counties, a large measure of independence and Home Rule for the different parts of the United Kingdom while leaving the supremacy of the Imperial Parliament unimpaired, graduated taxation (mainly by way of death duties), and a levy on the 'unearned increment of land in the vicinity of great cities', disestablishment of the Churches of England, Scotland and Wales, universal manhood suffrage and payment of members and land reforms in virtue of which labourers would be enabled to acquire smallholdings through the action of local authorities.(12) It was this last proposal which gave rise to the cry for 'Three acres and a cow' with which Chamberlain's name was widely associated.

In the course of this campaign, Chamberlain made a number of speeches which achieved wide notoriety and aroused still further the animosity and apprehension of the wealthier elements in the community generally and of the landed aristocracy in particular. Addressing a huge meeting in Birmingham, he said:

'What is to be the nature of the domestic legislation of the future? I cannot help thinking that it will be more directed to what are called social subjects than has hitherto been the case. How to promote the greater happiness of the masses of the people, how to increase their enjoyment of life, that is the problem of the future; and just as there are politicians who would occupy all the world and leave nothing for the ambition of anybody else, so we have their counterpart at home in the men who, having already annexed nearly everything that is worth having, expect everybody else to be content with the crumbs that fall from their table. . . . If you will go back to the early history of our social system you will find that . . . every man was born into the world with natural rights, with a right to a share in the great inheritance of the community, with a right to a part of the land of his birth. . . . Private ownership has taken the place of these communal rights and this system has become so interwoven with our habit and usages, it has been so sanctioned by law and protected by custom, that it might be very difficult and perhaps impossible to reverse it. . . . But then I ask what ransom will property pay for the security which it enjoys. . . . There is a doctrine in many men's mouths and in few men's practice – property has obligations as well as rights. I think in the future we shall hear a great deal more about the obligations of property and we shall not hear quite so much about its rights.'(13)

It is difficult for us, living in the second half of the twentieth century, to understand the storm which these words provoked in the sedate Victorian epoch. In particular, the word 'ransom' seemed to have an ugly ring and it was immediately pounced on by Chamberlain's opponents and critics. In a later speech, at Ipswich, he moderated his language somewhat, explaining that what he had really meant was 'what insurance will wealth find it to its advantage to provide?', and going on to give his own ideas of sensible insurance, viz: Free education, County Councils, 'the provision of healthy, decent dwellings in our large towns at fair rents and, in the country, facilities for the labourer to obtain a small plot of land'. Soon, however, he returned to the attack.

'I have been the subject of torrents of abuse and whirlwinds of invective,' he declared at Birmingham at the end of January 1885. 'The working classes of this country are to continue in the future as they have in the past – to order themselves lowly and reverently to all their betters and to do their duty in the state of life to which it shall please God to call them. . . . All this clamour about confiscation and blackmail and plunder is so much dust raised by men who are interested in maintaining the present system and who are either too prejudiced to read my proposals or too stupid to understand them. . . . If it be blackmail to propose that the rich should pay taxation in equal proportion to the poor, what word is strong enough to describe the present system under which the poor pay more than the rich? If it be confiscation to suggest that land may be acquired at a fair value for public purposes, what language will fitly describe the operation of those who have wrongly appropriated the common land and have extended their boundaries at the expense of their poorer neighbours, too weak and too ignorant to resist them?'

He told another audience:

'The great problem of our civilization is still unsolved. 'We have to account for and grapple with the mass of misery and destitution in our midst, co-existent as it is with the evidence of abundant wealth and teeming prosperity. It is a problem which some men would put aside by references to the eternal laws of supply and demand, to the necessity of freedom of contract, and to the sanctity of every private right of property. But, gentlemen, these phrases are the convenient cant of selfish wealth.' (14)

In the course of his campaign, he crossed the border and he attracted enormous audiences in Scotland. Addressing a huge meeting in Glasgow he said:

'Politics is the science of human happiness, and the business of a statesman and of politicians is to find out how they can raise the general condition of the people; how they can increase the happiness of those who are less fortunate among them. . . . I sometimes think that we are so used to poverty and its consequences that we forget it or neglect it. Yet surely there is some reason to doubt the perfection of our system when in this, the richest country in the world, one in thirty of the population at every moment are unable to obtain the means of subsistence without recourse to the parish, and one in ten at the same time are on the verge of starvation.'

And he told a Highland audience, 'The history of Highland clearances is a black page in the account with private ownership in land. . . . Thousands of industrious, hard-working, God-fearing people were driven from the lands which had belonged to their ancestors and which for generations they had cultivated. . . . I ask you whether it is not time that we should submit to careful examination and review a system which places such vast powers for evil in the hands of private individuals. . . . Let us look this fetish in the face; let us examine these sacred rights of property; let us see upon what they are founded and let us see whether there ought not to be some limitation to the exorbitant pretensions with which they have been accomplished.' But he told a Yorkshire audience that 'considering the difference in the character and capacity of men I do not believe that there can ever be an absolute equality of conditions, and I think that nothing would be more undesirable than that we should remove the stimulus to industry and thrift and exertion which is afforded by the security given to every man in the enjoyment of the fruits of his exertions. I am opposed to confiscation in every form because I believe that it would destroy that security and lessen that stimulus.'

But still his speeches were occasionally interlarded with sneers and sarcasms as when he said in Birmingham, 'I dare say it is sickening to some of those old-fashioned Tories to see how those who were once their serfs are awakening to their new responsibilities and their new privileges.'(15)

In June 1885, the Liberal Government sustained a defeat in the House of Commons. This was largely due to Parnell's annoyance with Coercion and to the fact that he and a number of his supporters had voted with the Opposition. Gladstone resigned and Lord Salisbury formed his 'caretaker Government'. In the General Election which took place in the autumn the Liberals, thanks largely to the support which they received from the newly enfranchised agricultural labourers, returned as the largest single Party, having easily defeated the Conservatives. The Liberals did not, however, have a majority over all other parties. The Irish still held the balance of power.

One thing was transparently clear from the election; that was that the overwhelming majority of Southern Ireland was solidly behind Parnell in his demand for complete Irish independence. The Irish Nationalist Party had returned eighty-six strong, having won all but five seats, and the Liberals in Ireland were almost obliterated. Gladstone was convinced from these results that the only satisfactory solution to the Irish problem was Home Rule in some form. On this, he was unquestionably right, though it is possible to argue that he acted with undue haste. Chamberlain, on the other hand, had made it clear, both during the election and for some time before it, that he was unalterably opposed to a Parliament in Dublin but that he would agree to a National Council in the Irish capital which should have the fullest possible powers to deal with Irish affairs. Chamberlain was on strong ground on two aspects of the Irish question – the first was Ulster and the second was Imperial defence. There is no reason to doubt, however, that, if Chamberlain had shown rather more deference to Gladstone, he could have obtained from him important concessions on both these points. Equally it is conceivable that if Gladstone had shown rather more tact in his handling of Chamberlain he might have carried him with him. The Irish problem was admittedly an extremely difficult one but it need not and should not have taken thirty-five years to find the right solution.

In January 1886, Gladstone started to form his third Government. He sent for Chamberlain and asked him what post he would like; Chamberlain replied that he would like to be Secretary for the Colonies, at which Gladstone is reputed to have remarked, 'Oh a Secretary of State'.(10) He then refused to give him this particular position but on learning that Chamberlain was willing to accept the Presidency of the Local Government Board he offered him that and Chamberlain agreed, but he expressed a strong wish that his faithful ally and life-long friend Jesse Collings should be the Parliamentary Secretary. Gladstone agreed but was tactless enough to stipulate that the salary should be reduced. Chamberlain was extremely annoyed about this.

Gladstone declared some time later that, before he submitted his Home Rule Scheme to the Cabinet, 'the subject of the Bill, and its leading details had been a matter of anxious consideration between himself and his nearest political friends'.(17) Chamberlain was not included in this number and this was part of the trouble between the two men, for, equally, Chamberlain had not consulted Gladstone before enunciating his 'Unauthorized Programme'.

In an important letter which he wrote at the beginning of March 1886, Chamberlain revealed his innermost thoughts to his brother Arthur:

'As regards Ireland I have quite made up my mind – indeed I have never felt the slightest hesitation. If Mr. Gladstone's scheme goes too far, as I expect it will, I shall leave him. The immediate result will be considerable unpopularity and temporary estrangement from the Radical Party. There is little backbone in politics and the great majority are prepared to swallow anything and stick to the machine and the Cabinet. I have no support worth mentioning and the only person who will go with me is Trevelyan and he is very weak generally but in this matter he is pledged up to the eyes.

I shall be left almost alone for a time. I cannot of course work with the Tories and Hartington is quite as much hostile to my radical views as to Mr. Gladstone's Irish plan.

But in time the situation will clear. Either Mr. Gladstone will succeed and get the Irish question out of the way or he will not.

In either case he will retire from politics and I do not suppose the Liberal Party will accept Childers or J. M. [Morley] as its permanent leader.'(18)

In February, he had written to John Morley:

'My determination is to maintain unimpaired all guarantees for the integrity of the Empire and the supremacy of Parliament and I do not believe that these can be obtained in connection with a legislative body sitting in Dublin or in connection with your proposals to put Ireland in the position of Canada.'(19)

And he told Lord Randolph Churchill towards the middle of March that from what he had heard of Gladstone's plans for Irish Home Rule they were 'absurd beyond belief' and such that 'a decently educated child in a National School would not propose such absurdities'.(20)

The final rupture occurred at a Cabinet meeting on March 26th, 1886. Chamberlain declared later that when he entered the Cabinet room that day, he intended to be conciliatory but, according to Morley, 'the Prime Minister made little attempt in that direction' (21) and there would appear to be little doubt that a tense and painful scene followed, fraught with considerable bitterness between the two leading participants.(22) Chamberlain's main objection to Gladstone's proposals was that they involved the cessation of the Irish representation at Westminster. Considering the unmitigated nuisance that the Irish members were, this seems strange indeed. When Gladstone was unable to satisfy him on this and a number of other points but made it clear, on the other hand, that, under his plans, Irish representation at Westminster, including that of Ulster, would cease, Chamberlain said 'Then I resign', picked up his papers and walked out of the room, followed by his friend and fellow Radical, Sir George Trevelyan, the Secretary for Scotland. Gladstone made no effort to detain them and told Lord Rosebery afterwards that 'nothing that had happened since the Government was formed had given him comparable satisfaction with Chamberlain's resignation'.(23)

And, in a conversation with Lord Bryce, shortly after this, Gladstone described Chamberlain as 'a most dangerous man – restless, ambitious and unscrupulous' and as one from whom the 'country would suffer'. Gladstone added, 'It does not much affect me but those of you who will be in public life during the next twenty years will get some experience of the mischief he can do.'(24)

There is no doubt that Chamberlain showed both courage and a spirit of self-sacrifice in the choice he made. Lord Hartington, heir apparent to the Leadership of the Liberal Party, also parted company with Gladstone on this issue, and, if Chamberlain had decided to remain, he might easily have taken Hartington's place. As it was, Chamberlain's whole political future was clouded over with uncertainty. Everything now depended on Birmingham and it was here that he was to be given the final proof of the loyalty and affection in which he was held by his fellow-citizens. But the victory was not won without a hard fight and there was one man in particular who seemed to be working hard to prevent it.

Francis Schnadhorst had been amongst the first Liberals in Birmingham to sense the trouble between Gladstone and Chamberlain and to foresee the possibility that the latter might resign. He knew that this would split the Party in Birmingham from top to bottom and he did his best to prevent it from happening. Schnadhorst seems to have become convinced as early as February 1886 that Chamberlain was determined to pick a quarrel with Gladstone because in that month he wrote to Chamberlain, trying to dissuade him from doing so and telling him, 'If you went out on three acres and a cow you would have to depend on one kind of people; if you went out on Ireland you would have to depend on another'.(25) After Chamberlain's resignation had become effective, Schnadhorst's one idea was to seek a compromise solution of the problem. He wrote to him on April 15th, 1886:

'I give it to you as my opinion that if it were not for personal loyalty to yourself an overwhelming majority of Birm-

ingham Liberals would support the Government. I have no
doubt that your influence will carry the 2,000 but it will leave a
divided Party. An elector for North Birmingham has just asked
me "cannot the breach be healed". This is the question in many
minds. I cannot describe to you the distress which many who
have followed you for years are in. I venture to ask you myself
whether it is not possible for you to take such a position as will
enable your friends to support the principle of the Bill while
every effort may be made to amend it in your direction. . . . Mr.
Gladstone has given up something. . . . he may give more. I
know how much you have had to contend with but . . . every
consideration points to . . . securing the unity of the Party.'(26)

Chamberlain suspected, however, that Schnadhorst, who had
recently become the secretary of the National Liberal Federation,
was working against him. Chamberlain wrote to J. T. Bunce, editor of the *Birmingham Daily Post*, on April 11th:

> 'When I see you at Easter I will tell you all I know about
> Schnadhorst's proceedings. Meanwhile I fear it is absolutely
> certain he is working against us and as a result we shall have
> trouble in Birmingham as well as in the Federation. . . . It is
> desirable to postpone an open breach as long as possible but
> under the circumstances I can no longer regard Schnadhorst as
> a safe or a friendly guide. He is now doing his best to prejudice
> opinion in Birmingham. Can you manage to get an invitation
> from the Association to me to address them on the Irish
> question?'(27)

But if Schnadhorst was working against him, there were others
who were working *for* him in Birmingham and foremost amongst
these were his own relations, particularly his brothers. Indeed so
great was the solidarity of the Chamberlain–Kenrick fraternity
behind Joseph that they became known amongst his opponents
as 'The Clique' (pronounced *Click*) and 'The Clique' became a
frequent toast at the family party at Christmas.(28)

Of all Joseph's relations, it was his brother Arthur who was his
strongest supporter at that particular time, though they were to
part company politically later. Arthur was a man of strong
emotions and at that time he was incensed with Gladstone and he

managed to persuade a considerable number of other people to share his feelings. 'I think Gladstone behaved like a blackguard to you but he has cut his own throat,' Arthur wrote to Joseph in April 1886. 'I don't know of course the impression in London, but here at all events the feeling is turned against him because of his double dealing with you in the matter of the "Queen's permission".'(29) This referred to Gladstone's thwarting of Chamberlain's speech explaining his resignation to the House when Gladstone prevented him from dealing with certain aspects of the Home Rule problem on the ground that they were matters requiring the Queen's permission and Chamberlain had not obtained it. 'That old blackguard the G.O.M. is capable of trying to trip you up on any formality,' Lord Randolph Churchill had warned Chamberlain before he made his speech.(30)

Arthur was no respecter of persons and was furthermore extremely apt to be quarrelsome. Thus he wrote of J. T. Bunce, the powerful Editor of the '*Birmingham Daily Post*', and a friend and supporter of Joseph: 'I have just spent an hour with J. T. Bunce – of course he is a poor creature and with all his bullying very timid for the circulation of his paper. But he does not mean to go to Gladstone unless Gladstone maintains an Irish representation at Westminster. I pointed out that your demand was the Irish representation.'(31)

The Kenricks, too, and the rest of 'the Clique' were solidly behind Chamberlain and in this way a body of opinion was soon made to manifest itself which Schnadhorst could not ignore. What he now hoped for was a resolution by the Committee of Two Thousand which would pay lip service to Chamberlain but stress the need for Party unity and make it clear that Chamberlain must not push Gladstone to a point at which that unity was endangered. It now became important to consider tactics and here Chamberlain soon showed himself to be the equal of Schnadhorst. He made it clear that he was not an 'irreconcilable opponent' and was more than willing to compromise over non-essentials provided that Gladstone would show a similarly accommodating spirit. But he was not willing to compromise over the safety of the nation, the future of Ulster, or the sovereignty of the Imperial Parliament. All his energies and ingenuity were now thrown into getting from the Committee of Two Thousand a resolution approving these principles, for he knew that Gladstone would defy such a resolution at his peril.

April 21st was the day fixed for the meeting of the Committee. That evening, Chamberlain addressed them in the Town Hall. For him it was one of the most critical speeches of his life, for he knew that failure to get their support meant the end of his political career. 'Fifteen or sixteen years ago,' he began, 'I was drawn into politics by my interest in social questions and by my desire to promote the welfare of the great majority of the population . . . and I looked to the Liberal Party as the great instrument of progress and reform. . . . And even now I entreat you so to conduct this discussion that when this time of trial is past we may once more unite without embittered memories . . . to carry forward the great work upon which hitherto we have been absolutely unanimous.' Then he went on to ask what had brought about the change in the happy and united state of the Party. 'The whole change,' he declared, 'is due to the force of character, to the determination and to the courage of one illustrious man and, although I regret the object for which these qualities have been displayed, I will say to you that never before has my admiration for them been so sincere and profound.' Then he said slowly and emphatically, 'No I have not changed,' and the great roar of applause which followed immediately showed that he had the meeting with him. Then he went on to review in detail Gladstone's proposals. With great foresight, he reminded his audience of the deadly peril in which Home Rule might involve the whole of Britain in the event of war. 'If that happens where shall we be?' he demanded. 'England may be struggling for its very existence; it may be in the throes of death; but Ireland will be unconcerned.'

Then, like his friend Lord Randolph Churchill, he 'played the orange card' vigorously, demanding that special consideration should be accorded to Ulster. He assured the meeting that his opposition to the Home Rule Bill was 'only conditional' but stressed that the retention of the Irish representatives at Westminster was essential. If Gladstone would show some sign of willingness to agree to an amendment on this vital point, he (Chamberlain) would meet him 'with delight'. He assured them that he was not going to join any 'combination of discordant parties', and concluded, 'You would justly despise and condemn me now if, for the sake of private interests and personal ambition, I were false to my convictions and disregarded what I believe to be the vital interests of my country.'

The vote of 'unabated confidence' in Chamberlain was actually moved by Schnadhorst. It was carried with acclamation. By then it was ten o'clock and Schnadhorst tried hard to get the meeting adjourned. But Chamberlain insisted on the all important vote on Irish policy being taken that night. The resolution was moved from the chair by Dr. Dale for whom the last few weeks had been a time of great heart-searching. Old friend and staunch supporter of Chamberlain though he was, Dale was also a fervent admirer of Gladstone. In his speech, while critical of the proposal to end Irish representation at Westminster, Dale was careful to make it clear that he was not moving a vote of censure on the Liberal leader. 'This great subject should not be treated as if it were a question whether we should follow the leadership of Mr. Chamberlain or of Mr. Gladstone,' he said. 'We need them both . . . The Liberal Party has the right to demand his [Chamberlain's] judgment at such a time as this – his frank and honest judgment. He has given it. He would have been a traitor to us, a traitor to his chief, a traitor to his country, if he had not given it frankly. But the question of leadership is not raised. Mr. Gladstone is leader of the party.'(32)

Gladstone, who knew the enormous influence which Dale wielded in Birmingham, immediately wrote him a highly propitiatory letter in which he congratulated him on 'the masterly manner in which you have confronted a most difficult situation', and added, 'It is only by a temper like yours, conjoined with ability (which in such a case cannot of itself suffice, whatever its amount), that the Irish question can be satisfactorily dealt with.' To this Dale replied:

'Accept my thanks for your generous letter. I am deeply sensible of the honour of receiving a letter from you when there is so much to occupy your time and strength.

I wonder whether it would be very presumptuous for me to state in a few sentences the grounds on which I think it is desirable to keep the Irish members – or some of them – at Westminster.'

Highbury
The Hall, Highbury

The Library, Highbury
Joseph Chamberlain's desk in the Library

He then proceeded at considerable length to develop his arguments on this aspect and concluded with an interesting reference to Chamberlain:

'I need not say how great a grief it is to me that Mr. Chamberlain should have been bound in honour – as I think he was – to leave your Ministry at such a time as this. I have worked with him for eighteen years and, though, of course, I have seen less of him since he became a Minister, our relations, which have often been extremely intimate, have been maintained. As the result of his temperament, education and environment – all so different from your own – he was certain to approach nearly every political question with different assumptions and in a different spirit. . . . But I know that when he entered the Ministry he was drawn to you very strongly and it seems to me a calamity that his future political life should miss the benefit it would derive from . . . your leadership. As yet I have had no talk with him except for a few moments on the platform of the Town Hall last Wednesday. . . . But from my long knowledge of him I can hardly believe that he is irreconcilable.'(34)

Gladstone replied cordially, but without any hint of willingness to yield on the important question of Irish representation.

On the second reading of the Home Rule Bill in June 1886 the Government were defeated, Chamberlain and his Radical followers voting with the Conservatives. In addition to the Radical Unionists, a number of Whig dissentients followed Lord Hartington into the opposition lobby. Gladstone immediately resigned and Parliament was dissolved.

In the ensuing election campaign, Chamberlain, at the very top of his form, rose to great heights of oratory. He addressed a huge meeting in Birmingham Town Hall on the eve of the Poll in the Bordesley Division. Shortly before, Gladstone had referred to his great friend and ally as 'a certain Mr. Jesse Collings . . . who is now engaged in an endeavour to obstruct beneficent legislation'. This slighting reference to one of the most prominent Radicals in the country, a man who, as Gladstone must have known, had done an enormous amount to win over the agricultural labourers to the Liberal cause at the previous election, did not do Gladstone any good or make it any easier for his friends to heal the breach with the Radical Unionists. Referring to this matter in his speech at the Town Hall, Chamberlain said, 'I do not care to dwell upon this. I hope it may be forgotten when the smoke of the battle clears away.' Then in concluding, he turned to the main issue.

'These two islands have always played a great part in the history of the world. Again and again, outnumbered, overmatched, confronted with difficulties and dangers, they have held their own against a world in arms. They have proudly, stubbornly resisted all their enemies and have scattered them like chaff before the wind. And, if in the future, if now you are going to yield to the threat of obstruction and agitation – if you tremble at the thought of responsibility, if you shrink from the duty which is cast upon you, if you are willing to wash your hands of your obligations, if you will desert those who trust to your loyalty and honour, if British courage and pluck are dead within your hearts, if you are going to quail before the dagger of the assassin and the threats (*cries of 'never' and loud and prolonged cheering as the whole audience rose like one man*) – and the threats of conspirators and rebels, then I say indeed the sceptre of dominion will have passed from our grasp, and this great Empire will perish with the loss of the qualities which have hitherto sustained it.'(35)

The result of the General Election which took place in July 1886 was that the Conservatives were returned with 316 seats, the Irish Nationalists 85, the Gladstonian Liberals 191 and the Liberal Unionists 78. Meanwhile, Schnadhorst, now openly a Gladstonian, had succeeded in getting the National Liberal Federation transferred from Birmingham to London, where a resolution giving unqualified support to Gladstone and his Irish policy was duly passed. Chamberlain resigned from the Federation and formed in Birmingham his own National Radical Union, of which Arthur Chamberlain became the secretary.

The Conservatives, though the biggest individual Party, still did not have a clear majority over all the others. In these circumstances, their leader, Lord Salisbury, suggested to Lord Hartington that the latter should become Prime Minister and that he [Salisbury] should take office under him as Foreign Secretary. On Hartington's rejection of this plan Lord Salisbury accepted the Queen's commission to form a Government.

In Chamberlain's mind there was no thought of joining any coalition or of taking office in a purely Conservative administration. At this stage, he still hoped that the Liberal Party would soon be re-united; indeed in his view there was only one obstacle to such re-unity – Gladstone. Shortly after the election, Chamberlain wrote to Jesse Collings.

'If he [Gladstone] retired, all would come right pretty quickly. If he remains, it is no use issuing manifestoes or anything else. . . . I believe we must "lie low" till the inevitable disappearance of the G.O.M. from the scene.' But the G.O.M. was to remain an effective, indeed a dominating figure in British politics for more than eight years.

In the autumn of 1887, Chamberlain was appointed by Lord Salisbury one of three Commissioners to go to the United States and take part in an Arbitration over the Fisheries dispute between that country and Canada. He sailed from Liverpool in the Cunard Liner *Etruria*, on an October day in 1887, little realizing that this visit would transform his whole life.

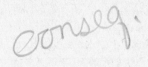

6

The Fisheries Commission and
its Sequel

It was a very rough passage – one of the roughest that the captain of that particular vessel ever remembered, but Chamberlain was a good sailor and, almost alone among the passengers, indulged a hearty appetite throughout. They reached New York on November 7th, 1887, and the British statesman was immediately pounced upon by reporters. He was fully their equal. He soon gained their goodwill because of the good-humoured manner in which he answered their numerous questions and by his obvious understanding of their calling and his willingness to provide them with as much 'copy' as possible. It was not long before he was known among them as 'the reporters' friend'.

Of course, his reputation had gone before him and the authorities, anticipating trouble, had taken elaborate precautions. He was loathed and detested by the Irish Americans, who, like Parnell, looked on him as 'the man who killed Home Rule'. He was, therefore, given police protection and a squad of detectives known as 'Mr. Chamberlain's friends' followed him wherever he went. Before his arrival, rumours had spread about him and he had been depicted in most unflattering colours, and the impression which he made when it was found that he was well-dressed, well-read, witty and charming, was all the more favourable for being so unexpected. About a week after his arrival, he was entertained to dinner by the New York Chamber of Commerce and his speech that evening (the first he had made in America) was a great success. The speaker who introduced him, misquoting Cowper, had referred to an English poem which contained the line '*Commerce* is the golden girdle of the globe'. Chamberlain, in his reply, displayed surprising literary prowess by not only correcting but completing the quotation:

> 'Again the band of commerce was designed
> To associate all the branches of mankind,
> And if a bounteous plenty be the robe,
> Trade is the golden girdle of the globe.'

He enjoyed himself thoroughly in New York where he spent ten days, leaving on November 17th for Washington.

In the capital, also, the arrival of the distinguished English Radical had been awaited with great interest, not unmixed in certain influential quarters with apprehension. A young diplomat at the British Legation whose name was Cecil Spring Rice had written shortly before, 'What does the Government mean by sending Joe here? They might as well send Judas Iscariot as Ambassador to Heaven as Chamberlain to America; and he pegs away as if his name wasn't enough to send them mad here, but he must needs rub it in as deeply as possible.'(1) And again: 'We are all in the expectation of Joseph Chamberlain's arrival. Why did Lord Salisbury send him? What an idea – worthy of Canning himself.' (2) Spring Rice himself was not at the time prejudiced in favour of Chamberlain for he tells, in one of his letters, how a mutual friend had said of the Radical leader that 'he had been brought up to believe in one God and now it had become himself'. But Spring Rice soon changed his views, relating in December that 'Chamberlain is making himself very popular here. He is always on the smile and especially kind to ladies. He has won the hearts of his enemies as far as his pleasantness is concerned, and he has a fine way of talking, short and frank, which is new and surprising to the Americans.'(3)

At Washington Chamberlain and his party took up their quarters at the Arlington Hotel. On the morning of November 19th, Sir Lionel Sackville West, the British Minister, took them over to the State Department, where they met Mr. Bayard, the Secretary of State. It was he who escorted Chamberlain to the White House and introduced him to the President of the United States, who, seated in a revolving chair in his office, chatted with them pleasantly on a number of commonplace topics, but without making any specific reference to their mission.

Grover Cleveland was then fifty years old and in the third year of his first term as President of the United States. Unlike his visitor,

Cleveland had known the meaning of poverty and hardship. His father (a Presbyterian minister) had died when he was only a child, so that, at fifteen, Cleveland had had to leave school to earn his living. After a number of early vicissitudes, he got work in a law office in Buffalo, and ultimately became a member of the Bar in that city. He owed his rapid rise in the political field to a series of fortuitous circumstances and to a reputation for rugged honesty at a time when that quality was conspicuous by its absence in most political quarters in the United States. He and Chamberlain were almost exact contemporaries, Cleveland being, in fact, the older by about eight months. They had both made their way into national politics by way of local government, each having been the Mayor of his own home town. It is significant of the difference in the political systems of their two countries that, whereas Chamberlain had been a national figure for more than ten years, but had still so far only achieved a minor Cabinet appointment, Cleveland, within four years of getting his foot on to the first rung of the political ladder as Mayor of Buffalo, had, without any of Chamberlain's brilliance, become President of the United States.(4) The two men took to one another immediately and continued to get on well together and, during his visit, Chamberlain dined two or three times at the White House.

The first meeting of the conference summoned to deal with the fisheries dispute took place on November 21st in a large room in the State Department. The Plenipotentiaries consisted, on the British side, of Joseph Chamberlain, Sir Charles Tupper and Sir Lionel Sackville West, the American representatives being Messrs. Bayard, Putnam and Angell. The dispute arose out of certain provisions in the Treaties made between the two countries in 1783 and 1818. These treaties restricted the right of American fishermen to operate in Canadian territorial waters. There was, however, scope for considerable argument over the precise nature and extent of these, and particularly whether the 'three-mile limit' was to be taken from a line drawn across the mouths of all creeks and bays or whether it was to follow the coast line round. For a number of years, New England fishermen had been fishing indiscriminately in Canadian territorial waters and a good deal of ill-feeling had been aroused because from time to time the Canadians had seized a number of American vessels. A compromise solution was clearly called for in the form of a new treaty but any such treaty would of course have to be ratified by the United States Senate. On this complicated question the commissioners laboured for nearly three months in a room in the State Department which commanded a view of the Washington Memorial and the River Potomac. The room, besides being large, was well furnished; it had ebony furniture, a polished oak floor and Bokhara rugs. Above the seat occupied by Joseph Chamberlain was a large portrait of J. G. Blaine, Cleveland's opponent in what had been one of the closest and most scurrilously conducted fights for the Presidency in the whole of American history.

That evening (November 21st) Chamberlain, accompanied by Sir William Maycock and a number of others of his party, went to Albaugh's theatre to see Richard Mansfield in *Dr. Jekyll and Mr. Hyde*. Here for the first time Chamberlain saw the young and very lovely First Lady, for the President and Mrs. Cleveland were sitting in a box immediately opposite theirs.(5)

Florence Folsom Cleveland, then twenty-four years old, had been married for rather less than eighteen months. She had been Cleveland's ward and her mother may well have had misgivings when she had learnt, a year or two previously, that her daughter, then still at College, was being courted by the corpulent and middle-aged Grover Cleveland, then Governor of New York. But it had all worked splendidly and President and First Lady were both radiantly happy. And, as far as Cleveland was concerned the marriage had increased not only his happiness but also his popularity with the country, for it was universally agreed that not since Dolly Madison had America had a sweeter or more charming First Lady. Not only did she brighten and enliven the White House; she brightened the President himself. Many had been the satyrical shafts directed by journalists at the clumsiness of the Bachelor President. One of these, in a Chicago newspaper, was called 'The tying of the Tie'.

> 'Now was Sir Grover passing wroth
> A murrain on the man he quoth
>   Who first invented ties.
> Egad, they are a grievous bore
> And tying of them vexeth sore
>   A person of my size.'

No one would have dreamt of applying this kind of criticism to Joseph Chamberlain, whose sartorial elegance was always beyond reproach, but Cleveland's new-found happiness was shortly to have great significance for him also.

On the evening of November 26th, Sir Lionel Sackville West gave a reception in honour of Chamberlain and his party at the headquarters of the British Legation. For some time the parties given by Sir Lionel and his three charming and intelligent daughters had far surpassed in brilliance and splendour those which took place at the White House, where, until very recently, a distinctly sombre atmosphere had prevailed. In view of its importance to Chamberlain's whole future, it is worth quoting a contemporary description of this particular party.

'The reception last night at the British Legation to Mr. Chamberlain and the members of the Fisheries Commission was the most brilliant event of the season. The Legation was aglow with light and extremely elegant in its new adornments and comfortably crowded from ten o'clock to midnight with a gathering of the most representative people in society. Sir Lionel and Miss West stood at the right of the entrance to the drawing-room to receive their guests, presenting each to Mr. Chamberlain and the other gentlemen. The younger Miss West soon led the dancers to the drawing-room, where excellent music, a well-waxed floor, plenty of partners and every other incentive to enjoyment awaited all. Miss West wore a dainty costume of pink satin veiled in tulle, Miss Flora West was in black tulle garlanded with flowers and Miss Amelia West in pink tulle sprayed with white blossoms. Light refreshments were served during the evening. The supper table had a centre of maidenhair ferns, tied crosswise with pink ribbons. Miss West was, as usual, the gentle and thoughtful hostess.'(7)

But it was not any one of the three Miss Wests who excited Chamberlain's admiration. Throughout the evening, he hardly left the side of a tall, demure looking, fair-haired girl, whom he had in fact already met a day or two previously at an afternoon reception given in his honour by a prominent Washington hostess. Mary Endicott, the daughter of Cleveland's Secretary of War, was then twenty-three years of age.

The Endicotts were an old New England family. Their ancestor who had been appointed by an English company to watch over their interests in Massachusetts had left Devonshire in the summer of 1628 and sailed across the Atlantic, later becoming Governor of the colony. The Endicotts had married into some of the leading New England families and they were now looked on as among the leaders of Washington society.

Chamberlain soon found that he had much to talk about to Mary; indeed it was clear to them both from the very beginning that they were affinities. About five years before, Mary had accompanied her parents on a trip to Europe and this had included England where she had met amongst others Lord Herschell, a prominent Liberal and at one time Gladstone's Lord Chancellor. In this way she had learnt a good deal about English politics (including the Home Rule controversy) and, though she had not met Chamberlain himself while in England, she could talk intelligently about his problems. So deeply absorbed did he become in his conversation with her and so charming did he find her that, during the early part of the evening, he hardly left her side and seemed oblivious of everything and everybody else – so much so that Miss West had to call him away to talk to some of the others in the party, which lasted until after midnight.(8)

After it was over, Chamberlain returned to the Arlington Hotel. It was a warm night, exceptionally warm for the time of year, the thermometer registering nearly eighty degrees.(9) Chamberlain threw open his window and lit one of his large black cigars. Now and again he leant out of the window and gazed at the starlit sky and at the dim outline of the Potomac River and the Washington Monument in the distance. He knew it had happened; he knew he was in love again, deeply, violently in love and that neither his career, nor the Fisheries Commission, nor Gladstone, nor Home Rule nor being Prime Minister mattered one iota to him compared with this. In spite of a somewhat hard and cold exterior, he was, at heart, a romantic. But even now, stirred though he undoubtedly was to the very depth of his being, he did not entirely lose his sense of the practical and the fitness of things. His mind was a welter of conflicting emotions. There was more than twenty-five years between them and he would be taking her away from her home and family – even from her own country. Would it all be fair to her? Would she not be far happier married to a young American with the same background as herself? And then there was the question of children. He had lost two wives in childbirth and he did not intend to risk losing a third. But to have no children – would *that* be fair to her?

It would not be surprising if, as he leant out of the window, his thoughts as well as his gaze turned in the direction of the White House. Everything that he had seen and heard tended to confirm that the President's marriage had been a great success and that it had brought them both great happiness. He knew himself to be unusually young looking, whereas Cleveland looked every day of his age. If the forthright, corpulent, middle-aged President could arouse the love of a young girl, why could not he? And on his side he now realized how deeply, how desperately he needed not so much the physical side of marriage as the love and sympathy and companionship it would bring. Only once or twice in his life had he been as miserable as during the few weeks before he left England. He had felt keenly the loss of valued friendships (Morley's in particular) brought about by the line which he had felt compelled to take in politics. He had become very lonely indeed.

Far into the night he sat smoking and thinking of all these things.

During the days and weeks that followed, great demands were made on his time not only for the work of the Commission but also for sight-seeing expeditions in the daytime and almost every night there were dinner-parties and receptions. The day after the party at the Legation, he and his friends drove out to see the Falls of the Potomac and, a few evenings later, the American members of the Commission gave a large dinner-party in his honour, the dinner-table being decorated with orchids, his favourite flower. A few days later, on December 10th, Chamberlain gave a return party at the Arlington. The menu cards which gave details of the very sumptuous eight course dinner had been designed by the host himself. At the top there appeared the 'Star Spangled Banner' and the 'Union Jack' and at the bottom the words 'Blood is thicker than water'. Apart from these official engagements there were numerous private parties to which he was invited, for he was soon in great demand in Washington society. He was taken by a Government boat down the Potomac to Mount Vernon to see the home of George Washington and for innumerable drives through the Virginia countryside and round Washington itself.(10)

In spite of all these activities, however, he managed to see a good deal of Miss Endicott. Her parents invited him to stay with them and it was probably during this short visit that a strong attraction became a certainty, on both sides, that fate intended them for one another. He told some of his friends later that, while in America, he had met 'a Lady by Reynolds or Gainsborough walking out of her frame'. Of course, Mary was by no means without other admirers. But it was noticed with amusement at the time that Chamberlain 'fairly chased all the young men away'. As for Mary, she confessed later that she had found him so gay, so interesting and – to use her own expression – so 'light in hand' that the thought of the age difference of more than twenty-five years never entered her head.

About the middle of December, the conference adjourned for about three weeks. Chamberlain had arranged to devote this interval to a visit to Canada. Accordingly, he travelled to Ottawa, spending Christmas at Government House with the Lansdownes. While in Canada, he made a speech of great significance. Addressing the Board of Trade dinner at the end of December he said:

'I am an Englishman. I am proud of the old country from which I come. I am not unmindful of the glorious traditions attached to it, of those institutions moulded by slow centuries of noble endeavour; but I should think our patriotism was warped and stunted indeed if it did not embrace the Greater Britain beyond the seas – the young and vigorous nations carrying everywhere a knowledge of the English tongue and English love of liberty and law. With these feelings I refuse to speak or to think of the United States as a foreign nation. They are our flesh and blood. . . . It may be that the Federation of Canada may be the lamp lighting our path to the Federation of the British Empire. If it is a dream . . . let us do all in our power to promote it and enlarge the relations and goodwill which ought always to exist between sons of England throughout the world and the old folks at home.'(11)

Returning to Washington early in the New Year, he turned once more with zeal to the work of the Commission and with greater zeal still to the far more delightful business of courtship, with the result that two highly satisfactory Treaties were arranged – the one public, the other private. The public Treaty constituted a sensible compromise. It provided firstly that all bays were to be regarded as part of Canadian territory unless more than ten miles in width and secondly that Americans were to have the right to fish in Canadian territorial waters if and so long as the United States allowed the unrestricted sale in America of fish caught in Canadian waters whether by Canadians or Americans. By the private Treaty, Chamberlain became secretly engaged to Miss Endicott about the end of January. There was, however, this difference between the two Treaties that the one required the consent of the United States Senate and the other did not. The Senate could and did later refuse to ratify the Fisheries Treaty but they had no such power over the Chamberlain–Endicott Treaty. Curiously enough, however, politics did enter into this latter Treaty also. The year 1888 was the last year of Grover Cleveland's first term and so unpopular was Chamberlain with the Irish that it was believed that Cleveland's chances of re-election would be seriously jeopardized if it became known that the daughter of his Secretary of War was engaged to 'the man that killed Home Rule'. So Chamberlain reluctantly agreed to the engagement being postponed until after the election.

At the end of February, Chamberlain left Washington for New York. He had thoroughly enjoyed himself in the American capital. 'I never saw so many bright and pretty women,' he wrote. 'I have taken to dancing and revised my waltzing and polking. . . . All anxious they say to have the secret of perpetual youth. I give them my receipt freely, "No exercise and smoke all day."' He also told his daughter that at one party 'a young lady asked which was the Chief Commissioner. On that distinguished individual being pointed out she said, "Wal I think he's just lovely."' But he said to Spring Rice that he had found dullness rampant everywhere particularly in politics. His view was that 'if you want to be rich and then richer' America was the country to live in, but if you wanted 'real life and not the means of living' England was the place.(12) As to his official work, he said to *The Times* correspondent, 'I am thoroughly satisfied with the result. I do not claim to have gained a victory. No sensible man wishes to obtain a triumph over friends.

I have regarded this difference as one between friends, but what I do claim is that we have arrived at a just and honourable settlement.' A contemporary article in a Washington journal shortly before he left declared that:

'The Hon. Joseph Chamberlain is about to leave Washington and I shall not be contradicted if I say that a very considerable part of Washington is sorry. Never has there been such a diner-out and a giver of dinners in this town as the gentleman who is going back in a few days to his seat in the House of Commons. To him chiefly is it attributable that the present winter has been the greatest season for dinner-parties that Washington has ever known. And they have been gay and enjoyable feats too for the Honourable Joseph has his wits about him and does not ask any odds from the keenest of Yankee combatants in a contest of wit and persiflage, any more than he needs to do in matters of State. The ladies especially will miss him, for rarely have they had such a guest. It may be mentioned, by the way, that Mr. Chamberlain has not been so exclusively devoted to the daughter of a Cabinet officer as some of the correspondents have reported, in evidence of which statement I have only to refer to the fact that he gave a box party to Miss Gwynn, one of the most charming and accomplished young ladies in Washington society.'(13)

It must be stated here that journalistic standards in the United States were certainly not at that time the highest they have ever been. The newspaper men had had a field day over the Cleveland romance and had greatly annoyed the President by following him in swarms to the scene of his honeymoon in Deer Creek Park, Maryland. 'Oh those reporters,' Cleveland would exclaim when he saw a group of them on occasions when he and Mrs. Cleveland were together, 'How I hate them.'(14) Now that Cleveland's love life had ceased to be quite the 'good copy' that it had once been they turned with almost equal enthusiasm to that of Chamberlain and the British statesman, on his side, became almost equally annoyed.

There is no doubt that Chamberlain's new-found happiness had transformed him and, on the whole, he made an excellent impression on the Americans. His appeals for Anglo-American

77

friendship and understanding were made with such warmth and obvious sincerity that they not only convinced but charmed his listeners. More than one contemporary account refers to the fact that he seemed to radiate warmth and happiness. Occasionally, however, there were flashes of the old sarcasm and irony. There was one particular reception which he gave while in Washington in the course of which he relapsed into his old form. It had been intimated to him that a certain Senator would appreciate an invitation. Chamberlain had not much liked what he had seen and heard of the man but he reluctantly agreed. In the course of the evening the Senator rose in his seat and addressed his host as follows:

'Mr Chamberlain, Sir. I'm pleased to know you, Sir, and I am proud to be your guest this evening. But there is one thing, Sir, I should like to say to you right here. Sir, neither I nor my colleagues have ever been able to understand how you came to desert the banner of that great man Mr. Gladstone (pronounced Glad-*stone*). People, Sir, who do that kind of thing in my country are known as "Mugwumps".' This latter term was the one applied to those Republicans who had abandoned their normal party allegiance during the Blaine–Cleveland fight and voted with the Democrats. Chamberlain carefully adjusted his eyeglass, bestowed an icy look upon his guest and then replied with the utmost acidity: 'From the remarks that have fallen from my friend the Senator I can readily understand that he is wholly incapable of appreciating the motives which have influenced me in severing myself from Mr. Gladstone.'(15)

After leaving Washington, Chamberlain spent a few days in Philadelphia and New York, in each of which cities he made speeches which were well received. He embarked on the Cunard liner *Umbria* early in March 1888.

A civic reception awaited him at Liverpool. He got back to Birmingham late on the evening of Saturday, March 10th, where a considerable gathering was present at what he later described as 'this home-coming of mine'. A few days later, he called on the Prime Minister to give him a full report on the result of his mission. Lord Salisbury, who handled Chamberlain with a great deal more understanding and tact than ever Gladstone had, gave him a most cordial welcome and this helped to improve still further the friendly relations between the two men. Chamberlain was particularly pleased when Salisbury told him it was the Queen's wish that he should be offered the Grand Cross of the Bath, in recognition for his services. He said, however, that he did not want any honours for himself but only for the members of his staff, though he added that he would very deeply appreciate an autographed portrait of Her Majesty. The Queen was graciously pleased to accede to his request on both these points. In spite of Lord Salisbury's blandishments, however, he had no intention of joining the Government at that stage; he cared a great deal more for power than he did for office and he felt that he could exert greater influence in favour of the causes which he had at heart by remaining outside the Administration.

At the end of March, Chamberlain was given the Freedom of Birmingham, an event which afforded him deep satisfaction. He was the first citizen to receive this great distinction; there have been twenty-five Freemen since, including Chamberlain's two sons Austen and Neville, the former being made a Freeman in 1926, and the latter in 1932. Thanking the Birmingham Town Council, Chamberlain said in the course of his speech, 'I can never forget that my apprenticeship to public life was served in Birmingham in company with many of those I see around me today and in connection with the municipal work which you are still carrying on.' There was a great banquet in the Town Hall that evening and Chamberlain was able to tell his audience something of the wonderful hospitality he had received in the United States and he spoke in glowing terms of the need for 'perpetual amity and goodwill between all the members of the English-speaking race'. The evening was made particularly memorable by the fact that it was the last occasion on which John Bright spoke in that famous building. He followed Chamberlain and added his own tribute to his Parliamentary colleague. 'I think it is a matter of which Birmingham may be proud', he said 'that my friend here near me, your eminent citizen, has been able by a good fortune which statesmen may envy, and by an exertion of abilities which are peculiar and singular, and not in many cases excelled or equalled – that he has been able to render a service to his country and to the blessed cause of peace which will give him pleasure, I hope, to the last hour of his life.'

The general political position in Birmingham was not, however, from Chamberlain's point of view entirely satisfactory. When Schnadhorst went over openly and whole-heartedly to Gladstone and succeeded in getting the National Liberal Federation moved to London, Chamberlain had formed a new national organization – the National Radical Union – with its Headquarters in Birmingham. His brother, Arthur, became the secretary of this. But Schnadhorst had taken advantage of Chamberlain's absence in the United States to make a determined assault on the Birmingham citadel. His aim had been to capture all the places in the Birmingham Liberal Association, to control the ward committees and to oust the 'Chamberlainites' from the divisional councils, installing Gladstonians in their place. At first, Schnadhorst looked like achieving a considerable success. . . . On his return from America Chamberlain reported that the Gladstonians were 'much more malignant' and that 'last night they secured a large majority of the Liberal Association in my division'. Drastic action on his part was clearly called for and it was soon forthcoming. Chamberlain decided to form a new Birmingham Liberal Association in Birmingham. Like its predecessor, the new organization was founded on the 'caucus' principle, its scope including municipal as well as Parliamentary affairs. By Easter, Chamberlain could declare that it was 'going like wild fire' and, a little later, that he would not be satisfied until he had purged the Council of every Gladstonian. Once more he expressed his feelings and his intentions by the Chamberlain motto '*Je tiens ferme*'. From then on it was clear that, certainly so far as Birmingham was concerned, an unbridgeable gulf divided the Liberals and the Liberal Unionists.

In thus weaning most of his old supporters from the Gladstonian fold, however, Chamberlain had accomplished only half his task; the other, far the more difficult, remained. This was to build up a satisfactory working alliance between the Liberal Unionists and the Conservatives. More and more Chamberlain was becoming convinced that Gladstone was the main danger so far as those broad schemes of social reform which Chamberlain had at heart were concerned. This was not because Gladstone was opposed to these but because, Chamberlain feared, so long as the Liberal leader remained committed to Home Rule they would be pushed into the background of his thinking and his programme.

Joseph Chamberlain by Frank Holl, 1886

A FAMILY GROUP AT HIGHBURY 1889

From the left: Neville Chamberlain, Ethel Chamberlain, Hilda Chamberlain Mrs.
Endicott, Beatrice Chamberlain, Mr. Endicott. Mrs. Endicott. Mrs. Joseph Chamberlain, Ida
Chamberlain

'Why not give our own people a turn?' was one of Chamberlain's most frequent and most telling cries. The difficulty was to convince his supporters that Conservatism was to be preferred to Gladstonianism so long as the latter involved Home Rule. On May 8th, he wrote that:

'In Birmingham a contest of much interest is going on. . . . A Conservative had been offered the vacancy, and was opposed by a Gladstonian with the whole strength of the old Liberal Association. . . . The difficulty is to get the rank and file to vote for a "Tory" . . . The issue is doubtful at present, and we are risking a good deal by thus burning our boats and throwing in our lot with the Conservatives.'

In this particular struggle, Chamberlain was greatly assisted by his two brothers, Arthur and Richard, and by his son Austen. On May 13th, he was able to report that 'we have knocked the enemy into a cocked hat and carried our man. . . . It will be a facer for the Gladstonians and a triumph for the family party, to which Austen contributed last night by a very good speech. . . .'(7) And Arthur's efforts brought a complimentary reference from Lord Randolph Churchill who wrote to Joseph, 'Certainly Schnadhorst is a child, but your brother's letter to Cook was the deciding stratagem of the battle.'(8)

During all this time, Miss Endicott was never far from his thoughts. Week after week, however busy he was, and in spite of the enormous amount of political correspondence that he had to get through, he continued to write long letters to her in which he poured out his love for her and in which he told her everything that was happening to him. These letters, often written long after midnight, show that he thought of everything he saw and almost everyone he met in terms of her. 'I cannot help contrasting the spirit in which I now go into society with what it was formerly. Then it was a distraction and amusement and helped to fill my time, but it had no relation to anything else. Now it is all in relation to you. . . . I catch myself continually thinking how would she like this. . . .'(19) Above all he is continually pre-occupied with what she will think of Highbury. 'I hope that you will be pleased with your new home, he wrote, 'it has quite a new interest for me now that I constantly connect it with you and see you in imagination in every room.' And again 'Did I tell you that I have arranged a rose house for you at Highbury? It is to be sixty feet long and on the best and latest model, but I fear we shall never equal the American roses, as our winter has so little sunshine in comparison. Still we try and grow the American beauties to remind you of the country you have given up for me.' And on his fifty-second birthday he wrote telling her how he had been thinking of the great change since his previous birthday. 'How much I owe you. Then I was much harder, striving to steel myself and to play the game of life till the cards fell from my hands and caring little how soon that time came. Now all this artificial insensibility is broken down: my youth has come back to me. . . .' And five days later, 'I hope that you will keep me to my work. Sometimes I feel as if I should like to give up my public life and devote myself to you, but it would not be right or wise, and, if you find me inclined to give myself entirely to the new happiness of my life, you must recall me to a sense of duty and you must *order* me back to the battlefield. . . . It is extraordinary how civil I am to every American and all because they are countrymen of somebody.'(20) And in the third week in September he again tells her of the change in him which she has already made. 'I do wish,' he told her, 'that . . . I could give myself up entirely to the thought of the future, for like you, I am changed. How much even you can hardly tell. I look back on the last thirteen years as a bad dream and yet during that time everything has gone well for me so that outsiders might think me the happiest man in the world. . . . I have had every comfort that money could give; my public life has been one of striking success and my political influence and reputation have grown constantly. Meanwhile, my children have been all that the most exacting father could desire; my tastes, my ambition and my affections have all been gratified; and yet in spite of all this I have been so lonely, there has never been a time when I would not have accepted a sentence of death as a relief. You have made life once more a glorious and a hopeful thing.'(21)

A few days before writing this letter, Chamberlain had booked his passage to the United States, using for this purpose the name of his Assistant Secretary, Sir Willoughby Maycock. They sailed from Liverpool in the Cunard liner *Aurania* on November 3rd, arriving in New York on November 12th. When they left England, the Americans were just about to vote for a new President. By the time they disembarked the election was over; Grover Cleveland had been beaten by Benjamin Harrison. So the postponement of the marriage had been unnecessary after all.

From New York they went to Washington, where Cleveland was still at the White House and would remain until the following March. But, at the British Legation, an important change had taken place. Sir Lionel Sackville West had been foolish enough to fall into a trap set by the Republicans by replying to an elector who had written for advice as to how to vote, telling his correspondent that on the whole the best choice was Cleveland. The Democrats were furious, feeling that the suggestion that the President was pro-British might lose them thousands of Irish votes. Cleveland insisted on the unfortunate West being recalled.

Joseph Chamberlain and Mary Endicott were married on November 15th, 1888. The ceremony took place in St. John's Church, Washington. The President was there as were also nearly all the members of his Cabinet and several Congressmen and Senators and members of the diplomatic corps. There were a number of American officers present in uniform to honour the bride's father, the Secretary of War. Needless to say, newspaper men were there in great numbers and they made the most of the occasion, reporting, amongst many other details, that the bridegroom wore, at the request of the bride, white violets on his black coat and looked radiant. After the ceremony there was a reception at the Endicotts' house in the course of which Grover Cleveland proposed the health of the bride and bridegroom.(22)

7

Mary Meets the Clan

It had been their intention originally to go for their honeymoon to the West Indies, passing *en route* through South Carolina. But an outbreak of yellow fever in the latter state forced them to alter their plans and they decided, instead, to spend their holiday in Paris and the South of France. They disembarked at Havre early in December and travelled straight to the French capital, for the exploration of which Mary could scarcely have found a better guide than her husband, who already knew it well. Indeed, any misgivings which Mrs. Endicott may have had must soon have been dispelled by the steady stream of ecstatic letters which she got from her daughter. 'If possible you are all more precious to me now than before,' Mary wrote shortly after reaching France. 'This new love only binds the old one all the more closely and makes me realize all that you are to me.' She told her mother that the weather in Paris was 'simply perfect', adding, 'Our first dissipation was a dinner at the Lyon d'or, one of the best restaurants, which is attached to this hotel.' They went more than once to the theatre and lunched at the British Embassy with the Ambassador, Lord Lytton, who found Chamberlain 'very pleasant and interesting' and Mary 'really charming, very young, very pretty, very ladylike and without any American accent or idiom.(1)

From Paris, they went to Cannes, where the weather was even kinder to them. 'This morning,' Mary wrote, 'it was enchanting to come into the parlour and find it filled with . . . roses and violets, the windows wide open and the sun shining on the Mediterranean.'(2) They soon found how much they had in common in the love of fine scenery and the beauties of nature. Mary thought Cannes 'beautifully situated and having much more country about it than Nice it is much more attractive .(3) Through all this delightful country they went for walks and drives together, revelling in the bright sunshine and wonderful views. 'On one side,' as

Mary wrote, 'the Mediterranean dancing in the sunshine and on the other the snow mountains with the peasants trudging along the road with every kind of pack and bundle' and with 'the olive and orange trees and the general atmosphere of southern brilliance' all of which she found 'enchanting'.(4) Mary derived great enjoyment from the shops and made numerous purchases of clothes, jewellery, and pottery and antiques for her new home, her husband almost invariably accompanying her and taking a great interest in her purchases. Once, after they had bought some pottery at a little shop near Cannes, the proprietor followed them out and exclaimed, '*Puisque vous êtes Lord Chamberlain je prendrai la liberté de vous expédier une autre pièce comme cadeau pour Madame.*' On Mary accepting the present, the shopkeeper insisted on them both following him back into the shop where her distinguished husband was asked to sign his name in a book, which he did.(5)

They returned to England in the third week in December 1888, for Joseph was determined that Christmas should be spent at Highbury. 'Austen met us in London,' Mary wrote, 'and I was charmed with him. He is tall and very good-looking . . . and with a most attractive manner. We had a pleasant, quiet dinner together.'(6) She was also delighted with the house in Prince's Gardens where considerable alterations and great preparations had been made in her honour. After spending a few days there, they left London for Birmingham.

It was 4.30 p.m. on a winter evening and already dark when they got to Birmingham. There were not many people about and they drove out to Highbury in a carriage. When they reached Mary's new home they found Beatrice (Chamberlain's eldest daughter) and the rest of the family all at the door and in Mary's words, 'They were lovely in the way they greeted me.'(7) She added:

'Beatrice was especially tender in her greeting and touched me very much by it. The younger girls are very attractive and after we had had some tea they came up to my room and clustered round me while I opened some presents which were awaiting me. The evening passed delightfully and they certainly did their part most fully in making me feel they were glad to welcome me to my new home. I am sure that Beatrice and I will be great friends. She is so bright and her expression is so charming. . . . She has a fine face and is full of feeling which one can see is all the stronger for having a reserved nature. Mr. and Mrs. Arthur Chamberlain and Joe's sister Mrs. James have just been here. They were all very nice and Joe told me to tell you that when they went off after their visit Mrs. Arthur Chamberlain said, "Now, I really do congratulate you".'(8)

Within the next few days she met all Chamberlain's brothers and sisters and their wives and husbands with the exception of Richard and his wife who were away. On New Year's Eve, she wrote to her mother, 'A great, great happiness has come to me for which I am more grateful than I can express.' And a day or two later:

'In the evening [New Year] the family all dined with us – Mr. and Mrs. Arthur Chamberlain, Mr. and Mrs. Walter Chamberlain, Mr. and Mrs. Herbert Chamberlain, Mr. and Mrs. Kenrick, Mr. and Mrs. Ryland, Mrs. James, etc. They were all as nice as could be and enjoyed the evening. Mr. Kenrick took me in and was again very pleasant and Mr. Herbert Chamberlain was on the other side. All the presents were exhibited . . . and a very good show they made. . . . Every day streams of callers arrive. Now I am in a thoroughly bewildered state as to whom I have seen.'(9) And a day or two later, she wrote 'We went to the Walter Chamberlains who had a large dinner in our honour. . . . The hall which is very pretty was decorated with evergreens and the first thing which greeted my sight was the American flag. When we entered the room the music struck up the wedding march which we had heard played exactly seven weeks before in St. John's Church [Washington]. . . . Walter took me in. . . . I wore my green silk dress which turns out most satisfactory. . . . In my hair was Papa's crescent – around my throat the pearl necklace and the opal bracelet bought with my legacy. . . . The shades of the stones harmonized beautifully with the green and yellow of the dress.' (10)

To this letter, Joseph Chamberlain added the following postscript:

'Mary has already captured all my relations, male and female. They say all kinds of nice things about her and what is more they mean them. One of my sisters-in-law told me with tears in her eyes that Mary was as charming as her photographs and yesterday my favourite sister-in-law, Lady Martineau, said, "I do not wonder you fell in love with her. I should have done so myself." They are all of the same mind and you may rest assured that your daughter is already as completely one of the family as she is of the other across the water.'

It may be added to this that the dinner given by the Walter Chamberlains was an eight course meal and one of the menu cards in which the different items were written out in French is still preserved among the Chamberlain papers. It included – *Tortue clair, Filets de Sole a la Monté, épinards au jambon, Ris de veace Sthubert, mouton galloise, canards sauvages, salade de homard, croutes a la Rochelle, Kirsch au Parmesan.*(12)

On the evening of January 8th, 1889, a great reception in honour of Joseph and Mary Chamberlain was given in Birmingham Town Hall. An excellent description of this unique occasion is available from the columns of the *Birmingham Daily Post.*

'Not only all classes but all parties were there. . . . The Town Hall itself – so gaunt and cold at other times – presented unquestionably the most brilliant spectacle it has ever had occasion to afford. The floor of the hall had the resemblance of a great drawing-room. Its walls were brightened with mirrors and sideboards and draped with a blue fabric and oriental curtains and it was furnished not only . . . as is customary on such occasions beneath the great gallery but over the whole floor space, large and numerous rugs softening the footfall. In the corners below and above and across the whole front of the orchestra . . . there was a charming arrangement of palms and poinsettias . . . and of cyclamens, marguerites . . . lilies of the valley and ericas. Some choice orchids set off the narrow ledge which runs along the top of the orchestra entablature.'(13)

The two chief guests were accompanied by all Joseph's children – Beatrice, Austen, Neville, Ida, Hilda and Ethel. As they entered the hall, the organ pealed forth 'Hail Columbia'. The newspaper reported that Mary 'was dressed with much simplicity and taste in a robe of pale pink corded silk with a plain bodice and festooned skirt. The dress was set off with a bow of satin ribbon of the same colour ... for ornaments she wore, upon a close coiffure, a crescent of sapphires and diamonds, upon the left breast a diamond star and round the neck a string of diamonds,' and that 'the applause brought a singularly pleasing smile' to her, appearing as she did to be 'armed against the universal scrutiny by her own sense of admiration for the bright scene before her'.(14) In the speech in which he expressed his own and Mary's gratitude for the welcoming addresses and presentations, Chamberlain said:

'While in America I was fortunate enough to make two Treaties. I had my secret document as well as the public document with which you are all familiar, and I am glad to say that even the august Senate of the United States had nothing to say to my private negotiations which you have ratified tonight by your presents and proceedings. ... I have done all in my power to promote union between the two countries. ... I know she [Mary] is prepared to take up her life among us, in the country of her adoption, in all its fullness, and that she will say like Ruth of old "Thy people shall be my people." [*Loud cheers*]. 'In America ... it is almost unheard of that any man should sit either for the House of Representatives or the Senate except as representing the district in which he resides. Here the contrary rule has almost prevailed ... but I can only say that in my own case all the pleasure that I have ever felt in political life, all the strength that has been given me to pursue it, have been increased by the sense which has never failed me that I have always had behind me the support of the people who have known me best, who have made me what I am, and whose support has never failed me in every time of difficulty and has laid me under an obligation which I am only too anxious to acknowledge and which I can never adequately repay.'

Then he spoke of the cordiality and kindness of Birmingham people and added:

'I have been touched and gratified by a note which I received from a Birmingham man in the wilds of Canada who sent me his congratulations and good wishes, and a little token of regard and gratitude in the shape of a sample of his skill. I am prouder of it – of having excited this feeling amongst my fellow-towns-men – than I am of anything else in my public life.'(15)

It is now time to take a rather closer look at the family of which Mary had now become a member. The 'Chamberlain Clan' in Birmingham was then at its zenith numerically for the time was not far distant when many of them would leave for other parts of the country, but, at that particular time, not only all Joseph's children but his three married sisters and three of his brothers and their families were all based on Birmingham. Richard had just left to live in London, having recently been elected Member of Parliament for Islington.

All the Chamberlain brothers were capable business men. Walter and Herbert had joined Joseph in the screw business of Chamberlain and Nettlefold, while Richard and Arthur had joined their father in the brassfounding business of Smith and Chamberlain. In due course both these businesses were sold and each of the brothers found themselves in possession of a substantial fortune, but none of them used this as an opportunity to live a luxurious and idle life. Herbert and Walter, the two youngest, had gone round the world together and in the course of their travels had met and married two very attractive Canadian girls. Herbert's wife, Lilian, whose father was a certain Col. Williams, was politically minded and later became the President of the Birmingham Women's Liberal Unionist League. The Herbert and Walter Chamberlains now lived close to one another in Edgbaston, the Herberts at Penrhyn and the Walters at Southbourne in Augustus Road, which had been Joseph's home before he built Highbury. Later, Walter moved from Birmingham, to live first at Ledbury in Herefordshire and later at Cobham in Surrey. Richard had combined business activities with a highly successful municipal career. He was an extremely popular Lord Mayor of Birmingham, and held that office in 1880, the year in which his brother Joseph became President of the Board of Trade and in which also the public memorial to Joseph, in the form of the fountain in Chamberlain Square, was erected. When this memorial was formally inaugurated on October 26th, 1880, Richard, as Mayor, gave a banquet in honour of Joseph at the Town Hall.

Besides his work on the Town Council, Richard had had a

number of business interests and he had also served the community well and faithfully in other ways. He had been Deputy Bailiff of the Grammar School Board; he also took a keen interest in the Birmingham Art Gallery and School of Art, securing for the former gifts in money and kind amounting to £100,000. He had been President of the Birmingham Sunday Lecture Society and the Footpaths and Open Spaces Preservation Society. While Mayor, he founded the Council House Library and provided for free organ recitals in the Town Hall. Like Joseph, Richard had lost his first wife and later remarried.(16) He remained a member of the Birmingham Council for two or three years after ceasing to be Lord Mayor and then resigned on being elected Member of Parliament for Islington. In the House, he supported his brother as a Liberal Unionist. He had a wife who was very keen on singing and for her benefit he bought an Opera House in Brussels, but this venture was not a great success.

Walter, the youngest of the brothers, was a man of considerable business ability and acumen. He became chairman of a number of famous companies – Guest, Keen and Nettlefold, Averys Ltd., the Soho Trust and the Fore Street Warehouse – and was also a director of a number of others. But he never took a great deal of interest in politics. He was undoubtedly a brilliant man with great charm and an excellent conversationalist. He was fond of travel and at one time owned an island in the South Seas. He was always fascinated by new inventions and later on became the owner of some of the earliest cars and also of one of the first X-ray sets, with which latter he practised on his butler in the cellar. He collected very fine Chelsea, Worcester and Sevres china, grew orchids and had a small zoo. He was extremely fond of hunting.(17)

The one of all his brothers who was closest to and whose activities had the greatest effect on Joseph was undoubtedly Arthur, who had married Louisa Kenrick, the twin sister of Joseph's second wife. They lived at Moor Green Hall and had a family of two sons and seven daughters. After the sale of Smith and Chamberlain, Arthur entered into partnership with a man called Hookham in a firm which specialized in electrical engineering, including the provision of electric lighting, dynamos and accessories. He had never been trained as an electrical engineer but it was one of his characteristics that he could rapidly master the essentials of a new business and pick up the necessary technical knowledge as he went along; to do so was one of his great delights. He hated waste and always swore to eliminate it from any business with which he was associated.(18)

Just about the time that Joseph Chamberlain's life was being transformed by his courtship of, and marriage to Mary Endicott, an important transformation was about to take place in the business life of his brother. The new venture upon which Arthur was now about to enter was of such importance in its ultimate effects, not only on Arthur himself but also on Joseph and his two sons as well as on Birmingham and the country as a whole, that the events which led up to it are worthy of a brief examination.

Around the same time as Joseph Chamberlain, there arrived in Birmingham a young Scotsman called George Kynoch, who had, however, none of Chamberlain's advantages, being of humble origin, the son of a journeyman tailor and entirely without money or influence or connections of any kind. His first employment in Birmingham was that of a bank clerk, but he soon found that this did not offer sufficient scope for his venturesome spirit and he left the bank in favour of a small business in Whittall Street, Birmingham, whose chief product was 'percussion caps', the forerunner of the modern cartridge. Kynoch knew nothing about gunpowder or explosives at the time but he had intelligence, shrewdness, plausibility and an intense desire to get on. Soon he was in charge not only of the premises in Whittall Street, but of a large factory and powder magazine constructed under licence from the West Bromwich magistrates. He took over this factory and enlarged it into a business of his own called Kynoch & Co. He obtained valuable contracts for cartridges from the British War Office and the Turkish Government and the business prospered greatly. By the time he was a little over forty, Kynoch was a wealthy man, owning a large factory, buildings and machinery and with a personal fortune estimated to have then amounted to between £60,000 and £80,000. Unfortunately, however, he soon overreached himself. He acquired a large mansion called Hamstead Hall at Handsworth, which stood in a park of about three hundred acres, and proceeded to furnish and decorate it with great elegance and luxury. Here he set himself up as a country squire, throwing open his house and grounds in aid of the Aston Conservative

Association and other bodies, which he thought worthy of support. He contributed liberally to local charities, travelled extensively and luxuriously and entered Parliament. All these activities made considerable inroads into his time and money at the expense of the business, which soon needed further finance. In order to raise this, Kynoch, in the year 1884, sold the business to a company called George Kynoch & Co. The company acquired the factory, plant, machinery, stock and raw materials formerly owned by Kynoch who, in return, got £70,000 in cash and 4,000 shares of £10 each.(19)

There was to be a board of six directors of whom the chairman was a certain Viscount Bury and Kynoch was to be the managing director; the other directors all had civil or military titles, but none of them knew anything about that or any other business. The company made a profit in its first year's trading but after that the situation started to deteriorate rapidly and the bank overdraft assumed alarming proportions. Methods of supervision were defective and a number of contracts were cancelled because the company's cartridges were not up to standard. Meanwhile Kynoch himself had acquired a rolling mill from which the company was caused to buy all its metal at prices fixed by himself and agencies in South Africa which were given the exclusive right to handle the company's products in that area on a commission basis. (20) It was not long before a number of the shareholders became disturbed by what they heard was happening to their investment. Early in the year 1888 they decided to take action.(26) An avenging angel was at hand.

Arthur Chamberlain, ascetic and serious looking, and permeated through and through with a deep and abiding integrity, was the exact opposite in every respect to George Kynoch. Someone once said of the leading Unitarian families that if they only believed in one God they paid 100 per cent. To none of them could this be applied with greater accuracy than to Arthur Chamberlain, who also believed in and obeyed implicitly Dr. Dale's commandment that 'Thou shalt always prepare a balance sheet'. As a result, he had a high reputation in business circles and when he started to campaign vigorously for a change of management at Kynochs he received a great deal of support. He became a pioneer in the vindication of shareholders' rights and the 'taking over' of inefficiently run companies. He was voted on to the board in the year 1888 and the following year became the chairman. Kynoch, Lord Bury and two of their co-directors were persuaded to resign. Later Arthur became the chairman of Tubes Ltd., the forerunner of the present Tube Investments. He was also a pioneer of the investment trust movement for he founded the Birmingham Trust of which he became the chairman.

It was a serious position with which Arthur Chamberlain was confronted when he took control of Kynochs – a trading loss of £18,000, and a bank overdraft of more than £50,000 and a stock list which was misleading in the extreme. Furthermore, many large contracts had been cancelled because of the poor quality of the goods, this, in turn, being due to faulty or non-existent supervision. The company had acquired a reputation for poor workmanship, dismissals had been rampant and morale in the factory was very low. Moreover, there had recently been a diversification of the company's business into expensive sidelines, all of which were losing money,(22) but Arthur Chamberlain started to pull the business round with calmness, imperturbability and quiet efficiency. He cut out the sidelines and concentrated on the company's main business, that of military ammunition and cartridges; this he decided to expand vigorously. Hitherto, the company had been dependent for its raw material on metal supplied from a mill owned by Kynoch and run by him entirely for his own benefit. On Arthur Chamberlain's advice, the company acquired this mill and also another and larger one so that, as he told shareholders, 'With these two mills under their control your directors are able not only to ensure a regular supply of metal at a fair price, but also generally to improve the quality of the rolling'.(23) A new factory, fresh plant for the manufacture of ·303 ammunition and a fuse-making department were all added before the end of the year. Furthermore, the inspection department was completely reorganized and eighty-five additional acres of land acquired at Witton and Streetly, the purpose of this acquisition being to set up improved magazines and adequate proof ranges.(24)

It was inevitable that Arthur should discuss the business with Joseph and tell his brother something of his plans for the future. The two were at that time fast friends, they went away together for fishing holidays and were frequent visitors at each other's houses, for though they were both obstinate and often differed profoundly they thoroughly enjoyed each other's company for both were excellent conversationalists. Often Joseph's children had been kept awake at night by the roars of laughter which would follow the witticisms of 'Uncle Arthur' in the room below.(25)

8

Sisal

By the year 1890, all but two of Joseph Chamberlain's children were grown up. The eldest, Beatrice, was actually two years older than Mary. The next in order of age was Austen. He was then twenty-five and the apple of his father's eye. By becoming adopted as Liberal Candidate for Hawick, Austen had already got his feet on to the first rung of that political ladder up which he was to climb a long way, without, however, getting right to the top.

Austen had had a very different kind of education to his father. A good preparatory school had been followed by Rugby, where his House Master was a certain Mr. Lee Warner, a man to whom Austen remained devoted throughout his life. Joseph Chamberlain had written to Lee Warner, 'I have never been anxious that he [Austen] should distinguish himself exceptionally at school and college but have always looked to general character and intelligence as the points of real importance.' But, on learning that Austen had only escaped a flogging from the Headmaster through the personal intervention of Lee Warner, Chamberlain wrote to the latter:

'I know that this brutal punishment is still in vogue at our public schools, after having almost disappeared from the army and navy and being reserved in our gaols for outrages of a particularly savage character, but it never entered my head that it would be applied for any but the worst offences, as for lying, stealing or indecency. If it is to be incurred for a simple neglect of rules, a mere thoughtless boy's lark, I cannot think of such punishment without disgust and indignation. It is this kind of treatment which destroys all sense of proportion in a boy's notion of offences, making gross immorality no worse than some slight breach of discipline while the ready appeal to physical force is a mental preparation for the rowdy jingoism which is the characteristic of many educated middle-class Englishmen. I do not intend to have my son flogged for trivial offences and I must therefore beg of you if unfortunately he should be sentenced to such a punishment by the Headmaster to let me know in order that I may at once remove him from the school.'(2)

Austen, however, was never again sentenced to a flogging but, on the contrary, did well at Rugby, becoming Head of his House and playing for it at football. When he left, Lee Warner wrote to his father:

'I never parted from a boy with greater reluctance; he has been more and more a power for good in my House ever since he first came. He has always been educating himself intellectually as much as any master could and withal he has been so companionable personally that I shall feel his going very much.'(3)

From Rugby, Austen went to Trinity College, Cambridge, where he remained for three years, taking his degree in June 1885. After this he spent nearly two years in France and Germany, meeting several distinguished politicians in both countries including Clemenceau, Ribot and Bismarck. It was during this time in France and Germany that Austen laid the foundation of that deep interest in and knowledge of foreign affairs which were his through life. He had an abiding love for France, for her people and for all things French, while his time in Germany implanted in him, on the whole, a dislike for and a distrust of the people of that country. He attended Treitschke's lectures and wrote of this experience:

'Treitsche has opened to me a new side of the German character – a narrow-minded, proud, intolerant Prussian chauvinism. . . . If you preach to the youth of a country that they stand on a higher step of creation to all other nations they are only too ready to believe it. . . . I fear my generation of Germans, and those a little younger, will be far more high-handed and will presume far more on the victories of '66 and '70 than those who won them. . . . They are likely to find a friend in Prince William, who is said to be thirsting for warlike distinction and is the idol of the military party and the youth.'(4)

Neville, the younger son, loathed Rugby, to which he was sent after a preparatory school at Southport. His dislike was partly due to the fact that he was bullied by an older boy who had been flogged by Austen while the latter was the Head of the House. Evidently Joseph's interdict did not prevent Austen from exercising the right of chastisement when he himself reached a position of authority and this fact may have aroused the resentment of the bully who was resolved to revenge himself on the younger brother when the older was safely out of the way. Neville had probably felt the loss of his mother more keenly than Austen had felt the loss of his, for Florence had been a second mother to Austen, whereas Neville had had to rely during his most impressionable and formative years on 'Aunt Clara', his father's younger sister, and she had not always been very good at supplying either. Once, when he returned from Rugby, where he had been thoroughly miserable and flung himself into her arms, all she said was, 'Neville, your cap's crooked.'(5)

But Neville's childhood and early youth were by no means universally unhappy. He was already developing those inner resources and that delight in music and in wild nature which were to be such a solace and source of strength to him through life. While at Rugby he joined the Natural History Society, became co-curator of the *vivarium*, keeper of the entomological album, and made a list of the *lepidoptera* which he had noticed in the area and presented them to the Society. In the summer he managed occasionally to escape from cricket, which he disliked, and to go off into the country with one of the few boys at Rugby with whom he really made friends. 'He seemed to know by instinct,' wrote Sir Leslie Scott later, 'just which bush we ought to beat on a woodland path to make a rare moth fly out.'(16) Austen too was at all times intensely appreciative of the beauties of nature and his knowledge of wild flowers was almost as great as Neville's of birds. Flowers were a passion with Austen throughout his life.

While at Rugby, Austen was a shining light in the school debating society but, though he joined it, nothing would induce Neville to take part in the debates. 'I don't take any interest in politics and never shall,' he said to another boy and, on being asked why not, he replied, 'You don't know what our house is like for days before my father makes one of his big speeches. Everybody has to be quiet and even at meals conversation is subdued.' Then he added, 'Wretched man, he never knows what he

is going to say'.(7) But Neville did take part in at least one of the
debates before he left Rugby. Years later, Joseph, speaking of his
two sons, said that Neville was the abler and that if he could be
persuaded to enter Parliament he would not be surprised if one
day he became Prime Minister.(8)

Unlike Austen, Neville did not go to the University or on to the
Continent on leaving Rugby. His father intended that he should go
into business and he had been sent to Mason's College, Birmingham, there to learn something of science, metallurgy and engineering. He was just about to leave the college and start with a firm
of Chartered Accountants in Birmingham when his father returned from his second visit to the United States; Neville had been
attending the college for about two years, living all the time at
home.

Neville spent a great deal more of his youth and early manhood
in Birmingham than did Austen and the city's influence on Neville
was correspondingly greater, though Austen retained through
life a deep affection for and pride in the town of his birth. Neville
did not make as many outside friendships as did Austen during
this period and one reason for this was the self-sufficiency of the
'Chamberlain clan'. Two of Neville's uncles had a particularly
strong influence on him at this time. They were George Kenrick
and Arthur Chamberlain. Both were men of great public spirit.

Arthur had become a member of Birmingham Town Council in
1872, was a member and staunch supporter of the Education
League from its inception and had become secretary of the National
Radical Union in 1886. He also played a leading part in starting
the Birmingham Hospital for Women. He was an extremely
zealous temperance reformer and had been made Chairman of the
Licensing Committee of the Birmingham City Council and in the
year 1885 had unsuccessfully contested the Evesham division of
Worcestershire in the Liberal interest.

Joseph Chamberlain was a shareholder in Kynochs and no
doubt Arthur reassured him about the long-term prospects for his
investment. Joseph's general financial position had, however, deteriorated considerably within the last year or two because he had
invested heavily in South American securities which had turned
out very badly. But a worse financial misfortune still was in store
for him.

Sisal

In the early autumn of 1890, Joseph and Mary returned to the United States to pay a visit to the latter's parents. On this occasion they were accompanied by Austen and, after staying for a short time in New England, they all three decided to go on to Canada and it was while they were in Montreal that they met Sir Ambrose Shea, who was staying in the same hotel. Shea at that time was the Governor of the Bahamas, but before entering the Colonial service he had been in business and Chamberlain took to him immediately. Into Joseph Chamberlain's attentive and receptive ears, Sir Ambrose poured forth the story of sisal, a plant which grew dark green leaves whose fibrous content could, in the view of Sir Ambrose, be used to make excellent rope. Furthermore, Shea explained, the soil and climate of the Bahamas were both ideally suited to the growth of sisal and it was Shea's great dream to make of sisal-growing a new industry for the colony over which he then presided, bringing untold wealth to its poverty stricken inhabitants as well as to anyone who was fortunate enough to get in on the ground floor of such a wonderful investment. A substantial outlay was necessary, however, in order to ensure success.

Joseph Chamberlain was very interested but before he committed himself he decided to do two things. The first was to have a thorough investigation carried out of conditions on the spot; the second was to consult Arthur. As his investigators he chose his two sons.

So Austen telegraphed to Neville telling him to meet him in New York on urgent business, while Joseph returned to England from Canada. Austen and Neville arrived in Nassau on November 10th, 1890. Six weeks later, Joseph received a letter from Austen telling him that 'The capital required for the cultivation of one thousand acres is £12,000 and the cost per ton of the fibre will be £11 10s. od. Assuming £20 as the selling price of the fibre, this leaves a profit of £8 10s. od. per ton after all expenses including 7½ per cent on capital have been paid – that is a profit of £8,500 on a capital of £12,000 or over 70 per cent. . . . These results are so fabulously good that they appear impossible. . . . If we are right Bahama hemp cultivation is nearly as good as the Governor thinks it.'(9)

Meanwhile Joseph had consulted Arthur who immediately and unhesitatingly advised against the project. But the letters which

Joseph had received and continued to receive from his two sons had fired him with enthusiasm. Furthermore, he was already starting to turn his eyes towards the Empire and the prospect of contributing substantially to one of the outposts of that Empire while at the same time re-habilitating his own fortune was attractive. Added to all this was the importance of finding a business opening for Neville. He recalled both his sons for consultation and they arrived back in January 1891. Lengthy discussions were held at Highbury and Joseph made up his mind to go into the venture. By April, Neville had arrived back in the Bahamas.

In the nature of things it would clearly be months if not years before any idea of the likely financial results could be obtained for land had not only to be acquired but cleared and planted. At first, things seemed to be going quite well. After some extremely arduous prospecting, Neville acquired a tract of some ten thousand acres on Andros Island near to Mastic Point, with an option on another ten thousand. He described this site as the best on the island.

He toiled unremittingly. For the first three months, he lived under extremely primitive conditions in a native hut, starting work at five o'clock every morning and never finishing before four. There was no society whatever in the district; apart from his overseer the nearest white man was an eccentric Scotsman who lived nearly half a day's journey away. Neville's life consisted of work all day and writing letters and reading books all evening. For nearly five years, he hardly saw anyone except his overseer and negro workmen. To these latter he was extremely good, attending to their wants and comfort in every way that he could. He was greatly beloved by the negro population on the island in consequence. In due time he acquired a house with a lovely view and a staff of black servants who cooked and looked after him. His garden soon became a real show, with vincas, roses and hibiscus, gloxinia and golden rod and he established a large tank with water orchids in it; his kitchen garden was replete with a wide variety of vegetables and fruit. Many of the seeds had come from Highbury. In September, his father wrote to him, 'I feel that this experience, whatever its ultimate result on our fortunes, will have had a beneficial and formative effect on your character. At times, in spite of all the hardships and annoyances you have to bear, I am inclined to envy you the opportunity you are having to show your manhood.'(10)

Neville sent his father regular fortnightly reports of his progress and the general picture which these gave was, at first, fairly satisfactory. By the end of the first year more than a thousand acres had been cut and planted. A number of important questions still remained unanswered, however. These included the likely yield per acre, the quality and marketability of the finished product and the likely trend of future prices. None of these questions had received a satisfactory answer when, in the autumn of 1893, Joseph Chamberlain paid his first visit to the island.

By that time his total commitment amounted to about £13,000. There certainly had not so far been anything like the return on capital which Austen had originally forecast and a very hard look at the economics of the business by the man whose money was involved was clearly called for. Instead of this, Joseph cast caution to the winds. During most of the time that he was in the Bahamas he was unwell and compelled to remain indoors nearly every day. Yet he authorized the construction at very great cost of a railway track across the territory, a new baling machine, the building of new roads, the blasting away of an entire hillside to clear a way for the roads and the track, the erection of further buildings and the purchase of more machinery and plant. Neville was told to go to Cuba and inspect the sugar plantations in order to get further ideas.(11)

The Andros Fibre Company, as the Chamberlain project had now become, soon became the surprise and pride of the Bahamas. From far and wide, drawn by what they had heard, people came to see it. These visitors were amazed by what they saw – new houses springing up everywhere, fine roads in all directions, a railway being laid down seven miles into the forest, and a long jetty stretching out into the deep water. A number of missionaries also came, greatly to Neville's irritation. 'I wish all the reverends in the Bahamas were at the bottom of the sea,' he wrote. There were exceptions, however, for at least one clergyman found him extremely polite and hospitable and well disposed towards the Church.

It was not long before signs of trouble started to appear. The ground was infested with weeds and the clearance of these was a great deal more costly than had been anticipated. At no time did the crop come up to expectation either in quality or quantity. Here and there quite good plants were grown, in spots where the soil was particularly favourable. But there were vast areas in which nothing that Neville and his workmen could do seemed to result in a really satisfactory product. Finally, to crown all these difficulties, that relatively small proportion of the total growth which was saleable had to be unloaded on to a continually falling market. Neville's letters became increasingly despondent. Then, in December 1896, a disastrous fire broke out and destroyed the new baling shed and most of the stored fibre. Samples of what was left were rejected by the New York buyers as being too stiff and harsh. About the end of April 1896, Neville, after making a thorough survey of the whole area, came finally to the conclusion that the enterprise could not possibly be made to pay. He told his father that he was bitterly disappointed and blamed himself entirely for his want of judgement and for not having, as the man on the spot, detected the signs of trouble earlier.(12)

Neville was called back to England and a family conclave took place; Joseph and Austen had already told Neville that they were just as much to blame as he was and that he must not take it all too much to heart. But it was clear that Joseph could not possibly afford to go on losing money on the present scale. There being no chance at all of a profit, only one decision was possible and that was to liquidate the enterprise. In the result, Joseph Chamberlain lost about £50,000.(13) This, coming on the top of his South American losses, was serious. But it was not calamitous. He still had a fortune left which was substantial for those days. He would have to draw in his horns and live quietly but he would still be in a position to gratify all or almost all his tastes which, with the possible exception of orchid growing, were fairly simple. He never indulged in vain recriminations but made up his mind that he would be satisfied with what he had got left. 'It will last my time,' he would say.(14)

9

The Cry of 'Judas' and the Downfall of Parnell

It was inevitable that his marriage should touch Joseph Chamberlain's life at every point. It affected profoundly his relations with his family. One of the truest and most touching things he ever said about Mary was that 'she brought my children near to me'. As, year by year, they saw the happiness she had brought to him and the changes she made in him, so more and more his children came to appreciate her. This applied particularly to Austen who both liked and admired her and with whom these feelings grew stronger as the years went by, as his numerous letters to her bear eloquent witness. And when Austen himself, after years of loneliness, found a similar happiness he appreciated Mary even more. Years later, Austen wrote to his own wife:

'As I read the second volume of Father's life,(1) I feel all the time how you have done for me what Mary did for Father. You have made life worth living and made of me a new man. I had of course never suffered the agony that Father had twice, but I suffered deeply in '95 and had come to feel that all that was best in life was somehow forbidden or refused to me and that as the years passed I was doomed to become ever more lonely. I can never, never give you back a tithe of what you have given to me.'(2)

His marriage also profoundly affected Joseph's political future. His new-found happiness both mellowed and softened him and gave him a steadier and more balanced approach to the whole political scene. But Mary affected his future in more subtle ways still. From the moment that he broke with Gladstone, the Conservatives had of course welcomed him as an ally. But socially a great gulf divided him both from the leaders and the rank and file of the Conservative Party. And the Whigs also never regarded the Chamberlains as their social equals. Two of Joseph's brothers, on applying for membership of a London Club, were 'blackballed' as a result of Whig opposition to them.(3)

Already before he met Mary, a change had started to take place in the attitude of the aristocracy towards Joseph Chamberlain. By some of them he was beginning not only to be tolerated but actually to be liked. Amongst the first to take him up had been Lord and Lady Jersey. He was invited to their house in Great Stanhope Street in 1886 and both the family and his fellow-guests seem to have enjoyed his company, though the butler thoroughly disapproved. In June 1887 and again a year later he went to stay at Osterley Park, the Jerseys' country house. On both occasions he was accompanied by Beatrice, and his fellow-guests on the second visit included Lady Lathom and her daughter, George Curzon, Lord and Lady Kintor, Sir John Sterling Maxwell and Prince Esterhazy. Some of them were amused to find Chamberlain one afternoon rowing on the lake with a tall hat on his head and a pipe in his mouth.(4) He soon showed that he could relax completely and thoroughly enjoy himself in the company of people like this. Thus, in the course of another of these country house parties he was discovered in the long gallery joining in a game which involved him in trying to balance a poker on the end of his nose. And Sir Edward Hamilton described in his diary a party given by the Duchess of Manchester in July 1887 when Chamberlain, having absented himself from the dancing floor, was to be found, complete with eye glass and orchid, playing baccarat with Lord Randolph Churchill and the Prince of Wales.(5)

Other friends of those early days were the Francis Jeunes (later Lord and Lady St. Helier) and Lady Dorothy Neville. Lady Dorothy found him 'gifted with a strong sense of humour' which made him 'a most delightful friend'. Amongst the many interesting things which he told her in the course of their long friendship was the fact that he did not care for clubs at all because 'the bores that infest them spoil his temper'.(6) He once told Sir Cecil Spring Rice that he had come to the conclusion when he got to know them that the so-called 'upper classes' were a very different set of individuals from the 'idle, selfish, self-indulgent and generally pernicious people whom he had denounced'. Still there were formidable barriers between himself and these people which his resignation from Gladstone's Government might not by itself have cleared away.

Mary helped greatly to remove these barriers. She was American and the aristocracy took to her from the start, for she represented something quite new to them. Furthermore, she was intelligent, quiet, demure and utterly without 'push' or ostentation in any shape or form. Socially she was an immediate and enormous success and invitations were soon being showered on the Chamberlains by the Whig and Tory aristocracy to their country houses and to parties in London. Mary's intense and unaffected interest and delight in these great houses made her all the more acceptable as a guest, and were also a source of great pleasure to Joseph. 'One expects to see Lords and Ladies in ruffs and hoops descend from their walls and take up their old lives,' she wrote from Hardwick Hall, whither they had gone to stay with the Hartingtons. 'We arrived just before a very late dinner. The other guests were the Duchess of Manchester, Lady Charles Beresford, Mr. and Mrs. Sassoon and Mr. Calcraft, at present head of the Board of Trade. . . . Lord Hartington took me in to dinner. . . . I was taken up to bed through the long gallery hung with tapestry.' (7) She was presented to the Queen who noted in her journal that 'Mrs. Chamberlain is very pretty and young-looking and is very lady-like with a nice, frank open manner'.(8) And, five years later, after meeting her again, Her Majesty noted that 'Mrs. Chamberlain looked lovely and was as charming as ever'.(9)

It was not long before Mary's letters to her mother started to bristle with the news of the titled people by whom she was entertained or whom she and Joseph themselves had entertained at Highbury.(10)

Other threads were drawing Chamberlain ever closer to the Conservatives during the years which followed his return from the United States. One was Gladstonian obstinacy and another was the surprisingly sensible and progressive attitude of the Conservative leaders and their readiness to listen to his ideas for reform and social amelioration. Joseph Chamberlain was resolved that so long as Gladstone remained committed to Irish Home Rule the Conservatives must be kept in power at all cost. So he concentrated on persuading the Government to adopt some of the measures which were dearest to his heart and he was surprised and pleased at the relative ease with which he was able to do so. Thanks largely to him, Free Education and County Councils were both established during this period – that of Lord Salisbury's second Government.

Chamberlain's former colleagues and associates of the Liberal Party had watched his political gravitation to the right with interest and some of them with a good deal of malevolence. Both their resentment and their opportunities for invective were increased by some of his own speeches. He had become much less acid and more human, it is true, but he still could not resist the temptation to indulge in the occasional sharp thrust of the rapier.

An opportunity occurred in the course of the debate on the subject of the Royal Grants in the summer of 1889. 'I say that the sum taken by the Queen is reasonable and even moderate,' he declared. 'We are told that the People – the People with a capital "P" [*laughter*] – think it exorbitant. We are told this by hon. members who profess on all occasions to speak for the People with a capital "P".... These hon. members tell us it is a shameful thing to fawn upon a monarch. So it is; but it is a much more shameful thing to truckle to a multitude.'(11) Again, having discovered that certain of the Irish members were paid from a fund collected by Parnell in America, he suggested that these were payments which owed their origin at least partly to subscriptions from servant girls in the United States and then he went on to say that at least he and his Radical Unionist colleagues were allied with English gentlemen and not, like the Gladstonians, with the members of a 'kept Party'. These were not very wise things for him to say and of course his enemies seized on them. Not only by the Irish but by the Gladstonians as well the cry of 'Judas' was raised. 'Judas Iscariot betrayed his Master,' said one well-known Liberal, 'and so has Mr. Chamberlain.' Labouchere went further than that. 'I have not come down here to defend Judas,' he said at Bury. 'Still there was something to be said for Judas. After betraying his Master, Judas did not attend public meetings; he did not revile his associates; he did not sponge upon the priests, the pharisees and the Sadducees in order to be received into their society; he did not go swaggering about Judea saying he had now joined the gentlemen of Jerusalem. No, Judas was contrite; he was ashamed; he went out and hanged himself. In some things Judas appears advantageously with Mr. Chamberlain.'(12) And, later in the same speech, Labouchere described, 'this ex-radical, donning as he did the Tory livery, first putting on the coat and then pulling on the breeches, until he stood forward boldly and proudly in the character of a full-blown Tory flunkey'.(13)

Marriage may have mellowed but it did not entirely alter Joseph Chamberlain. There is no doubt that at times he was ruthless and even brutal and that there were occasions when he showed little or no consideration for the feelings and points of view of other people. John Morley had been one of the first friends that he made through politics. They had got to know each other during the days of the Birmingham Education League before either of them entered the House of Commons. For years they had taken an annual holiday abroad together and Morley had frequently stayed at Highbury. It really appeared that they were kindred spirits. Yet, in October 1891, Chamberlain wrote to Morley:

'Your letter justifies and therefore aggravates the offence of your original attack. . . . I do not wish to prolong this correspondence. You promised not to attack me personally, my motives or my character. You have failed to keep the agreement. . . . At least in the future I shall not be under any limitations which I feel bound strictly to observe but which you think yourself at liberty to disregard whenever you consider that Mr. Gladstone's sacred personality is being treated with insufficient reverence.' (14)

So an old friendship was brought summarily to an end. It was years before the breach even began to be healed. And to another Liberal who for years had been his friend and supporter he wrote:

'Your references to the leadership of what you now call "the party of progress" lead me to say how deeply I have been grieved and wounded by your defection from the Unionist ranks. I cannot justify it and when you invented the description of a "Stalwart" to apply to yourself especially and a few others of the strongest opponents of Mr. Gladstone's Home Rule Bill I could not possibly have conceived that a few years' struggle would exhaust your patience and drive you back a penitent to the party whose policy you had repudiated and whose political morality you had most strongly condemned.'(15)

If as time went on Chamberlain and the Conservative leaders tended to draw nearer to one another, relations between their respective supporters in the constituencies were nothing like so cordial. In Birmingham the position was particularly delicate. Chamberlain was still of the opinion that there must be a working alliance between the Liberal Unionists and the Conservatives and that this should extend not only to Parliamentary elections but to municipal contests as well. At first it had been his own supporters with whom he had had the greatest difficulty over this. Now it was the Conservatives' turn to prove awkward. And here the situation was complicated by the influence of Lord Randolph Churchill, that fascinating but unstable personality, who, like a brilliant meteor, flashed briefly across the political scene in the latter part of the nineteenth century.

Lord Randolph had many enthusiastic admirers amongst the Conservatives of Birmingham, by whom he was looked on as the leader of 'Tory democracy'. He had certainly done a great deal to earn that title, particularly in Birmingham. When, in the year 1883, the Conservative Party held their annual conference in Birmingham, Churchill suggested that they too should have a thoroughly democratically elected policy-making body. 'If you want to gain the confidence of the working classes,' he declared, 'let them have a share and a large share – a real share and not a sham share – in your party councils and in your party government.'(16) And again, 'The Caucus may perhaps be a name of evil sound and omen in the ears of aristocratic or privileged classes, but it is undeniably the only form of political organization which can collect, guide and control for common objects large masses of electors.'(17) So impressed with Lord Randolph were the local Conservatives that they invited him to become one of their candidates at the next General Election. In 1885, he fought a hard and brilliant fight against John Bright in the very heart of the enemy citadel and lost by less than eight hundred votes – not a bad result in view of Bright's enormous prestige and long association with Birmingham. Meanwhile, largely as a result of Lord Randolph's influence, the local Conservative Association had gained greatly in strength; the Conservatives were making great headway in the municipal contests, many of which they fought on party lines and won.

Chamberlain always liked and at times had greatly admired Lord Randolph. They became friends and there was at one time some talk of a working alliance between them but, in the end, each decided to go his own way. In 1886, however, immediately after the split in the Liberal Party over Home Rule, Lord Randolph was of inestimable help to Chamberlain in securing the unity of Tory and Liberal Unionists in the General Election of that year. Churchill went specially to Birmingham in June 1886, to appeal to the local Tories to support Liberal Unionists. In this he was extremely successful and, on his return to London, he wrote that 'we shall run no other candidates except Mathews, and we shall give all our support to the Liberal Unionists, asking for no return and making no boast or taunt'.

In the year 1889, however, there arose a serious source of disunion. It was known that John Bright had not long to live and the local Conservatives were extremely anxious that Lord Randolph should be Bright's successor and they felt that the Liberal Unionists should agree to this. Churchill was at that time Member for Paddington and had made it clear that he would not leave that division unless it was 'the strong and unanimous wish' of both Tories and Liberal Unionists in the central division of Birmingham (Bright's constituency) that he should fight. Chamberlain had made it clear to him that if he (Lord Randolph) should decide to stand in Birmingham, he would have his (Chamberlain's) support.

John Bright died on March 27th, 1889, and the local Conservatives immediately called for the unanimous adoption of Lord Randolph as the Unionist candidate. At the beginning of April, a body of enthusiastic Conservatives hurried up to London to throw themselves at their idol's feet. But the Liberal Unionists (including Chamberlain) were less enthusiastic. In this situation, Churchill decided to abide by the decision of three people, namely, Sir Michael Hicks Beach, Lord Hartington and Chamberlain. They unanimously advised him not to stand, though Chamberlain added that if he did decide to do so he would 'feel pledged to give him any support in my power'. After listening to this advice, Churchill decided not to stand in Birmingham.

The Birmingham Tories were furious and it was only the combined influence of Arthur Balfour and Sir Michael Hicks Beach, two of the most influential leaders of their party, that dissuaded them from running their own candidate. Balfour went specially to Birmingham to intercede with them and, in the end, managed to persuade them to support Arthur Bright, the Liberal Unionist candidate. Nevertheless, relations between the two Unionist parties in Birmingham were strained for quite a considerable time afterwards and the Gladstonians took full advantage of the situation. But the national leaders of the Unionist Parties worked hard to restore the breach and, in the end, they were successful.

In January 1891, the Birmingham Liberal Unionists and Conservatives held a joint meeting in the Town Hall. Towards the end of the same year, the Conservative National Union held their annual meeting in Birmingham and the next day Chamberlain sat next to Lord Salisbury at the luncheon given in honour of the Prime Minister and proposed the toast of 'The Unionist cause'. There was one passage in his speech which was particularly significant:

> 'It is not for a mere personal or private question that one can repudiate one's old leaders. It is only when, as in this case, the existence or at least the security of the Empire is in question. Even after the rupture had taken place there were many of us – I was one of them – who hoped that it would be only temporary, who believed that the Gladstonians would speedily abandon the path upon which we knew, and they had good cause for knowing, they had most reluctantly entered; and we looked forward, therefore, to a speedy reunion. If I refer to that now it is to say that since then the gulf has widened and deepened. Now I neither look for nor desire reunion.'

So far as the country as a whole was concerned, the basis of the compact worked out between the Unionist Leaders was that the determining factor should be the state of affairs immediately prior to the election of 1886, i.e. where a seat was held by a Liberal Unionist at that date that Party was to have the right to choose the candidate at all subsequent elections and the Conservatives would support him; similarly, Liberal Unionists would support the candidate chosen by the Conservatives in seats which that Party had held at that date. On the whole, this bargain caused less friction in other parts of the country than it did in Birmingham.

At the beginning of the last decade of the nineteenth century, the Parliamentary scene was transformed by Parnell's triumphant vindication in the matter of the Piggott forgeries, followed by his downfall at the hands of O'Shea. During the year 1887 *The Times* had published a series of articles under the heading 'Parnellism and Crime'. Included in these was a facsimile copy of a letter purporting to have been signed by Parnell and implying sympathy with and complicity in the Phoenix Park murders. Parnell immediately denounced the letter as a forgery. He first saw it in *The Times* when he was having breakfast with Mrs. O'Shea with whom he was living at the cottage at Eltham and, having read it, he tossed the newspaper over to her with the remark, 'Wouldn't you hide your head with shame if your King were so stupid as that, my Queen?' (18) Later, *The Times* produced another letter, also purporting to have been signed by Parnell which contained the words, 'let there be an end of this hesitency'. The mistake in spelling proved to be the newspaper's undoing. There came a dramatic moment in the course of the Judicial Commission ordered by the Government when Sir Charles Russell asked Piggott to write down a number of words including 'hesitancy' and when he saw that Piggott had spelt it 'hesitency' he pointed his finger at him and exclaimed, 'There stands the forger, My Lord.' Piggott disappeared soon afterwards and later committed suicide.

Parnell's triumph was now complete. When he appeared in the House of Commons for the first time after the Commission had issued its report in February 1890 vindicating him completely, the whole Liberal Party, led by Gladstone, rose in a body and bowed to him. He was asked to stay at Hawarden and his visit was a great success. One day Miss Gladstone asked him who his favourite actor was. 'Your father,' replied Parnell and the 'Grand Old Man' chuckled.(19) For them both the future at that moment seemed rosy indeed but Parnell's doom was not far distant.

It is not certain at what stage the various characters chiefly involved in the Parnell drama – in particular O'Shea, Gladstone and Joseph Chamberlain – first became aware of Parnell's liaison with Mrs. O'Shea. According to Sir Charles Dilke, Sir William Harcourt referred to the fact of Mrs. O'Shea being Parnell's mistress in the course of a Cabinet meeting held as early as May 1882.(20) A more cunning politician than Joseph Chamberlain would have dropped O'Shea like a hot pair of tongs as soon as the first signs of trouble started to loom up on the horizon. But Chamberlain, who could never resist an exciting situation, continued to correspond with him for years after Mrs. O'Shea's adulterous relationship with Parnell had become public knowledge, and his friendship with O'Shea, like his friendship with Dilke, provided his enemies with ammunition with which to attack him. There was no more foundation for their charges in the one case than in the other.

In the year 1889, Mrs. Wood died leaving a fortune of about £200,000 to Mrs. O'Shea, whose husband now found himself in a state of complete dependence on herself and her lover. This was not a state of affairs which appealed to him at all and he decided to strike. First he tried to extract for himself a substantial portion of the £200,000. Having failed in this, he instituted proceedings for divorce, citing Parnell as the co-respondent. The suit was undefended.

At first Parnell did not take the divorce case particularly seriously. He affirmed his determination to retain the leadership of the Irish Party and in this, at first, the majority of the members of that Party seemed to be willing to support him. But the embattled might of the Nonconformist conscience was to prove too much for him. From Liberal platforms all over the country there came denunciations of any further truck with the adulterer. Gladstone made it clear that the continuance of Parnell as head of the Irish Party would be fatal to his own [Gladstone's] leadership of the Liberals and, therefore, to the prospects of Home Rule. There was a dramatic sequel in Committee Room 15 of the House of Commons when, after a fierce battle, Parnell was finally removed from the leadership of the Irish Party. He married Mrs. O'Shea and, a few months later, in October 1891, he died.

At the end of the year 1891, the Liberal Unionist member for East Worcestershire, a certain Mr. G. W. Hastings, was declared no longer competent to sit in the House of Commons owing to fraudulent conduct of which he had been found guilty. The local Liberal Unionists at once claimed the seat and asked Austen Chamberlain to be their candidate. The Conservatives, however, at first objected, partly on the ground that the other side, their previous candidate having disgraced himself, had forfeited the right of choice, and partly because Austen did not at that time appear to have anything to commend him except the fact that he was his father's son. But they soon changed their minds after they had met and listened to Austen. By then, he had developed into an excellent platform speaker. After meeting and corresponding with Austen, Colonel Milward (the Chairman of the local Conservative Party), was delighted with him and the local Conservative Association as a whole soon came to the conclusion that they themselves could not possibly have discovered a better man. They joined with enthusiasm in adopting him. It was obvious that East Worcestershire, being much nearer to Birmingham, would be better for Austen than Hawick and, his supporters in the latter constituency appreciating this and making no objection, he accepted the new offer. He was returned unopposed as member for East Worcestershire on March 30th, 1892. A day or two later, escorted by his father and his uncle, Richard Chamberlain, then M.P. for Islington, Austen took the oath and then took his seat.

The Parliament of which Austen found himself a member when he entered the House of Commons for the first time was moribund; it was clear that there must be a new one within the next twelve months. In fact, the dissolution came about ten weeks later, namely in June 1892, though Joseph Chamberlain had been in favour of waiting until the autumn. This time, both Joseph and Austen had to fight for their seats, both being returned with satisfactory majorities. The General Election gave the Gladstonian and Irish Nationalist forces together a majority of forty over the Conservatives and Liberal Unionists though the combined total of the two latter was greater than that of the Gladstonians. Lord Salisbury decided that his Government should face Parliament but they were defeated in August on a motion of 'no confidence' moved by a rising barrister who had recently entered Parliament and whose name was Herbert Henry Asquith. Lord Salisbury then resigned and the Queen sent for Gladstone.

The octogenarian statesman was not in a particularly enviable position because he was completely dependent on Irish support and the price of that support was Home Rule. The Irish were factious, rowdy, disruptive and difficult in every way. Their present leader was John Redmond but nobody knew how far he could control the wild men who surrounded him or what kind of a Home Rule Bill he or they would demand. Joseph Chamberlain seized on this in his speeches both in the House and in the country. What brand of Home Rule would be produced this time, he demanded. He flayed Gladstone, he flayed his supporters and he flayed the Irish. Gladstone hit back hard, accusing Chamberlain of using 'language of habitual, gross and enormous exaggeration' and adding that Chamberlain 'constantly and deliberately and with the utmost confidence and infallibility ascribes to men who have a right to stand on a level with him, and who were at one time his colleagues, and supposed to be his friends, motives for their acts the direct contrary of that which they state themselves and motives which they indignantly disclaim'. But, in the spring of 1892, a pleasant interlude occurred to interrupt these diatribes. It was during the second reading of Gladstone's second Home Rule Bill that Austen made his maiden speech. He spoke well, criticizing Gladstone's proposals forcefully and carefully, but without any element of rancour or bitterness. In his report of the debate to the Queen, Gladstone wrote that, 'A little later in the evening Mr. Austen Chamberlain, son of Mr. Chamberlain, took part for the first time in the debates of the House. He delivered one of the best speeches which has been made against the Bill and exhibited himself as a person of whom high political anticipations may reasonably be entertained.'(21)

Three days later, Gladstone again referred to Austen's speech – this time in the House. Looking across at Joseph Chamberlain he said that 'it was a speech which must have been dear and refreshing to a father's heart'.(32) Joseph Chamberlain was deeply touched by this graceful tribute, coming as it did from the man whose career he had done his best to blight and whose dearest political hopes he had done so much to thwart. He rose in his place and bowed low to the Prime Minister. After Gladstone had retired from public life in March 1894, Chamberlain wrote to ask him whether he might call to see him. He received a cordial reply and Mr. and Mrs. Chamberlain called on the Gladstones at Dollis Hill where they were given a warm welcome. Gladstone thanked them for coming. 'You are very kind,' he said to Chamberlain. 'You have often been very kind to me.' Then they talked together in a very friendly way about politics, past and present. They met again and for the last time at Cannes about six months later and here again there was a pleasant and friendly atmosphere between them.(23) In a speech which he made at Birmingham Town Hall shortly after Gladstone's retirement, Chamberlain said, 'The active life of the greatest parliamentary orator and statesman of our time has been terminated. . . . I will say for myself here in your presence that, although, to my deep regret, during the last few years, I have felt it my duty to oppose to the utmost Mr. Gladstone's policy, I have never, either in public or private, said one single word derogatory to his transcendent abilities and to his personal worth.'(24)

Meanwhile, the House of Lords had thrown out the Home Rule Bill, but the Liberal leaders had not dared to face the country on this issue. On the retirement of Gladstone, Lord Rosebery became Prime Minister.

During the winter of 1894-5, Chamberlain suffered from the worst fit of depression, in fact probably the only really bad one, that he had had since his third marriage. The weather was atrocious and his wife was away in the South of France where both her parents were ill. His financial affairs were going from bad to worse. To the enormous loss on the Bahamas venture and on his South American investments there was now added a substantial decline in the value of a number of his other securities.

He wrote to his wife in February 1895:

'The last thing is the failure of Canadian Pacific to pay its dividend. The shares have fallen five in consequence and may, I suppose, go lower. They are thirteen lower than they were at Christmas. I well know that you will meet any trouble of this kind as bravely as possible, but it is a constant anxiety to me, all the more that I can see nothing to be done. If we were in ordinary circumstances it would not be difficult to cut down expenses but I do not know how to retrench without giving up London altogether. It is no use thinking about it now, we must wait and see.'(25)

His position was undoubtedly serious. In London he maintained a large and lavish establishment (considerably enlarged since his marriage) including a butler, two footmen and numerous other indoor servants. In those days, Members of Parliament were not paid and neither he nor Austen were drawing any salary from any other source. He had two unmarried daughters and something would have to be done for Neville when he got back from the Bahamas. He decided that he would have to some extent to live on capital and started the process of realization. Amongst the holdings to be jettisoned was that in Canadian Pacific, his shares in which he sold at a heavy loss. This was the signal for the company to recover and, thereafter, it went from strength to strength. (26)

Within twelve months, however, a great change for the better had taken place in his financial position. The Government had fallen, Lord Salisbury had taken office and Joseph and Austen had both been given important posts in the new administration, for which, of course, they both received salaries. At the same time there had been a substantial improvement in the financial prospects of Kynoch Ltd., and therefore of Arthur Chamberlain. Curiously enough, both the fall of Lord Rosebery's Government and the brightening prospects at Kynochs had had one rather interesting factor in common. This was a substance, then little known, called cordite.

10

Cordite, Conservatives and Cleveland

Since he had assumed responsibility for the management of Kynochs, Arthur Chamberlain had shown that he could combine
ruthless efficiency, economy and the elimination of waste on the
one hand with vision and enterprise on the other. By the end of the
year 1892, he had got rid of the main sources of loss, including
particularly the lamp business and the gun factory, and he had instituted a thorough system of inspection in the ammunition factory, thereby insuring a really reliable product and reinstating
the company once more with the Government from whom a fairly
steady flow of orders was now secured.(1) Chamberlain knew,
however, that this period of consolidation was not, by itself,
enough. He knew that a business never stands still and that he must
be constantly on the look-out for fresh ideas and new products. It
was here particularly that he showed both his daring and his brilliance as a businessman, for he became one of the earliest pioneers
of cordite.

Arthur Chamberlain was on the whole benevolent in his attitude towards the workpeople for whom he soon secured sickness
benefits on a large and generous scale. Furthermore, almost alone
among the employers of that day and age, he was not a believer
in unduly long working hours and he did everything he could to
make those at Witton progressively shorter, being amongst the first
employers in the country to introduce a forty-eight hour week. This
reduction in the total number of hours worked, he said, 'does not
seriously, if at all, increase the percentage of wages to the cost of production while it diminishes loss through waste and improves the
general average of quality'. But he was insistent that during the
working week as thus reduced each man must give of his utmost;
he had no time for slackers. Furthermore, he was intolerant of
trade unions and of every other outside form of interference between employer and employed, including that of the Government.

The first serious stoppage to arise since he became chairman occurred in July 1891 when it was alleged by the union that the foreman in the fitting shop had engaged a number of low-paid apprentices at the expense of skilled toolmakers. The union announced that the men would strike unless the foreman was dismissed whereupon they were told firstly that he would not be, secondly that, thenceforward, no member of any 'Trade Society' would find employment at Witton. When a strike ensued Arthur addressed the strikers by letter in the following terms:

'You had absolutely no grievance of any kind sufficient to justify a strike. But you placed yourselves in the hands of political partisans and you imported paid agitators from outside to slander the company which for years past had been paying you better wages than the majority are ever likely to get again in your lives. For your own selfish purposes and by misrepresentations you induced a number of the men and women employed in the cartridge factory, who had no connection with your work and no grievance whatever against the company, to throw themselves out of employment. You are now responsible for the fact that 500 or 600 of these have lost for a time if not for ever an employment that supported their homes . . . After the way you have behaved to your directors, to your foremen and to your fellow-workpeople your return to work in the way you propose would interfere with the goodwill and harmony that now prevail.'(2)

Strange to relate, Arthur Chamberlain succeeded by these means in breaking the strike and in weakening for the time being the power of the union.

It was probably towards the end of 1892 that Arthur's thoughts turned seriously towards cordite, a new form of smokeless explosive which he felt sure would soon replace the older types of gunpowder, guncotton and nitroglycerine. He foresaw the likelihood of considerable expansion in the explosives industry for military and civilian purposes alike. He decided to build a large new factory in Ireland for the manufacture of cordite. In his address to shareholders for the year 1895, he told them that:

'In January, after careful consideration of all other available localities, a site was chosen on the east coast of Ireland . . . containing about 170 acres. All the necessary work for setting up a new industry has since been unceasingly pressed forward, and the place has been changed from barren sand hills into a completely equipped factory in the unprecedentedly short time of five months. The directors have every confidence in the future of cordite as the best all-round smokeless explosive on the market. . . .'(3)

Meanwhile, there were others who were beginning to appreciate the importance of cordite. On the evening of June 21st, 1895, a Conservative, Mr. Brodrick, moved in the House of Commons a vote of censure on the Secretary for War, Campbell-Bannerman, for not having ensured a sufficient supply of cordite and small arms ammunition for the army. The House was sparsely attended that evening, less than half the total number of Members being present, and, after a short debate, it divided. As they went into the Opposition lobby together, Arthur Balfour said to Chamberlain, 'Well, I suppose they'll have their usual majority.' 'Don't be too sure of that,' came the answer and, when the figures were announced, they showed that the Government were in a minority of seven. Two days later, Lord Rosebery resigned and the Queen sent for Lord Salisbury. The next day (Monday), Lord Salisbury and Balfour met Chamberlain and the Duke of Devonshire to discuss the position. It was decided that Salisbury should form a Government, that the two latter should join it and that there should be a dissolution as soon as possible. On being asked what position he would like in the new Government, Chamberlain replied that he would like to be Secretary of the Colonies. Balfour told him that he could have any department he wished, including the Exchequer, but Chamberlain repeated that he would prefer the colonies. Accordingly he once more entered the Cabinet but this time under a Conservative Prime Minister and as Colonial Secretary. Austen became Civil Lord of the Admiralty. A General Election soon followed and resulted in a substantial Unionist majority over all other parties.

Meanwhile, great consternation and annoyance had fallen on a large section of the Liberal Party. Seven Ministers had been absent from the critical division, as well as a large number of back bench members. Amongst these latter was a young Welsh solicitor whose name was David Lloyd George, elected for the first time at a by-election in Carnarvon Boroughs five years previously. In the ensuing General Election another Liberal candidate denounced Lloyd George for acting 'in sinister coalition with the Tories' by deliberately absenting himself from the 'cordite' division. Lloyd George decided that attack was the best form of defence. In a speech in his constituency, he said that he would tell his audience what really happened in the 'cordite' debate. A Tory M.P. had complained that there were not enough cartridges per soldier, he said: Mr. Campbell-Bannerman, the Secretary for War, had denied this. Then Mr. Joseph Chamberlain had got up and said that there should be four hundred rounds per man. Chamberlain had complained, declared Lloyd George, that there was not enough powder and bullets to kill people and, Lloyd George went on to assert, Chamberlain was evidently keen that further orders for cordite and other ammunition should be given to a firm called Kynoch and Co. of Birmingham. The chairman of that firm was Joseph Chamberlain's brother, Lloyd George pointed out, adding that there were four Chamberlains who had large holdings in the firm and two of Joseph Chamberlain's former partners in the screw trade were also shareholders in Kynochs. So much for Imperial Patriotism, Brummagem type, concluded Lloyd George. (4)

He was later to repeat these charges before much wider audiences and Chamberlain was most indignantly and strenuously to deny them.

Nearly a decade had elapsed since Joseph Chamberlain had first held office; in the interval, his interests had widened and his stature had increased. Striking evidence of this latter fact is to be found in the extent to which, in increasing measure, he was sought out by foreign statesmen. When, for instance, Theodore Roosevelt, then a rising member of the New York Assembly, came to England in the year 1887, he insisted on being introduced to Chamberlain who, he wrote, 'impressed me very greatly by his keenness, readiness and force and who, by the way was thoroughly the gentleman'.(5) And another Radical, even more prominent and equally patriotic, this time a Frenchman, had come to England and insisted on meeting him in July 1891. Georges Clemenceau and Joseph Chamberlain met at the house of a mutual friend, Admiral Maxse, and discussed the international situation in some detail. Clemenceau said that France needed the friendship of England, but that at that particular moment there was great irritation with England in France though this was only superficial. The two chief sources of irritation were Egypt and Newfoundland. Chamberlain said that he 'heartily desired a cordial friendship with France, and regretted the policy of *tracasserie* pursued in Egypt and elsewhere which had alienated English sympathy'. At the end of their conversation, Chamberlain asked Clemenceau whether he would like his views to be passed on to Lord Salisbury, and Clemenceau said that he would but it must be clearly understood that he had been talking purely as a private individual, though important members of the French Government knew of his visit and would be informed of what had transpired.(6)

It is interesting to notice the things that Joseph Chamberlain had in common with Theodore Roosevelt and Georges Clemenceau. Each was a Radical, each was ruthless, each was ambitious and each was destined to split parties, break up Cabinets and overthrow Governments. Each in his own way became the *enfant terrible* of political life in his country, each was intensely patriotic and for each belief in the greatness and destiny of his country was a consuming passion.

A friend of Roosevelt's, Henry Cabot Lodge(7) was staying with the Chamberlains at Highbury when the results of the General Election were being declared. The figures soon proclaimed a Unionist triumph. Shortly before the result in Derby, where Sir William Harcourt was standing, was announced, Lodge asked Chamberlain what would happen there and received the reply that Harcourt was 'safe enough'. In this, however, Chamberlain was mistaken; a few minutes later he got the news that his old friend had been beaten. He received it with surprise and regret. When all the results were known it was clear that the Unionist forces had achieved the greatest majority since the Reform Bill. Conservatives and Liberal Unionists together had a majority of 152 over all other parties.

Amongst the earliest problems with which the new Colonial Secretary had to deal was one which intimately concerned the United States and which, in less skilful hands, might easily have led to a rupture between the two countries. At this time, few, if any, British politicians had more friends or points of contact among leading members of both the great American parties than Chamberlain nor was there anyone more fitted to deal tactfully with the elected representatives of the great Republic across the ocean. And, curiously enough, the statesman who precipitated a crisis over this particular problem was none other than Chamberlain's old friend, the proposer of the toast of his wedding, Grover Cleveland. On leaving the White House in March 1889, Mrs. Cleveland had said to one of the servants, 'Now Jerry, mind you keep everything nice for us. We're coming back in exactly four years from today.'(8) And they had done so, Cleveland having been the only ex-President to be nominated and elected, after an interval out of office, in the history of the United States.

The particular matter which once more brought Chamberlain and Cleveland into touch with one another concerned the boundary between Venezuela and British Guiana. For years this question had been talked and argued about but nothing definite had been decided. Most of the area in dispute was jungle, forest and swamp and, at first, it did not seem to be worth anyone's while to worry a great deal about who it all belonged to. But, during the nineteenth century, swarms of immigrants had poured into South America. In this particular area (Venezuela: British Guiana) a great deal of very valuable reclamation and irrigation was carried out and many of the immigrants, not unnaturally, both desired and claimed British rule and protection rather than those of a South American State. It was this which gave rise to the idea in certain influential quarters that Britain was about to embark on an extension of colonialism in South America. Feelings soon started to run high and the Monroe Doctrine was invoked.

In July 1895, Richard Olney, Cleveland's Secretary of State, addressed a strong memorandum to the British Government protesting against the enlargement of British Guiana at the expense of Venezuela, invoking the Monroe doctrine and calling for immediate arbitration.(9) But Lord Salisbury was not used to being addressed in this manner by foreigners, nor did he take kindly to the 'twisting of the lion's tail' by Americans. He replied that the Monroe Doctrine had no place in the law of nations, that its interpretation and application to the present position were both extremely strange, and that he was not willing to submit to any arbitration at the behest of the United States. Then Grover

Cleveland himself came suddenly and dramatically into the picture. On December 17th, 1895, he sent a message to Congress requesting the appointment of a commission to make the necessary investigation and 'having ascertained the true boundary between British Guiana and Venezuela to report upon the matter with the least possible delay'. The President's message continued 'when such a report is made and accepted it will in my opinion be the duty of the United States to resist by every means in its power, as a wilful aggression upon its rights and interests, the appropriation by Great Britain of any lands or the exercise of governmental jurisdiction over any territory which, after investigation, we have determined of right belongs to Venezuela. In making these recommendations I am fully alive to the responsibility incurred and keenly realize all the consequences that may follow.'(6) There were those on both sides of the Atlantic who, reading this bellicose and defiant message, considered that war between the two countries was quite a possibility.

But Chamberlain thought otherwise. While he knew that England had many bitter enemies in the United States, particularly amongst the Irish, he knew also from his visits to and the friendships he had made in that country that at the heart of America there was a deep desire and need for the friendship of England. While, therefore, he was determined in no way to sacrifice the proved rights of British Guiana and of those who had settled within her borders he was equally determined to go to the extreme limit in making every reasonable concession to American feeling. He urged this point of view incessantly on his colleagues in the Cabinet and, in the end, received Lord Salisbury's permission to cross the Atlantic himself on an unofficial visit. Chamberlain had already met Olney on one of his previous expeditions and he was determined to take advantage of this fact. The two statesmen met unofficially in Boston in September 1896 and largely as a result of these conversations and of Chamberlain's efforts generally an amicable understanding was arrived at which led to the signing on February 2nd, 1897, of the Treaty of Washington under which the Venezuelan boundary question was submitted to the arbitration of five jurists – two British, two American and one neutral. The result was entirely satisfactory, the award safeguarding all those British Guianian interests on which Chamberlain had insisted.

I I

The Boer War

In February 1898, the American battleship *Maine* was blown up in
Havana harbour and there ensued the Cuban War between the
United States and Spain. In the following May, when Admiral
Dewey won a decisive victory over the Spanish fleet in the
Pacific, Chamberlain received news of the fact at the Colonial
Office before President McKinley. Chamberlain immediately com-
municated with the American Embassy and his message reached
the White House before the victory had been announced in the
American Press.

Chamberlain immediately grasped the significance of this emergence of the United States on to the stage of world affairs. In a
speech at Birmingham he said:

'They [the Americans] are a powerful and generous nation.
They speak our language, they are bred of our race [*loud cheers*].
Their laws, their literature, their standpoint on every question
are the same as ours; their feelings, their interest, in the cause of
humanity and the peaceful development of the world are identical with ours [*cheers*]. I do not know what the future has in store
for us, I do not know what arrangements may be possible with
the United States, but this I know and feel – that the closer, the
more cordial, the fuller and more definite these arrangements
are with the consent of both people, the better it will be for both
and for the world [*loud cheers*]. And I even go so far as to say
that, terrible as war may be, even war itself would be cheaply
purchased if, in a great and noble cause, the Stars and Stripes
and the Union Jack should wave together [*loud and prolonged
cheers*] over an Anglo-Saxon alliance.'(1)

Meanwhile, dark clouds were looming over the African continent. During the first half of the nineteenth century, the area which
became known as the Transvaal Republic was inhabited partly

by native Africans and partly by Dutch farmers (Boers) who had trekked northwards largely in order to escape British rule. During the seventh and eighth decades of the century, however, gold and diamonds were discovered in large quantities on the Rand and this had led to a flood of immigrants, mainly British. The President of the Transvaal was an obstinate, narrow minded and autocratic old man of Dutch extraction whose name was Johannes Paul Kruger. He thoroughly disliked and at all times ill-treated the immigrants who became known as 'Uitlanders'. In spite of the fact that it was largely by their industry and with their money that the mines had been developed and that they soon came to outnumber the native Dutch by more than two to one, they were treated throughout the Kruger régime as complete outcasts. They were not allowed to vote either in municipal or national affairs. They were subjected to heavy and discriminatory taxation without any representation or voice in the manner in which the money was spent. Their children were forced to attend schools in which Dutch was the only language. Another grievance was the 'monopolies' (e.g. the dynamite monopoly) created by Kruger in favour of his friends as a further means of extortion from the 'Uitlanders'.

The problem of the 'Uitlanders' was amongst the earliest and most serious with which Chamberlain had to deal after he became Colonial Secretary. It was no new problem; for more than twenty years they had been chafing under Kruger's despotic rule and smarting from his insults and Chamberlain's Liberal predecessor, Lord Ripon, had been warned more than once by the Colonial Office that they might attempt a rebellion.

Christmas 1895 was spent by Mr. and Mrs. Chamberlain as usual with their family at Highbury. On the evening of December 30th, the annual servants ball was to take place. This was always a great event and the whole family generally took part in it. While Chamberlain was about to dress for dinner, a special messenger who had arrived suddenly with an important message from the Colonial Office was shown into his room. The message informed him that, the day before, Dr. Jameson, with a force of several hundred men armed with maxim-guns and field artillery, had crossed into the Transvaal. It was noticed at the time that, as soon as he had read the dispatch, Chamberlain clenched his hands. Then he turned to one of his family who was in the room and said, 'If this succeeds, it will ruin me. . . . I am going up to London to crush it.'(2) He had dinner at Highbury, though without changing, and then had a telegram sent off to South Africa fully endorsing the action already taken by the High Commissioner, Sir A. Milner, in condemning the raid, and adding, 'Leave no stone unturned to prevent mischief.' He would not allow the ball to be interfered with in any way and even insisted that the coachman, who, he knew, would enjoy it, should stay behind. When he thought it was time to go, he sent for a cab, which, however, was late in arriving and he only just caught the 12.50 a.m. train to London.(3)

The Jameson raid was a complete failure. Jameson and his followers were surrounded by the Boers and captured. Jameson himself was sent to England for trial where he was convicted and sent to prison. Kruger was triumphant. Rapidly, he continued to pile up arms in the Transvaal and the plight of the 'Uitlanders' got worse. A young English workman called Edgar was shot in his own home by two Boer police in circumstances which amounted to murder. The criminals, after having been admitted to jail, were fined by a Boer Court. As a result of this and other outrages, the wrath of the British people at home, roused also as it had been by a congratulatory telegram sent by the Kaiser to Kruger, mounted steadily. Milner had warned Chamberlain that there were only two alternatives in the Transvaal – either Reform or War. To the discerning, it was becoming increasingly obvious that it was the second of Milner's two alternatives which would, in fact, eventuate – and before long.

Amongst the discerning was Arthur Chamberlain. Addressing the shareholders of Kynochs in 1896, he told them that 'the time must shortly come when the extensive development of the company's business will require larger cash resources. The directors wish the shareholders to know that the condition of the business already justifies, and will soon demand, an important increase and re-arrangement of the company's capital.'

Their confidence in Arthur Chamberlain was such that the shareholders speedily and eagerly subscribed an addition of £500,000 to the company's capital. With this substantial finance, the chairman was able to embark on a vigorous expansion of the company's activities. The Lion Works at Witton were extended and re-equipped to such an extent as to enable the company to make all its own cartridge brass; more than 100 tons were soon being rolled weekly. Already, in 1887, Chamberlain was able to report:

'We have acquired a black gunpowder mill at Worsboro' dale and 180 acres of freehold land at Arklow in Co. Dublin, half covered by a most perfect and complete explosives factory making cordite and dynamite, together with a large and important chemical works, and 750 acres freehold on the Thames, which it is proposed to develop into a 'second Witton'. The black gunpowder trade, cordite and dynamite are all going well – in fact we cannot make dynamite fast enough.'

An important new enterprise which was also announced around this time was the Kynoch machine-gun – 'now recognized as one of the necessities of modern armament'. In the development of this, Kynochs had acquired certain patent rights but they had added an invention of their own for 'automatically cooling the barrel without the use of water'.(4)

It was while these changes were taking place at Kynochs that the sisal enterprise in the Bahamas was finally liquidated and Neville returned home. On him had devolved the melancholy task of disposing of the assets and attending the auction sale when there was only one bidder for the whole of the plant and machinery which went for £560. In March 1897, the time came to say 'good-bye'. 'People,' he wrote later, 'came and sat in my office and sobbed.' Amongst other tributes that he received was one that particularly touched him. It took the form of a letter from thirty-three of the hands, thanking him for all he had done for them.(5) He arrived back in time for Queen Victoria's Diamond Jubilee.

Neville was now twenty-eight years old – without money, without a profession and without employment. He decided to settle down in Birmingham where he could live at home and he soon started to look around for a business opening. Arthur was quite willing to take him into Kynochs where he considered that there was an excellent opening. But Joseph thought this would be too dangerous politically. So Neville had to look round for a business of his own. The difficulty here was finance. It was not a very convenient moment for Joseph to find capital, for, on the top of all his expenses, the Diamond Jubilee was proving inordinately expensive.(6) But the Jubilee, with the representatives of Her Majesty's colonies and dominions gathered from every corner of the globe to do her honour, had fired his imagination and he was determined to play his full part whatever the cost.

In the end, Neville got himself established in business partly with the help of his two uncles, Arthur and Walter, and partly with that of his father. Arthur got him a directorship in a company called Elliott and Co. which made copper, brass and other metal products at Selly Oak. This company was at the time quite separate from and independent of Kynochs, though it is interesting to notice that, over thirty years later, both companies were absorbed into Imperial Chemical Industries. But Neville's main business was a firm called Hoskins & Co. which owned a workshop in Lower Trinity Street, Bordesley, and made cabin berths for ships. Neville himself acquired most of the shares in this company, but other members of the Chamberlain family, including Arthur, Austen and Mary (Mrs. J. Chamberlain) were also shareholders.

The outlook in South Africa continued to deteriorate and, early in October 1899, Kruger told the Volksraad to read psalm 108, verse 7, 'God hath spoken in his holiness; I will rejoice. I will divide Shechem, and mete out the valley of Succoth,' which, he said 'came to my mind while I was struggling in prayer'. The Raad approved war and then adjourned. On October 9th Kruger addressed to the British Government an ultimatum demanding the withdrawal of all troops from the borders of the Transvaal, the removal within a reasonable time of all British troops sent as reinforcements to South Africa, and that none of Her Majesty's forces then on the high seas should be landed at any port in South Africa. Two days later, the Orange Free State declared herself on the side of the Transvaal and the day after that, Thursday, October 2nd, Boer Commandos started to pour across the border into Natal and, on the other side, entering Bechuanaland, a number of them captured an armoured train near Mafeking. The South African War had begun.

Meanwhile, on October 5th, Chamberlain had written to the High Commissioner, Sir Alfred Milner:

'I am sending a line to anticipate a probable visit from Winston Churchill, the son of Lord Randolph Churchill, who is going out as correspondent for the *Morning Post*. I have declined to give any introductions to you to newspaper correspondents, and I do not introduce Churchill as such, but only as the son of my old friend to whom I should be glad at any time to do a kindness. He is a very clever young fellow with many of his father's qualities. He has the reputation of being bumptious, but I have not myself found him so, and time will no doubt get rid of the defect if he has it. . . . He is a good writer and full of energy. He hopes to be in Parliament but want of means stands in the way. If, when he comes, you can help him with any introductions to people who will put him on the right lines I shall be very much obliged. . . .'(7)

Shortly after arriving in South Africa, Churchill was taken prisoner by the Boers.

For the first three months of the war the British public got nothing but bad news. British forces were compelled to fall back on Ladysmith and Kimberley, both of which were besieged. Then, during one week in December 1899 (black week), the army suffered three crushing defeats at Magersfontein (December 11th), Stormberg (December 10th) and Colenso (December 15th). One good piece of news reached England to relieve the gloom caused by 'black week'. This was that Winston Churchill had arrived in Durban having escaped from the prisoner of war camp at Pretoria in which he had been incarcerated by the Boers.

Early in the New Year, Roberts arrived as Commander-in-Chief, with Kitchener as his chief of staff, and large reinforcements started to pour into South Africa, not only from the United Kingdom, but also from Canada, Australia and New Zealand, and Chamberlain himself found particularly encouraging the reinforcements from the Empire. It was remarkable how soon after the arrival of Roberts and Kitchener the whole scene changed. On February 15th, 1900, Kimberley was relieved by a large force of cavalry under General French, and twelve days later the same force surrounded four thousand Boers at Paardeburg and compelled them to surrender. Meanwhile, Roberts had been sweeping northwards through the Orange Free State. He entered its capital, Bloemfontein, on March 13th. After pausing to re-establish his transport, he continued his march on the Transvaal on May

1st. He forced his way over the Sand River and on May 12th occupied Kronstadt. He entered Johannesburg on May 31st and Pretoria on June 5th. Meanwhile, on May 17th, Mafeking was relieved. There were scenes of wild enthusiasm when this news was received in London.

But if the Boers in South Africa were now in full retreat their friends in England had decided that the moment had arrived to go vigorously into the attack. The 'pro-Boers' were a small but extremely vocal section of the Liberal Opposition, the remaining members of which were either Liberal Imperialists or neutrals, the latter being neither particularly in favour of the war nor particularly against it. One of the leading 'pro-Boers' was Labouchere. His attitude was governed far more by hatred for Chamberlain than by sympathy for the Boers. Labouchere's venom had been greatly increased by a recent exposure of him made by Chamberlain. Amongst the documents seized by the British after Roberts had entered Bloemfontein were a number of letters from Liberal politicians to correspondents in South Africa. Amongst these was one from Labouchere which contained the following significant passage, 'Don't for goodness' sake let Mr. Kruger make his first mistake by refusing this; a little skilful management and he will give Master Joe another fall.'(8)

From then on, the slogan of Labouchere and his friends was 'Go for Joe' . . . In looking round for a stick with which to beat Chamberlain their attention once more fastened itself on the growing expansion and prosperity of Kynochs. Most of them contented themselves with sly sneers and innuendoes and the propagation of such meaningful slogans as, 'While the British Empire expands, Kynochs contract.' But there was one man who was prepared to be a good deal more specific. In a speech in July, Lloyd George made a number of definite charges. The War Office, he declared, had invited tenders for cordite and in spite of the fact that Kynochs was the highest of seven tenders they were awarded the contract, though they had subsequently had to reduce their figure. Who controlled Kynochs? The Chamberlain family. Yet Joseph Chamberlain had started a war in South Africa because (amongst other things) Kruger and his friends had profited from a diamond monopoly.(9)

Joseph Chamberlain replied to this in a letter in which he said that the whole accusation was 'without a shadow of foundation'. He was not himself a shareholder in Kynochs and had no part in or control over its management in any way whatsoever. But Lloyd George was not prepared to leave the matter there. 'What about Charles Hoskins & Co.,' he demanded a few days later. This company were contractors to the Admiralty. Who were its shareholders? The first name on the list was Mrs. Mary Endicott Chamberlain, wife of the Right Hon. Joseph Chamberlain of Highbury, Birmingham. The next name was Arthur Neville Chamberlain of the same address, a son of the Right Hon. gentleman. Then came another son, Joseph Austen Chamberlain, with six hundred shares. He lived at the same address and *was himself a Civil Lord of the Admiralty*. There were other Chamberlains amongst the shareholders. In fact, except for one or two shares evidently taken by clerks, the company was entirely owned by the Chamberlain family. Yet Joseph Chamberlain had declared that he had no interest, direct or indirect, in any firm dealing with the Government.(10)

The fact was that Admiralty work had never formed more than an infinitesimal part of Hoskins & Co.'s business and the company had ceased to do such work some time before the Chamberlains acquired control of it.

In the spring of 1900, Lloyd George had expressed the view that there would be a General Election soon because 'you may rely upon Chamberlain forcing a dissolution in the height of the war fever'.(11) As to the proximity of the election Lloyd George was right. Chamberlain knew well that never again in that Parliament would the Government be so popular and the Opposition so disunited as they were then. Furthermore, with the clearance of the last Boer invaders from Cape Colony and the fall of Johannesburg and Pretoria, it looked as though the end of the war was in sight and Chamberlain urged upon his colleagues the importance of a fresh mandate to the Government which was to be responsible for the peace. His views prevailed and the Queen signed the proclamation dissolving Parliament on September 17th, 1900.

In the Khaki Election, two men were outstanding – they were Joseph Chamberlain and David Lloyd George. On the Government side, the Colonial Secretary was overwhelmingly the dominant figure. Everywhere he was in demand for Conservative platforms and he did his best not to disappoint more than he could help of the numerous applicants. There was one engagement however, that he was determined to keep. 'I have promised Winston Churchill to speak at Oldham,' he said. 'It is a long way outside my limit; but I could not say "No" to a son of Lord Randolph for whom I had a great regard.' He journeyed to Oldham on September 25th, leaving Birmingham at 2 p.m. and arriving at Clegg Street Station, Oldham, at about 4.30 p.m. Here he was met by Winston Churchill and together they travelled to Shaw, where they were to be the guests of Mr. and Mrs. Lees-Milne at Crompton Hall.(12) After dining there, they returned later in the evening to Oldham where Chamberlain was to address a great meeting in the Empire Theatre. The streets of Oldham were packed with people anxious to catch a glimpse of the famous Colonial Secretary; according to a local newspaper account 'many of the mill-owners in the district had decided to stop work earlier than usual in order to give their operatives an opportunity of welcoming suitably the man who crushed Kruger'.(13) Chamberlain and Churchill drove to the meeting in an open carriage and at the door of the theatre they were surrounded by an immense crowd, 'booing', yelling and shouting at the tops of their voices so that for several minutes neither the carriage itself nor any of its occupants could move. This was entirely to the liking both of the candidate and of his distinguished supporter.

The Empire Theatre was crammed to capacity, a crowd estimated at more than four thousand having been packed into it. There was wild enthusiasm as the speakers mounted the platform for Churchill, too, was already a popular figure because of his ex-exploits in South Africa. The band played a number of patriotic airs including 'Soldiers of the Queen'.(14) In the course of his speech, Chamberlain said:

> 'Before we go to business, I should like to say a word or two in regard to the occasion of my visit. . . . I hold, and I think you will agree with me, that a man's first duty is to his own district. We hold at the present 38 out of 44 seats in four counties surrounding Birmingham and I want to increase the number [*cheers*]. But as that will give me a great deal to do in the next fortnight, I have felt obliged, although greatly to my regret, to

refuse all the invitations which have been addressed to me from a distance except the one from Oldham [*cheers*]. I come here to-night in the first instance at the invitation of my friend Mr. Winston Churchill – his father was a great friend of mine. We quarrelled sometimes, the best of friends quarrel occasionally, but we always made it up quickly. And it is a pleasure to me to think that in what I believe was the last speech that the late Lord Randolph Churchill made in public in the course of that great campaign which he undertook when he was smitten by disease and when nothing but his own unparalleled courage could have carried him through – it is a pleasure to think that I stood by his side and supported him – well . . . I think his son has inherited some of the great qualities of his father – his originality and his courage.'(15)

In his speeches up and down the country, Chamberlain referred frequently to a telegram sent by the Mayor of Mafeking containing the words, 'A seat given to the Liberals is a seat given to the Boers.' As for Lloyd George he rained down blows upon the Colonial Secretary at any and every opportunity. The South African War was, in Lloyd George's view, entirely the work of one man. Joseph Chamberlain, he argued, had willed it, planned it, brought it about, profited by it and was now, in spite of the advice of the generals, unnecessarily prolonging it. But, in the General Election, it was Chamberlain who carried the day, the Conservative and Unionist forces returning with a decisive majority over all other Parties.

Joseph Chamberlain wrote to his wife of the campaign as a whole, 'It has been fought with the greatest malignity by the baser sort on the other side.' But now it was over he could relax for a few days at Highbury. 'We are hard at work in the garden,' he told his wife in another letter. 'Austen has been indefatigable, when he has had any time to spare, in pruning trees and there has been a great deal of lopping of the old oaks. There is also a great deal of planting still to be done and the rhododendron borders which were left last year to be re-made, and the lower garden to be re-planted, so there is plenty of occupation. . . .'(16)

The campaign had taken its toll of him and he wrote to Jesse Collings on October 10th, 1900, after it was over, 'I have felt a little sick at the abominable flood of slanders that have been poured out on my unfortunate head.' He now felt justified, in order to recuperate, in taking a short holiday abroad and he and Austen embarked on a short Mediterranean cruise. At Gibraltar he learnt of the composition of the new Government. He himself, by his own desire, remained Colonial Secretary but Austen got promotion, becoming Financial Secretary to the Treasury. They met Mrs. Chamberlain and her mother at Naples and returned overland.

The new Parliament opened early in December and almost immediately the campaign of innuendo against the Chamberlains was resumed. On December 10th, Lloyd George moved the following amendment to the Address:

> 'That Ministers of the Crown and members of either House of Parliament holding subordinate office in any public department ought to have no interest direct or indirect in any firm or company competing for contracts with the Crown, unless, the nature and extent of such interest being first declared, your Majesty shall have directed such precautions to be taken as may effectually prevent any suspicion of influence or favouritism in the allocation of such contracts.'

In his speech, Chamberlain complained of the 'dreary flow of petty malignity' and the 'conspiracy of insinuation' which was 'so infinitely worse than a direct charge'. He continued:

> 'When I went into public life I gave up business altogether. I withdrew my capital such as it was. I had to invest it somehow, but I have endeavoured in the whole course of my public life to be in the position in which Caesar's wife should have been – to give no cause even of suspicion to the most malicious of opponents. . . . I will take one case. I was a considerable shareholder in the Small Arms Company and in another company, Kynochs. Now, what did I do? I sold out of both companies and I sold out of them at a loss. . . .'

Austen Chamberlain also made a short speech in the same sense. Arthur Balfour warmly defended them both, exclaiming ironically, 'Wanted, a man to serve Her Majesty with no money and no relations.' He paid a warm tribute to his colleague and ended by saying that the Colonial Secretary had 'never stood higher in the general opinion of his countrymen than he does at this moment'. The amendment was rejected.

But this did not stop the calumnies from continuing both in speeches and in the Press. Arthur took proceedings for libel as did Neville and both were successful. Joseph considered doing so but was dissuaded by the advice of Counsel.

Meanwhile, the war dragged on; the Boer resistance lasted far longer than had been anticipated at the time of the election. This fact was used by certain of the Opposition and particularly by Lloyd George as a stick with which to beat Chamberlain. After the fall of Pretoria, Lloyd George argued, when the Governments of both Boer Republics had resigned but before the irregular guerilla warfare had started, there had been an ideal opportunity to offer generous peace terms and to arrive at a sensible settlement. Why, asked Lloyd George, had not this opportunity been seized? 'Because,' he answered, 'we had an electioneer and not a statesman at the head of affairs; a man who had his eye not on the destiny of Africa, but on the polling booths of Britain.'(17) 'There was a soldier who knew what war meant; he strove to make peace,' cried the same orator in the course of another speech. 'There was another man, who strolled among his orchids, six thousand miles away from the deadly bark of the Mauser rifle. He stopped Kitchener's peace.'(18)

In order to contain the Boer guerillas and to shorten the war, Kitchener and his staff had decided on the policy of Blockhouses and Concentration Camps. Lloyd George considered all this to be unspeakably cruel and laid the blame for all the suffering involved squarely at the door of Chamberlain:

'At this rate within a few years there will not be a child alive on the 'veldt'. And when the Boer prisoners of war return ... to look on the black embers of the house that has been burned to the ground, to hear from the lips of their wives how their children died in the disease-stricken camps – what then? A barrier of dead children's bodies will rise up between the British and the Boer races in South Africa. Herod of old tried such a thing as this. He sought to crush a little race by killing its young sons and daughters. He was not a success; and I would commend the story to Herod's modern imitator.'(19)

Chamberlain's own comment on this was that such speeches could not fail to encourage the Boers and thus help to prolong the war.

In season and out of season, in the House of Commons and on public platforms, Lloyd George continued to attack Chamberlain. In Wales his sallies brought delighted cheering as when, at Llanelly in October 1900, he described the progress of 'Chamberlain's war'. Last year, he said, the public had been relieved to hear that the war was over – 'how handily, just in time for the General Election in October!' Then 'hallo, what's this – still on in November – and another little bill for a few million pounds. That was *last* November. . . . Now after twelve months more fighting how did we stand? We had a Government which would not make peace and even yet did not know how to make war.' (20)

In December 1901, Lloyd George decided to carry the war right into the enemy's camp by going to Birmingham itself. The sequel is well known. So violent and threatening was the mob which raged round the Town Hall, where the Welsh orator and his party had assembled, that Lloyd George was compelled to escape from the building disguised as a policeman. Though reinforced from all the surrounding districts the police were unable to contain the mob which smashed all the windows, broke open the doors, and surged into the building and on to the platform and ransacked the rooms behind it, only to find that their quarry had escaped. This spontaneous demonstration of anger and rage was not due only or even mainly to the fact that Lloyd George was looked on as a 'Pro-Boer'; it was due far more to the calumnies he had directed at the Chamberlains. It was the City's answer to the man who had insulted its most famous and best-loved son. When a fellow-Member asked Chamberlain in the House of Commons why the people of Birmingham had allowed Lloyd George to escape he replied coldly, 'What's everybody's business is nobody's business.'(21)

12

Education, Food Taxes and the Liberal Landslide

On January 22nd, 1901, Queen Victoria died. The South African War dragged on for more than a year of Edward VII's reign. It was finally ended by the Treaty of Vereeniging on May 31st, 1902. The war had proved far more costly than had been originally anticipated and, as one means of paying for it, Sir Michael Hicks Beach had introduced into his Budget in April 1902 a corn registration duty of 3d. per cwt. on all imported corn. This was to have important consequences later.

On the afternoon of July 7th, while he was being driven by cab from the Colonial Office to the Athenaeum Club, Joseph Chamberlain had a most unpleasant accident. The horse shied and slipped, the strap which held the cab window broke and a heavy pane of glass crashed down on Chamberlain's head, from which blood poured while he stumbled out of the cab. A policeman bound up his wound and he was rushed to Charing Cross Hospital, where he remained for the next two days, having three stitches inserted without an anaesthetic.

On July 11th, 1902, Lord Salisbury resigned and the King sent for Arthur Balfour. Before going to the Palace, Balfour insisted on going to Princes Gardens where Chamberlain was lying in bed. He was asleep when his visitor arrived but Mary, realizing the importance of the visit, took the responsibility of waking him up. There had been those who had felt that Chamberlain should succeed Lord Salisbury but he himself was never of their number. He had always been deeply grateful for the loyalty which Balfour had given him, particularly over the 'smear campaign' directed against him and his family by Lloyd George and others during the war. It had always been his intention to give the fullest possible support to Balfour's succession to Lord Salisbury. He had lost over a pint of blood and the doctors insisted that he must remain in bed for at least a fortnight, but, as soon as he was able to sit up and put pen to paper, he wrote to the hospital, thanking them for what they had done for him and enclosing a cheque for fifty guineas 'in the hopes that it may serve to relieve others in worse case than myself'.

On July 12th, Balfour kissed hands on his appointment as Prime Minister. Two days later, he summoned all the Unionist members of Parliament to a meeting at the Foreign Office and Austen Chamberlain read out the following message from his father:

> 'I am to say how greatly disappointed my father is that he cannot be here today to welcome Mr. Balfour to the leadership [*cheers*] – and to say with what pride and pleasure he will give all the assistance in his power to Mr. Balfour in the responsible task which lies before him [*renewed cheers*]. ... My father bids me to say to you, Mr. Balfour, that you will find in him a colleague equally attached to you by private friendship and public regard, and, in offering you his own support, he feels that he may speak also in the name of the whole of the Liberal Unionist Party in the House of Commons. [*Hear, Hear and cheers*].'(1)

Nearly all Lord Salisbury's former ministers continued to serve under Balfour but there were two important changes. The first was that Sir Michael Hicks Beach resigned, his place at the Exchequer being taken by Mr. (later Lord) Ritchie, a rigid Free Trader. The second was that Austen Chamberlain became the new Postmaster General.

Joseph Chamberlain's accident and subsequent confinement to bed had come at a singularly inopportune moment, for two major events, both of which concerned him vitally, were taking place at the time. One was the Committee stage of the Government's Education Bill and the other was the Colonial Conference. The Education Bill was largely the result of the untiring efforts of Arthur Balfour, for whom education was probably the cause that was nearest to his heart, perhaps the only public cause for which he ever felt any enthusiasm at all. The Bill provided for the replacement of the old School Boards by Education Committees of each County and County Borough Council and of certain Urban

District Councils. These authorities would be responsible for all schools in their areas, of whatever denomination, and whether provided or non-provided, and they would have power to levy rates for the maintenance and upkeep of the schools. Joseph Chamberlain's position over all this was a difficult one. Personally, he had mellowed considerably and had now got over nearly all that prejudice against the established Church which had, originally, coloured so much of his thinking about education. Furthermore, he had great affection and admiration for Balfour and he knew what a lot education meant to his friend and colleague. It also meant a great deal to himself, though it did not occupy quite the pride of place in Chamberlain's mind that it did in Balfour's. But he was very conscious of its great importance to the whole future of the country and his enthusiasm had been kindled afresh by his recent work for and connection with Birmingham University. He realized fully that the whole system, particularly in its relationship to higher education, needed drastic overhaul if England was not to fall behind in the field of science and industry to countries such as Germany which had a more up-to-date education system.

But, though he was fundamentally sympathetic to the aims of the Bill, Chamberlain was also very conscious of its political dangers. He was particularly apprehensive of the effect of a provision that local Education Committees should be bound to maintain Church schools out of the rates. At his insistence, therefore, a provision was inserted in the Bill as originally promulgated which became known as the 'Local Option' clause. This made the extent to which and the terms on which any particular 'Voluntary School' received aid from the rates a matter for the discretion of each particular Education Committee. But when the Bill was in Committee (which stage was reached while Chamberlain was in bed suffering from the results of his accident) the local option clause was struck out. This was one of the first matters to concern Chamberlain as soon as he had recovered sufficiently to be able to take an interest in politics after his accident. What made matters worse was that the Bill provided that, in the case of Church schools, a majority of the Managers should be appointed by the 'Foundation Authority' – i.e. the Church. He knew well the appalling effect which all this would have on the 'Nonconformist conscience'. 'The political future seems to me – an optimist by profession – most gloomy,' he wrote to the Duke of Devonshire towards the end of September. 'I told you that your Education Bill would destroy your own party. It has done so. Our best friends are leaving us by scores and hundreds, and will not come back.'(2)

In Birmingham a first-class storm was threatening over the Bill and the way Chamberlain managed to quell it bears eloquent testimony not only to his great skill and powers of persuasion but also to his tremendous prestige and influence in the city: Accompanied by Austen and Neville, he appeared before a meeting of the Liberal Unionist Association at its offices in Birmingham and in the course of his speech he said:

> 'I hope the differences, if differences there be between us at the present time, may be composed. But if not . . . then, gentlemen, at least let us agree to differ upon this one contested and difficult point . . . but let us never consent to do anything that would assist the intrigues of those who . . . would hand over Ireland to the Home Rulers, would transfer the settlement of . . . South Africa to the . . . Pro-Boers, who would leave our interests in the hands of the Little Englanders. . . . believe me, gentlemen, if in this discussion we could hear a little more about the children and a little less about the sects we should make greater progress. . . . I attach the greatest importance to those conscientious scruples which I know exist . . . yet . . . if I had to go to my constituents . . . it is not upon . . . these paltry questions of sectarian competition that I should argue it . . . but . . . from the point of view of the children themselves – the future citizens of this country.'(3)

It was a very telling speech and by means of it Chamberlain succeeded in quelling what might otherwise have been a very dangerous revolt. Austen, too, had distinguished himself during this particular controversy, making some of the best speeches that he had ever made and emerging as a first-class performer in debate. He stressed the importance of 'one authority which should cover the whole field of education, which should be able to watch a child from the time it entered a primary school upwards through the higher learning, and see that those who were fitted to take advantage of it by scholarship and other means were enabled to benefit by all that school or college or university could give'. 'Those,' he declared, were 'objects on which every reasonable man might well be agreed' and he added that, if they would only look at the question a little more from the point of view of the children, there would be a good deal more agreement. He was, he affirmed, a Nonconformist himself but he told the House that he could not understand the attitude of those who would sooner that the larger number of children went uneducated than that a penny of public money should find its way to a voluntary school. He added that, in his view, in the great mass of schools, the religious difficulty was hardly felt.(4) And, in another speech, about a month later, he replied to the suggestion that the fact that the Church could appoint a majority of the school managers would give them complete control over the Church schools – 'The local authority,' he pointed out, 'is, by the terms of the Bill, to be responsible for, and have control over, not only all money which they thus provide but all the money which is provided out of national resources. The Managers of the school, in all matters of school instruction, are to take their directions from that local authority and, if they persistently and wilfully fail to carry out their instruction, the local authority may step in and do what they have ordered to be done. Is not that sufficiently complete control over all the public elementary secular instruction to satisfy even the most exacting judge?'(5)

For the Liberal Opposition, the Bill afforded a 'Bonanza'. To them it was like the first swallow which, after a long and dreary winter, proclaims the approach of spring. They knew that the Nonconformist conscience was now fully roused and they proposed to take full advantage of this fact. Both in the House and in the country they denounced the Bill with the utmost vigour. Asquith described it as 'a piece of reactionary domestic legislation' and as 'a Bill which absolutely upsets and revolutionizes the existing system of education. It abolishes the school boards and establishes in place of them a non-representative authority.' Lloyd George found in it another stick with which to beat Joseph Chamberlain of whom he said that 'his advocacy of the Bill is the last act of treachery in the career of one who has sold many of his convictions'.(6) But Lloyd George also said in the House, 'Give the children the Bible if you want to teach them the Christian faith. Let it be expounded to them by its Founder. Stop this brawling of priests in and around the schools, so that the children can hear him speak to them in his own words. I appeal to the House of Commons now, at the eleventh hour, to use its great influence and lift its commanding voice and say "Pray silence for the Master".'(7) Amongst the Liberal leaders, however, only Haldane remained throughout a firm and consistent supporter of the Bill.

The Colonial Conference had also reached a crucial stage at the time that Chamberlain met with his accident. The question of inter-colonial preference in the matter of tariffs and trade had been very much under discussion, but nothing definite so far as Britain was concerned had been decided by the time that Chamberlain was taken to hospital and the conference broke up in August, before he was fully recovered. It had, however, been resolved that the British Government should be urged to give preference to the colonies in the matter of any tariffs or duties which might be imposed. Chamberlain, particularly in his conversations with Canadian ministers, had agreed to give the matter his sympathetic consideration but he had made it clear that he could not bind the British Government. To him, the corn duty imposed by Hicks Beach seemed to offer an excellent opportunity to give preference to Canada by remitting the duty on that country's wheat and he urged this point of view on his colleagues in the Cabinet as soon as he was well enough to attend the meetings. Meanwhile, he had decided to embark on an extensive tour of South Africa, starting in the late autumn, and he had persuaded Balfour to agree to this.

Chamberlain was due to sail from Southampton on November 25th, 1902. He attended a Cabinet meeting on November 19th, the last before his departure. He again raised the question of preferential treatment for Canadian corn and it seems likely that he was supported over this by a majority of the Cabinet, though Ritchie made it clear that he was not willing to be committed as to what his next budget might or might not contain.

On November 17th, a farewell banquet was given in honour of Mr. and Mrs. Chamberlain in Birmingham Town Hall. It was nearly fourteen years since the last such banquet and Chamberlain's first words were of all that his wife had meant to him during that interval. 'I can never say, certainly not in a public gathering, what I owe to her,' he declared, 'but I know that, during fourteen years of arduous and sometimes excessive strain, she has sustained me by her courage and cheered me by her gracious companionship and I have found in her my best and truest counsellor.' Then, as on that former occasion, he said something of his affection for Birmingham:

'How should I do other than love it?' he asked. Then he went on 'Here is my home, here is my family life, and no man owes more than I do to the blessings of a family life. Here I have been happy, here also I have sorrowed; and, through good and evil, through all the vicissitudes of my career, the sympathy and the goodwill of the people have followed me and have bound me to them by links of steel and by the share which they have had in the precious memories of my life.'(8)

They drove back to Highbury between a long avenue of torch bearers and all the way along the route there were dense crowds, cheering all the way, though it was a bitterly cold night. Every now and then, Chamberlain stood up in his carriage and, each time he did so, there were shouts of 'There's Joey', 'Look at 'im now', ''Ere comes *our* Joe' and 'Wish you a pleasant journey, Joey'.(9)

They left London on the morning of November 25th, travelling by the royal train to Portsmouth, where they boarded H.M.S. *Good Hope*. After breaking the journey in Cairo, at Mombasa and in Zanzibar, they finally reached Durban on December 26th, 1902.

In the course of a very extensive tour of South Africa, which included Natal, the Transvaal, the Orange Free State and Cape Colony, Chamberlain studied the situation most carefully, making speeches in all the principal cities including Durban, Maritzburg, Pretoria, Johannesburg and Cape Town. The speech which he made at Durban provided the key note. 'The issue has been decided. The British flag is, and will be and must be, paramount throughout South Africa . . . reconciliation should be easy. We hold out our hand and we ask the Dutch to take it frankly, and in the spirit in which it is tendered.' And at Pretoria he said, 'Henceforth we are one nation under one flag. We have left the past behind.' He embarked from Cape Town on his return journey on February 25th, arriving back in England in March. When he got to Birmingham there was another torchlight procession to escort him to Highbury.

In the course of the voyage he had received disquieting news from Austen telling him that Ritchie had now expressed himself as being utterly opposed to any form of imperial preference and indeed determined on the repeal in his next Budget of the corn duty itself. Balfour had given Austen this piece of news at a levee and had suggested that he should get into touch with his father immediately. Joseph Chamberlain was bitterly disappointed when he got the news and, indeed, it was the repeal of the corn duty which finally precipitated him into a full-scale programme of Tariff Reform. He announced his advocacy of such a programme in an important speech at Birmingham on May 15th, 1903, in which he proposed the imposition of duties on a wide variety of imported goods, partly as a retaliation against foreign countries which had imposed tariffs on British goods, but mainly in order to bind the Empire more closely together by a system of imperial preference. Unless it could be held together by material ties, he told his audience, it would inevitably disintegrate. The choice lay between a policy of imperial unity, on the one hand, and 'an entirely artificial and wrong interpretation which has been placed upon the doctrines of Free Trade by a small remnant of Little Englanders of the Manchester School who now profess to be the sole repositories of the doctrine of Mr. Cobden and Mr. Bright' on the other.(10)

This speech brought consternation into the minds of many important Conservatives and Unionists who knew how unpopular any proposal to tax imported food would be likely to be with the electors. A Free Trade section rapidly developed itself within the Unionist ranks. Balfour was particularly disturbed and strove unremittingly to find some kind of 'half-way house' at which both sides could meet.

But the Liberals were jubilant. 'Wonderful news,' said Asquith, coming into his wife's bedroom on the morning of May 16th with a copy of *The Times* containing Chamberlain's speech. 'It is only a question of time when we shall sweep the country.'(11) As for Lloyd George, his comment was characteristic. 'The day of Mr. Chamberlain's ascendancy in British politics is drawing to a close,' he declared, 'and a fitting termination it is for such a career. It ends, as it began, with the split of a Party.'(12)

All that summer, the Liberal leaders, particularly Asquith and

Lloyd George, went in to the attack, doing their best to widen the rift in the Unionist ranks. In this they were largely successful for by the middle of September, not only Joseph Chamberlain himself but also Ritchie, Lord Balfour of Burleigh and Lord George Hamilton had resigned. The resignation of the Duke of Devonshire followed about three weeks later. Joseph Chamberlain had written to Balfour on September 9th, tendering his resignation so that he could devote himself 'to the work of explaining and popularizing those principles of imperial union' which in his view were so essential to the future well-being of the country and the Empire. But that privately he felt acutely and indeed bitterly resented the behaviour of his late colleagues is clear from a letter which he wrote to the Duke of Devonshire. 'What did I ask of you before I went to South Africa? That you should retain the one shilling corn duty and give a drawback to Canada. I thought you had all, except Ritchie, accepted this policy. While I was slaving my life out, you threw it over as of no importance and it is to the indifference to a great policy, which you had yourselves accepted, that you owe the present situation.'(13)

These resignations had an important effect on the political future of Austen. Balfour was most anxious to remain on as good terms as possible with Joseph Chamberlain. In order to assure this and further in order to provide a link between himself and his ex-Colonial Secretary, he decided to appoint Austen, then Postmaster General, to be Chancellor of the Exchequer. Austen thus jumped several rungs of the political ladder at once and stepped into one of the leading positions in the Government and in the Tory hierarchy. But he did not have either the power or the importance that some Chancellors of the Exchequer have had, for example Sir Michael Hicks-Beach, who had also been Leader of the House. Throughout the time that Balfour was Prime Minister and leader of the Conservative Party Austen had neither the importance nor the power of Lord Lansdowne.

Austen presented two Budgets as Chancellor. In his first he increased income tax from 11d. to 1s. and put an extra 3d. in the pound duty on tobacco and 2d. on tea. In his second Budget he reluctantly left income tax at 1s., though he took off the extra 2d. from the duty on tea. He was also responsible for the issue of £10,000,000 2¾ per cent Exchequer Bonds, repayable by equal instalments over ten years. This cheap form of borrowing by the Government was surprisingly successful and both Budgets were well received.

During all this time, Austen maintained his interest in foreign affairs. Balfour had, greatly to his credit, instituted the Committee of Imperial Defence and Austen, as Chancellor, became a member of it. He took an extremely keen interest in it and one paper which he circularized to the other members of the committee at the time of the Moroccan crisis in 1905 when war between France and Germany appeared a possibility is well worth quoting as showing his great prescience and knowledge of foreign affairs.

He had, he said, received reliable information that there was a widespread belief in France that Germany desired to persecute that country into an alliance against England. Germany was afraid to attack England with 900,000 soldiers on her flank, but if she could be certain of immunity from French interference, she would throw her troops across Belgium and Holland, seize the ports over against England and land an army on our shores. . . . The value of the English alliance to a continental power was greatly diminished by our reluctance to give definite engagements to be in a definite place at a definite time with a given force of ships and soldiers. The appalling swiftness of the blows in modern European warfare made it absolutely necessary to determine in time of peace all the steps to be taken if they were to be effectively helpful in time of war. France desired to avoid provocation but would not allow Germany to dictate her foreign policy. . . . In the event of a Franco-German war, it was now known with certainty in Paris that Germany would 'immediately violate the neutrality of Belgium'. (14)

Shortly after going to the Exchequer Austen left 40 Princes Gardens, where hitherto he had always lived with his father whenever Parliament was in session, and moved into No. 11 Downing Street, the official residence of the Chancellor of the Exchequer. On doing so, he wrote the following letter to his father:

My Dear Father,
I cannot close my first evening away from your roof . . . without writing a line to you. It is so great a change in my life, and all about me is so strange, that as yet I hardly realize it.

But what I do realize is how much I owe to you, and how very dear to me is the close friendship which you have encouraged between us. I do not think there are many fathers who have been and are to their sons all that you have been to me; and my prayer tonight is that the perfect confidence which I have enjoyed for so long may continue unimpaired by our separation, and that I may do something to help you in the great work which you have undertaken.

It is at once a great encouragement and a great responsibility to be heir to so fine a tradition of private honour and public duty, and I will do my best to be not unworthy of the name.

Ever your affectionate son,
Austen Chamberlain.' (15)

Meanwhile, Austen was finding his task of providing the link between Balfour and his father a very difficult one. Each went his own way. Balfour's attitude towards the whole question of Tariff Reform was baffling and inscrutable in the extreme. It certainly was not a subject on which he felt at all strongly. There were few political subjects on which he did so feel. Education was certainly one such subject and Defence and the Anglo-French Entente were perhaps others. The fiscal question interested but did not excite him. He recognized, however, the importance of strengthening inter-imperial ties and that, if foreign nations insisted on piling up tariffs against British goods, there might come a time when Britain would be left with no alternative but to retaliate. He spoke in this sense at Sheffield in October 1903, hoping that by his so-called Sheffield programme he would avoid the twin dangers of having to disown Joseph Chamberlain on the one hand, and of committing himself to taxes on food, which he knew would be electorally disastrous, on the other.

Joseph Chamberlain was not at all satisfied with this. As Balfour's speeches became more and more vague and academic, so did those of Chamberlain become more and more concrete, practical and specific and the gulf between the two men widened correspondingly. Austen did his best to close it. He wrote long and earnest letters to Balfour, begging him to adopt a more positive attitude on the Tariff issue.

Balfour's replies were a masterpiece of dialectical skill and polished evasion. He treated Austen (whom he genuinely liked and who liked him) rather as a kindly professor would treat a favourite pupil who was both able and industrious but had not yet arrived at a due recognition of the many-sidedness of truth.

Austen found Balfour's behaviour in the House even more exasperating than his answers to letters. As a walker along a parliamentary tight rope, Balfour displayed almost incredible skill. When the storm broke about him with Joseph Chamberlain's adoption of Tariff Reform and then his resignation as well as that of nearly all the most important members of his Cabinet, few competent observers thought that he could remain Prime Minister for more than a few months. Yet he succeeded in doing so for two and a half years. This was due in large measure to his great intellectual skill and debating powers which enabled him so successfully to remain for a long time 'all things to all men' both in the House and in the country.

The Liberal Opposition, however, were determined to exploit Balfour's dilemma to the full. At first he fenced so skilfully that he was able to parry their thrusts, though he lost some of the ablest among the younger members of his Party; it was during this period that Winston Churchill crossed the floor of the House. The time came, however, when the Liberals framed motions in such a way that if Balfour opposed them he would stand committed to the Chamberlain programme but annoy the Free Traders in his own Party, whereas if he supported them the opposite result would follow. Austen, who was a convinced supporter of his father, wanted Balfour to take a bold line in the House and come out wholeheartedly and unequivocally in favour of Tariff Reform. But Balfour was still uncertain how far Joseph Chamberlain's campaign was making headway in the country and he decided to abstain on these Liberal resolutions and he succeeded, greatly to Austen's chagrin, in persuading a majority of the Cabinet to adopt this course. Austen was deeply perturbed by this and wondered whether he ought to resign. Or would he serve the cause of Tariff Reform better by continuing to remain a member of the Government?

Extremely worried and torn by conflicting emotions, Austen decided to consult his father, who, however, told him that he must make his own decision. After a sleepless night, Austen decided to 'eat dirt' and follow the official Party line.

Meanwhile, Joseph Chamberlain's Tariff Reform campaign was proceeding apace. He had founded the Tariff Reform League and had engaged a staff of experts to feed him with information on the subject, industry by industry. He himself undertook a protracted speaking tour, covering as much of the country as possible, and including in the first few months of his campaign places as far apart as Glasgow, Greenock, Newcastle, Tynemouth, Liverpool, Cardiff and Leeds. Asquith and Lloyd George followed in his wake. In clarity of exposition and in the mastery of economic principles, Asquith excelled. Lloyd George relied more on rhetoric and declamation. At Oldham, in October 1903, replying to Chamberlain's speech at Glasgow a few days before, Lloyd George said:

> 'Mr. Chamberlain has appealed to the workmen and there were very fine specimens of the British workman on his platform. There were three Dukes, two Marquesses, three or four Earls, and as many Lords as there were ministerial resignations. They had gone to help the workman to tax his own bread. The corn laws meant high rents for them and, when a statesman of Mr. Chamberlain's position comes forward and proposes a return to the old corn law days, Lords and Dukes and Earls and Squires all come clucking towards him like a flock of fowls when they hear the corn shaken in the bin. . . . Mr. Chamberlain spoke of the day when every working man should have a pig. A few years ago the policy was three acres and a cow. Now it is three Dukes and a pig.'(16)

Referring to the position as between Balfour on the one hand and Joseph and Austen Chamberlain on the other, Lloyd George described the Government as 'like a worm, cut in half, but both ends still wriggling blindly', and declared that 'the Prime Minister tried to escape from the Birmingham compound but the overseer left in charge discovered him before he got very far from the fence'.(17) He described Austen as being like Casabianca 'bravely sinking with the ship on his father's orders', and said that Joseph Chamberlain's speeches were one long tale of woe: 'Our financial supremacy was going, our merchant trade was going, our industries were going. In fact,' said Lloyd George 'everything is going except the Government and that won't go.'(18)

Amongst the meetings which Joseph Chamberlain addressed

during those early months was one at Liverpool which was to have important consequences. Chamberlain attached great importance to winning over the working masses of industrial Lancashire. Here he had discovered an unexpected but extremely welcome ally in the person of Sir Archibald Salvidge, the leader of Tory democracy in Liverpool, a man who, though never in the House of Commons, wielded enormous influence which was by no means confined to that city. Salvidge had arranged a lunch-party in the Town Hall at which the Mayor and a number of other notables were present. After lunch, Chamberlain was introduced to a young man who, he was told, would be one of the speakers at the meeting.(19) The young man surprised him by immediately plunging into the political situation and addressing the great man in the following manner: 'Cannot you postpone the proposal to tax food until we are politically stronger? Cannot you in the first place use the Protectionist argument which has great value in the industrial constituencies – and postpone until we are stronger the full, and ultimately indispensable programme?' Utterly astonished, Chamberlain surveyed the young man through his eye-glass and then remarked coldly: 'My young friend, you have mistaken my purpose; all these matters were deeply considered by me before I conceived and declared my proposals.' The young man said afterwards that he would have liked to pursue the matter 'as I was entirely unconvinced'.(20)

The meeting was a great success. Chamberlain got an enormous ovation and his speech was very well received. When it was over, however, he was surprised to find that the young man who had been arguing with him that afternoon had been chosen to second the vote of thanks. He was still more surprised when, instead of the few perfunctory remarks usual on such occasions, this speech went on for nearly half an hour. But, though surprised, Chamberlain was not annoyed; on the contrary, his face soon became wreathed in smiles. For here was no half-hearted apology for Tariff Reform but a vigorous and brilliant defence of it, coupled with an attack on the Liberals which was quite as scathing as anything that Lloyd George could produce. Half-way through the speech, Chamberlain turned to Salvidge and whispered 'Who is this young man? He was arguing with me this afternoon.'

'He is a local barrister of whom we have a very high opinion,' replied Salvidge. 'His name is F. E. Smith. He is fighting the Scotland division at the next election.' 'The *Scotland* division,' said Chamberlain. 'He'll never win that.' A thoughtful expression came over his face and soon he was seen to whisper to Salvidge again.(21) After the meeting he went up to Smith, congratulated him on a brilliant speech and then said, 'I have told Salvidge that he must get you a seat that you can win. You will be returned to Parliament. Come up to me in the lobby of the House of Commons and recall yourself to my recollection.'(22)

Joseph Chamberlain was invariably kind and helpful to the younger generation and his kindness was by no means confined to his own supporters. Ever since he had gone to speak for Winston Churchill at Oldham in the Khaki Election, when he had smilingly told him that 'the last time I came here was to sell screws', Chamberlain had followed Churchill's carreer with interest and had more than once spoken with admiration and approval of him to Ausen. For his part, the brilliant young Winston, enthralled almost from the cradle by politics, had found Joseph Chamberlain a particularly fascinating figure and had engaged him in conversation whenever he could. They had met frequently not only in the House of Commons but also at dinner-parties in London and at country house parties. Churchill recalled later one occasion when they were both the guests of Lady St. Helier at her delightful house on the Thames. One afternoon, when they were all sailing down the river in a launch, they passed an old man sitting in a chair near the river. 'Look, there is Labouchere,' said Lady St. Helier. 'A bundle of old rags,' remarked Chamberlain, turning his head away but not before Churchill had noticed the expression of intense loathing which had come over Chamberlain's face.

Now they were opposed politically and Churchill was forcefully and ferociously attacking that programme of Tariff Reform which was so dear to Joseph Chamberlain's heart and to which he had committed his whole political future. Churchill had already developed considerable powers of invective and would castigate the Tory policy in such telling phrases as 'Patriotism by the Imperial Pint, an open hand with the public purse and an open door for the public house, cheap labour for the millionaire and dear food for the million.' He was now engaged on the biography of his father and wrote to Chamberlain (though with some trepidation) for help over letters, etc. He received an immediate invitation to spend the night at Highbury, where he dined alone with Joseph Chamberlain whom he found charming. Over a bottle of 1834 port they talked into the small hours of the morning and Chamberlain produced letters and diaries and memoranda and talked about them with a vivacity and sparkle which fascinated the younger man. All that Chamberlain said about their political differences was 'I think you are quite right feeling as you do to join the Liberals. You must expect to have the same sort of abuse flung at you as I have endured. But if a man is sure of himself, it only sharpens him and makes him more effective.'(23)

13

A Birthday and a Wedding

Though Chamberlain made many converts to Tariff Reform in the course of his campaign, not all the members of his own family were to be found in this number. Arthur Chamberlain, in particular, remained an unrepentant and militant Free Trader throughout. Nor did he keep his views to himself. On the contrary, he embodied them in speeches and pamphlets, some of which proved no inconsiderable embarrassment to Joseph. One of his pamphlets was entitled 'A Straight Talk on Free Trade and Protection', and Arthur caused it to be circulated among the workpeople employed by Kynochs, advising them in it to 'Vote Liberal for Free Trade and Spending Power'. So telling were some of Arthur's arguments that Asquith, in one of his speeches, quoted him with great effect against Joseph.

When Joseph Chamberlain took his career in his hands and broke with Gladstone, Arthur had been one of his chief lieutenants in the hard struggle he had had to maintain his position in Birmingham. But the consuming passion of Arthur's life was temperance reform. As chairman of the Birmingham Licensing Magistrates he had been responsible for the 'Surrender Scheme', a plan for reducing the number of licensed houses by agreement.(1) This had worked well but Arthur's zeal had met with ever-increasing opposition and, in the end, mainly owing to the efforts of a number of Conservative Magistrates, he was defeated in the election for the Chairmanship. This infuriated him and, furthermore, he utterly disapproved of the licensing policy of Balfour's Government. In a speech in Birmingham in 1904 Arthur had declared that:

'In these days too much importance is given to public opinion and too little importance is given to the duty of obeying our own consciences and of giving effect to our own convictions. . . .

I knew when I began (on the 'Surrender Scheme') that sooner or later I should find myself in opposition to the most powerful and the most frankly selfish trade in the country. I knew that I should make more enemies than friends and that the more successful I was the more unpopular I should be. . . . I visited public houses and saw their effect on the life of the people.'

He went on to say that his experience had been sufficient 'to prove the havoc wrought by drink'. He added that Balfour had succumbed to political pressure, and that the agitation which had preceded his own dismissal was 'identified with the Unionist Party', whose 'henchmen and wirepullers' brought down their trained Members of Parliament, 'men of the greatest influence in politics, but who had taken no part in our licensing work and knew nothing of its effect on the homes of the people. I cannot help thinking,' he said, 'that some people will pay a heavy price in the next world for having been Magistrates in this'. He continued:(2)

'I repudiate a Party that sinks so low, whose Imperial ideas end in making them slaves to the Empire of drink. Mr. Balfour's immoral bargain with the drink trade cannot succeed. . . . The Magistrates will not submit to the affront of having their discretionary powers taken away. The people will not consent to be taxed for the sake of the richest trade in the country. . . . After the next General Election we shall have a new Parliament and the new Government will once more lead the country in the paths of peace, prosperity and reform and in those days the temperance cause will certainly triumph. With me all personal considerations are absorbed in the hope that Birmingham will return to the principles that inspired it in the days of John Bright and will once more justify her old reputation of being the best governed city in the Kingdom.'(3)

Arthur's tirade may seem, at first sight, slightly absurd to the present generation. It was not so, however, in the circumstances of his own day and age. For this was the time of the 'gin palace', when enterprising publicans would advertise their ability to make a man 'drunk for a penny' and 'dead drunk for twopence'. In the Black Country the 'havoc wrought by drink' was particularly pronounced.

Throughout his life, Arthur Chamberlain had managed to combine, in a remarkable manner, business, philanthropic and public activities. He became chairman of the Birmingham Hospital for Women, an institution very dear to his heart, for which down the years he did wonderful work. His manner of dealing with shareholders in the various companies of which he became the chairman was all his own. Finding one shareholder, who continually asked him questions, extremely tiresome, Arthur turned to the secretary and asked him how many shares the man owned. 'Ten,' whispered the secretary. Arthur then extracted a ten-pound note from his wallet and turning a wrathful gaze on the shareholder, said to him 'There's your shareholding. Now leave the room.'(4)

As time went on Joseph Chamberlain became increasingly irritated with Balfour's procrastination over the fiscal issue and the rift in the Conservative Party continued to get worse and worse. Finally, towards the end of November 1905, addressing the annual meeting of the National Liberal Council at Bristol, Chamberlain gave public vent to his feelings of irritation, declared that he felt confident that he had the support of the overwhelming majority of Conservatives and Liberal Unionists and accused Balfour of evading the really important issues. It was a fighting speech in which Chamberlain gave notice that thenceforward he would wage war on anyone, including Balfour and the Duke of Devonshire, who sought in any way to water down his programme over Tariff Reform. 'No army was ever led successfully to battle on the principle that the lamest should govern its march,' he said. It was almost certainly as a result of this speech that Balfour decided that he could carry on no longer, and on December 4th, 1905, he tendered his resignation to the King, who accepted it and sent for Sir Henry Campbell-Bannerman, the then leader of the Liberal Party. Campbell-Bannerman agreed to form a Government, but, a few weeks later, asked for a dissolution and Parliament was, accordingly, dissolved in January 1906.

The General Election which followed ended in disaster for the Conservative and Liberal Unionist Parties. A number of factors contributed to this, but three were outstanding – the importation of Chinese coolies into the mines in the Transvaal, the fear of dear food, and the offence given to the Nonconformist conscience by the Education Act. The Liberals exploited each of these to the full and there were Nonconformist ministers on nearly every Liberal platform. There were also placards of Chinese coolies manacled together, and others displaying the little loaf labelled 'Protection' and the big loaf labelled 'Free Trade'.

Chamberlain had, sometime previously, ridiculed the 'big and little loaf' in the course of one of his speeches in Birmingham – 'I have had the curiosity to inquire what would be the exact difference in the size of the loaf if the whole tax which I propose to be put upon corn was met by a corresponding reduction in the size of the loaf. I asked my friend Mr. Alderman Bowkett to make me two loaves in order to test this question,' he said. He then drew out of a paper parcel two loaves, apparently identical in size, and held them up before the audience amidst laughter and cheers.(5)

The result of the General Election of 1906 was that the Liberals were returned with a total of 401 seats, the Irish Nationalists getting 83 and Labour (significantly) 29. Against these, the combined Conservative and Liberal Unionist strength was only 157 (132 Conservatives, 25 Liberal Unionists). Amongst the many casualties on the Conservative side was Arthur Balfour who was defeated in Manchester by Mr. (later Mr. Justice) Horridge. In those days the results did not all come out on the same day and the news of Balfour's defeat caused consternation among the Conservatives of nearby Liverpool which had still to go to the poll. But there was one Conservative candidate who proved equal to the occasion and in the Walton division of Liverpool placards appeared bearing the words 'Is Balfour out? Then all the more reason for putting *Smith* in.' F. E. Smith was returned with a small majority, one of the few Conservatives in industrial Lancashire to get in.

He had not forgotten Joseph Chamberlain's promise. On March 12th, 1906, a motion was put down by a Liberal Member – 'That this House, recognizing that in the recent General Election the people of the United Kingdom have demonstrated their unqualified fidelity to the principles and practice of Free Trade, deems it right to record its determination to resist any proposal . . . to create in this country a system of Protection.' The House was packed and everybody wanted to speak. But Smith had made up his mind that this was his opportunity and that he would make his maiden speech that night if he possibly could. He sought out Joseph Chamberlain, who had not forgotten him and promised to do what he could and who then went off in the direction of the Speaker's chair. A few minutes later, Chamberlain returned. 'I have spoken to the Speaker,' he said. 'You will be called on just before ten o'clock. This is the chance of your life, my friend. See that you use it.'

He used it fully and Joseph Chamberlain was delighted with the speech and particularly with the clever way in which his young protégé turned the tables on that past master of insult and invective, David Lloyd George, now President of the Board of Trade. Smith referred to a suggestion by Lloyd George 'to simple rustics' that 'if the Tories came into power, they would introduce slavery on the hills of Wales'. 'I did not say that,' Lloyd George immediately interrupted. 'The right hon. gentleman would no doubt be extremely anxious to forget it if he could,' said Smith, 'but, anticipating a temporary lapse of memory, I have in my hand the *Manchester Guardian* of January 16th. 1906, which contains a report of his speech. The right hon. gentleman said: "What would they say to introducing Chinamen at 1s. a day into the Welsh quarries? Slavery on the hills of Wales! Heaven forgive me for the suggestion." I have no means of judging how Heaven *will* deal with persons who think it decent to make such suggestions.'

Meanwhile, with Balfour no longer a member, Joseph Chamberlain had become, for the time being, Leader of the Opposition. There were some who would have liked to have taken advantage of Balfour's defeat to get rid of him from the Party leadership altogether, and to replace him with Joseph Chamberlain, but Chamberlain would have none of this. Intensely irritated though he had been at times with Balfour, he remained completely loyal to him throughout. 'Nothing would induce me to take the leadership, in his [Balfour's] place,' he wrote to Walter Long, 'and I have told all my friends, some of whom are no doubt as indiscreet as his supporters, that it is no use suggesting me for a position which would be entirely opposed to my personal sentiments and must inevitably lead to diaster. The leader of a Party mainly composed of Conservatives ought to be, and I think must be, a Conservative . . . I am told, though I do not think the matter was mentioned when I saw Balfour, that he is as much opposed to a third leadership (which would be quite acceptable to me) as he is to a definite platform or a union of organizations. In fact he is *non possumus* everywhere, and I confess I do not see my way out of the difficulties in which we are placed.'(6)

Austen, meanwhile, had not been feeling at all well, and he decided that, as soon as he could, he would seek rest and change. It was not, however, until April 1906 that he was able to get away for a holiday. Then he went abroad with his friend and contemporary Leverton Harris, who was Conservative Member for Tynemouth. The two friends went to Algiers. One afternoon, they were having tea in the garden of one of the leading hotels, when Austen drew the attention of his friend to a very attractive young lady who was sitting at a nearby table. She was tall, slender, fair-haired and in her middle twenties. 'You see that girl sitting over there,' said Austen, 'That's the girl I'm going to marry.'(7) Somehow he managed to scrape an aquaintance and there followed a whirlwind courtship. Her name was Ivy Dundas; her father was a Colonel in the regular army. In this and in other respects her background was quite different from Austen's, for her male relations on both sides had, for generations, either been Army officers or clergymen of the Church of England. Within ten days of their first meeting, Austen had announced the engagement. Congratulations poured in to them both. There were two which Ivy particularly treasured. The first was from Austen's father:

'My dear Miss Dundas,

Austen has just informed me of his engagement, and I feel that I must not lose a day in telling you how pleased we all are with the news, and how delighted we shall be to welcome you to what has been a very united family, and how grateful we are to you for all the prospects of increased happiness to him which your consent to be his wife has brought into his life.

May I say to you, as his father, that he has been the best of sons and the most affectionate and unselfish of brothers, and that I hope this will be some guarantee to you that he will be a loving and devoted husband ... you have it in your power to give him the one thing that has hitherto been wanting, to complete his life, the intimate sympathy and support which only a wife can afford.... With you at his side to share his feelings, and support and encourage him, he will find new courage in facing the anxieties which come to every public man, and his private happiness will increase the usefulness of his public life.

You will see how confidently we anticipate the good effects which your share in his future will have on him, but, believe me, we are not less confident that you will not regret the choice you have made, and that your life also will be broadened, your interests enlarged, and your happiness increased by the life companionship on which you are entering.

I hope that it may not be long before we meet again, and when I may express to you personally my delight at your engagement.

> Believe me,
> Most sincerely yours,
> J. Chamberlain.'(8)

The other was from Austen's sister Beatrice.

'Dear Miss Dundas,

I long to add another to the hearty welcomes that await you from Austen's family. I almost feel as though we owed you an apology for being so many, but we are all possessed by one feeling just now, and rejoicing at the happiness which you have brought into Austen's life. . . . I could sing his praises to you all day, and should much like to do so – not that I think you can need any telling to know what he is, but because I think you would like to hear nice things about him, and about his strength and his tenderness, his unselfishness and resourcefulness. . . .'(9)

To few men has marriage brought greater happiness than to Austen Chamberlain. The difference in background, far from being a drawback, was a great advantage. Ivy brought him out and broadened and widened his mind and outlook to a greater degree, and suited him far better than a member of the 'Kenrick clan' in Birmingham or any of that ilk could ever have done. Their devotion to one another grew and deepened as the years went by, and the extent of it may be gauged by some of the letters Austen wrote to her after they had been married for more than fifteen years. Thus, in 1922, on the occasion of one of their rare separations, he wrote:

'I have no news to send you except that I love you, and that is no news to you. Perhaps it is well that we should have been separated a few days, for otherwise we should never have known how much we were to one another . . . when a man has all he needs, he is apt to take his happiness too much for granted, and to think too lightly of his good fortune. When you are with me, I am surrounded with your love, so cushioned on the security and confidence that you bring, that I have nought to wish for, except a little more of this world's goods that I might leave you and those I love in greater comfort and security. But when you are absent, that which in your presence I feel without expression, and feed upon without thought, suddenly becomes a conscious need, an insistent thought, pounding and penetrating all I do and think and feel and say, and I long to have you near me, and to whisper in your ear how deeply, how passionately I love you and am bound up in you. These are the times when I would be a poet that I might sing my love to you and lay bare my heart, with the shamelessness of a poet's outpourings. In place of all that I would say, I can only echo I love you, love, love you. Heart and head, body and soul, I am yours my beloved. Near or far you possess me,' And again, 'My dearest when you are out of my reach, above all when you are not well, the world is a grim place even on the brightest and loveliest of days. It is you who have brought all the sunshine into my life and who fill my days with love and happiness and, when you are not near me, my heart is one great aching longing for you.'(10)

The news of Austen's engagement had been received with great interest and enthusiasm in Birmingham, and it was not long before large numbers of his own and his father's friends and supporters in that city had the opportunity of meeting his fiancée. One of the first public functions which Ivy and Austen attended together was the banquet given in the Town Hall to celebrate Joseph Chamberlain's seventieth birthday. Tremendous preparations had been made for this event. On July 7th, 1906, there was a civic lunch at the Council House, at which more than two hundred people were present, including all the civic dignitaries. In his speech of thanks during which it was noticed that there were tears in his eyes, Joseph Chamberlain said:

Mr. and Mrs. Joseph Chamberlain

Arthur Chamberlain, senior

'My Lord Mayor, I appreciate very highly your hospitality and the way in which you have made yourself the mouthpiece of my fellow-citizens in a manner which recalls so many personal and public associations and such a long course of un-broken friendships, and, above all, which fills my heart with pride and thankfulness that, with the greater part of my life behind me, I have been able to retain the distinction which I have most coveted and which I most prize, the affectionate regard of those among whom I live. . . . I feel that, if I have been permitted to serve this community, no man has ever had more generous masters. They have been my teachers also. What I am, for good or ill, they have made me. This is the city of my adoption, and of my affection. It has been the home of strong convictions, of great ideals, of frank expressions, of earnest endeavour to carry out its ideals, and I have tried to interpret what I believe to be the spirit of the town. I have found, in the affection of my own people, an overwhelming reward for a strenuous life of work and contest.'(11)

After the lunch, there was a motor-car procession to Birmingham's main parks – Victoria (King's Heath), Ward End, Aston, Victoria (Handsworth), Summerfield and Calthorpe. Enormous crowds were massed in these parks, in each of which there was a special enclosure, where Chamberlain was presented with an address of congratulation and welcome. It was not, however, the oratory of the civic leaders that was the chief feature of this great day. It was the enthusiasm of the common people, who turned out in their thousands and their cries of "'Ere comes Joe', 'Good old Joe', 'Best of luck to you Joey', touched Chamberlain most. The scenes were without precedent, and unforgettable. A contemporary journalist wrote:

'For 14 or 15 miles, Mr. Chamberlain rode beneath bunting . . . it seemed as if every house on the long route had its bay of banners. Thousands of strings of banners and flags and devices of all kinds were hung across from house to house. Each road and street was a bright vista of many colours and the sun shone gloriously on all. Hundreds of windows were bowers of flowers and greenery . . . the poorer class streets made as brave a show as the suburban roads lined with pretty houses . . . but the most memorable feature of the day was the endless crowds who cheered the great citizen. They numbered hundreds of thousands – probably more than half the population of Birmingham, Aston and Handsworth. They had one thought – to show Mr. Chamberlain their pride in him, and their good wishes for himself and his family . . . Mr. Chamberlain who witnessed the display in Calthorpe Park until half-past ten at night seemed as happy as all the hundreds of thousands of happy people who thronged the city.'(12)

Two days later, on July 9th, there was a large meeting at the Bingley Hall; Joseph Chamberlain was to be the chief speaker and Austen and Neville were there too. Joseph's entrance into the Hall provoked wild enthusiasm. As he mounted the platform the whole audience rose and sang a song composed specially for the occasion which included the words 'We'll follow Joe through weal and woe, for the sake of Auld Lang Syne'. An eye-witness said that the effect on the audience, as he rose to make his speech, was 'electrical', adding that 'it was one of those demonstrations which made one feel that there is a certain magnetism about Mr. Chamberlain's personality which influences all those who come within his presence'.(13)

He began by reviewing some of the great achievements of his alliance with the Conservatives: Extension of local government, free education, facilities for allotments and smallholdings, the development of factory legislation and workmen's compensation – these were only a small part of what had been done. 'People talk of a change of opinion as if it were a disgrace,' he said. 'To me it is a sign of life. If you are alive you must change. It is only the dead who remain the same [*laughter and cheers*]. And of all charges brought against a man or a party that of inconsistency because of changed opinion is the most inept.' Then he went on to speak of the Empire:

> 'The moral grandeur of a nation depends on its being some-times able to forget itself,' he said, '. . . to think of the race for which it stands. England without an Empire – can you conceive it? England in that case would not be the England we love. If the ties of sympathy which have gradually been woven between ourselves and our children, who are soon to become great

nations over the seas, if these ties were weakened or destroyed, if we suffered their affection to die, if we allowed them to drift apart, then this England of ours would soon sink from the comparative position it has enjoyed throughout the centuries . . . it would be a fifth-rate nation. We will not have it [*loud cheers*]. . . . The union of the Empire must be accompanied, as I have said, by a closer understanding, by a closer sympathy. To secure that is the highest object of statesmanship now at the beginning of the twentieth century, and if these were the last words I was permitted to utter to you, I would rejoice to utter them in your presence, and with your approval. I know that the fruition of our hopes is certain. I hope I may be able to live to congratulate you upon our common triumph but in any case I have faith in the people. I trust in the good sense, the intelligence and patriotism of the majority, the vast majority of my countrymen. I look forward to the future with hope and confidence and

> "Others I doubt not if not we
> The issue of our toil shall see."'(14)

Those were indeed the last words that he was ever to address to a great gathering of his fellow-citizens. He received a tremendous ovation when he sat down and then there were repeated calls for Austen. Rising to his feet at last, amid loud cheers, Austen said:

'I do not know how it is, but lately there seems to be some confusion in the public mind between those shows which are my right honourable friend's and those which are mine. This is not mine. Yet since you call upon me to say a few words there are two thoughts that have been chiefly present in my mind in these days to which I would like to give expression. You, the citizens of Birmingham, have placed every member of my family under new obligations. You have bound us to you by even closer ties of interest and affection, by the heartiness of the welcome that you have given to my father, by the generous recognition of his long and faithful service, and by the warmth of the welcome that you have given to all who are connected with him, or who are about to be connected with him. For my brother and myself, I would say that we recognize the obligations that you have laid us under, and that if, at any time, in any capacity, we can render any service to the city of our birth, we shall be proud to obey your summons.

There is another thought, perhaps less personal . . . which has dwelt much in my mind. It is that we who have met to celebrate this period in the career of a man who has given his life to his city and his race . . . are pledged by every tie of honour and gratitude to support him to the utmost of our power, and we are pledged that, come what may to any individual in the fight, we will never rest till victory crowns the cause for which he has laboured for so long.'(15)

The day after the Bingley Hall meeting, Joseph Chamberlain travelled to London. Two days later, while dressing for dinner, he had a stroke which paralysed the whole left side of his body, and from the effects of which he never recovered. He was taken straight to bed and remained there continuously for five weeks, at the end of which time he was carried downstairs and, shortly after that, he was able to be wheeled out of doors. But he remained an invalid for the rest of his life.

However, his brain continued to be perfectly active, and he could still take a keen interest not only in national politics, but also in local affairs, and in those municipal and charitable projects in Birmingham which had always been so dear to his heart. High amongst these latter was Birmingham University, a subject which had, in fact, been occupying his thoughts off and on for more than twenty years. As long ago as 1888, he had told his fellow-citizens that they must not confine their zeal for education to the elementary stage, but that the ultimate aim must be that of 'enabling the poorest amongst us if he has but the ability, if God has given him these gifts, to rise to the greatest heights of culture . . . I desire that we may crown the edifice by establishing here in Birmingham a true Midland University. I hope that every Birmingham man will keep it before him as one of the great objects of his life.'(16)

Another ten years passed, however, before he was able to take concrete steps towards the accomplishment of his ideal, and it was not until the year 1898 that a Petition for a Royal Charter incorporating the University was drafted. Chamberláin made many alterations in the original draft and it was not until 1900 that, the Petition having been presented, the Charter was granted and Chamberlain himself was appointed the first Chancellor of the University. In the speech which he made at the first meeting called to authorize the presentation of the Petition, he had set forth some of his aims:

> 'Our ideal may be stated, in a few words, to be the creation in Birmingham of a great school of universal teaching – an institution which shall provide for the intellectual cultivation of the mind in the broadest possible sense, and shall maintain for ever in this city the highest standard of intellectual eminence.'(17)

But he realized fully that Birmingham University, situated as it was at the very heart of one of England's most vital industrial districts, must have a practical content as well. Thus, in the course of his speech at the first meeting of the Court of Governors, he said:

> 'No one can read the reports which have recently appeared of the progress of manufacture in the United States . . . without being fully aware that we have somewhat fallen behind – that we have reached a critical stage, and that it depends very much on what we are doing now at the beginning of the twentieth century whether at its end we shall continue to maintain our supremacy, or even equality, with our great commercial and manufacturing rivals. . . . I would remind you that all history shows that progress of every kind depends upon certain individuals rather than on the mass.'

The 'great steps,' he told his audience, had been accomplished by 'individuals of superior quality and genius' and what they had to do was 'to produce more of these great men'. To the argument that genius was born and not made, he replied that, 'even if it were true, at least we can multiply tenfold the number of those who are qualified to be the assistants and interpreters of these men, who can take their ideas and carry them into practical operation. . . . That is the object . . . which I think the University of Birmingham must . . . deliberately set itself.'(18)

But high ideals were not by themselves enough. It was equally important to secure the material wherewithal for their realization. Originally it was felt that a start could be made with £100,000 but Chamberlain recognized from the beginning that this figure was utterly inadequate. His own first target was £250,000 which, by constant hard work and continual appeals to his friends and admirers in and around Birmingham, and to local pride, he managed to raise. He then proceeded to increase his target first to half a million, and then to a million pounds sterling. 'They must have,' he said at the second yearly meeting of the Court of Governors, 'a University second to none,' and that is what it would cost. He did, however, during his lifetime, see the fund rise to over £450,000 and most of this was due to his own untiring efforts. He managed to persuade Andrew Carnegie and Sir James Chance to give £50,000 each and one of his local admirers, Mr. Charles Hoocroft, to give £20,000. Carnegie's gift was not due to any love or admiration for Joseph Chamberlain himself whom Carnegie described in a letter to John Morley as 'a dangerous demagogue'. 'Your friend (Joseph Chamberlain),' Carnegie wrote, 'is the wrecker of harmony wherever he goes; mark that! Where Satan dwells, discord ever reigns. Never did I know of action so rash, so reckless, as this of his just now. These things show a man of keen, restless energy and drive, minus sane judgment.'(19)

Chamberlain also persuaded the Calthorpe family to give twenty-five acres of land to the University and this munificent gift was increased later by another twenty acres. In addition, by using his influence with the City Council and the local County Councils and with other local bodies and businesses, he managed to secure an annual income equal to the interest on another £200,000.

He himself gave £2,000. He would have liked to have given more, but even this was more than he could really afford, having regard to his earlier losses and the many other calls upon him. Arthur gave £500 to the University and became the chairman of an advisory committee on science and education.

Meanwhile the wedding of Austen and Ivy had taken place at St. Margaret's, Westminster, on Saturday, July 21st, 1906. This was one of the most widely publicized weddings of the year and a great crowd had gathered outside the church. Neville was the best man and nearly all the Chamberlains were there, but not

Joseph who, greatly to his disappointment, was still too ill to attend. Balfour, Asquith and the Morleys were amongst the guests.(20) After their honeymoon abroad, the newly married couple went for a short time to the Hans Crescent Hotel while their new house in Egerton Gardens was being got ready for them. Ivy was very artistic and took a great delight in the choosing and designing of the furniture and decorations. In this she was most successful, and there followed for her and Austen several very happy years during which all that Edwardian society had to offer (and it had a great deal) was at their command. Austen was not then, or at any other time, a rich man, and Ivy had very little of her own, but they managed to live most comfortably with a considerable staff of indoor servants, which included a butler. Being in Opposition, Austen drew no salary from public sources, though he was a director of the Standard Bank. But the letters which he wrote to his stepmother and others, around this time, are replete with descriptions of the lunch- and dinner-parties of eight or ten people which he and Ivy were constantly giving.

Throughout his period in Opposition, Austen maintained a close interest in foreign affairs. He had many friends in foreign countries, and amongst his guests distinguished foreigners were often included. Another of his informants on this subject was Sir Cecil Spring Rice. 'Springy', as he was called affectionately by his many friends and intimates, had been rather a favourite of the Endicotts, and their house in Washington had been one of those at which he had received much kindness and hospitality when he first joined the British Legation in the American capital. After Joseph Chamberlain's marriage to Mary Endicott he had become a fairly frequent and most welcome visitor at Highbury, where he and Chamberlain exchanged views on world topics. They had by no means always seen eye to eye. Chamberlain had for years favoured an Anglo–German–American alliance and had made considerable efforts to this end, including having conversations on the subject with Count von Bulow, when the latter had come to England with the Kaiser. Spring Rice, though agreeing fully with Chamberlain as far as America was concerned, did not agree with his ideas so far as they related to Germany. He knew that country far too well, having served two terms in the British Embassy at Berlin.

It had been Spring Rice's great hope, as he had written to Mrs. Roosevelt, whose husband was President of the United States and a great friend of his, that Chamberlain would lead a 'movement for the regeneration of national character, self-sacrifice, national defence, and devotion of all departments to the good of the nation'.(21) He considered that the time was ripe for such a movement. Now that Joseph Chamberlain had been removed almost completely from the political arena, by his stroke, Spring Rice had turned to Austen. At the time, Spring Rice was the Minister in Stockholm but he kept in touch with affairs in Germany and was fully aware of and seriously alarmed by the menace which that country constituted. Ever since they came to power, he had done his best to warn the Liberal Government of the German danger, but his warnings had fallen on deaf ears, and Asquith, who succeeded Campbell-Bannerman as Prime Minister in April 1908, had described his dispatches as 'hysterical'. (22) Having failed with Asquith, Spring Rice turned to Austen. He told him that all independence of thought in Germany was now gone, and that the whole machinery of German Government through the schools, the Universities and the public services was being used to bring up the younger generation in the same conviction that they must fight England that those of the 'sixties had had that they must fight France. The danger was that they would sow mines all round our coasts, leaving a strip known only to themselves, and having picked a quarrel over some trivial issue, send an ultimatum and immediately invade. Meanwhile they would lull Britain into a false security and do their best to prevent her training her citizens for home defence.(23) From Austen, this point of view received a great deal more sympathy and understanding than it had from Asquith.

Spring Rice went to see Joseph Chamberlain after he had had his stroke and wrote of his visit:

'I saw J.C. He looks all right but you know his situation. It was most touching to see the care taken of him by his wife, and the family affection which surrounds him. He spoke a great deal of C.B. [Campbell-Bannerman] whom he described as a clever man and a brave man and deprecated the attacks made on him by Balfour. He was kindly in all he said of his past associates. I almost wish I hadn't seen him; it is so sad to see that kind of power nearing its end.'(24)

The care and love which his wife lavished on Joseph Chamberlain was certainly beyond praise. For nearly twenty years, her smiling face had been a familiar sight on innumerable platforms up and down the country. Now there were no more speeches to listen to, no more meetings to attend, but her present task was quite as difficult and quite as arduous as any which she had had to face. It was that of keeping her husband cheerful and stopping him getting too depressed by his invalid condition, as well as running his home and looking after him generally. Every year, generally at the end of March or the beginning of April, they went to the South of France where they had rented a villa and the following extracts taken from Mary's letters to her mother give a picture of their life together on the Riviera.

'March 14th, 1907.

Today Joe has walked further than he ever has at all since we came here, a half-mile up the road and back, a trifle more as our drive is steep, and he has to walk down and then up, a steep long pull with only a short level piece in the whole walk. This is very good for he does it on end without sitting down and today the strong wind must have added to the mile in effort as well . . .'(25)

'March 12th, 1908.

Ida and I went for a long walk over the hills and found anemones, violets and other flowers, while the views were charming. Monday, Tuesday and Wednesday were brilliant but the *mistrale* was bad. Today was lovely again. This morning Joe made the most of it by walking out of the garden and along the sea-front where a boulevard has been made. He went a little distance to a seat and sat looking at the sea. Then we got him to come back to his chair, and he sat on the terrace and then the piazza until 4.30 . . . I wish there were more interesting people here, but on Sunday I brought Lord Brougham back from church and two days ago Lord Cadogan turned up; he is to lunch with us on Monday. If we can't get interesting people we must have dull ones for it would be very easy for him to relapse and I do not wish him to do so.'(26)

'March 19th, 1908.

We are jogging along most comfortably and Joe seems well and cheerful, in fact for a few days he has been at high-water mark. It is curious how he still fluctuates for no particular reason and in a way of which he himself is unconscious, but on the whole the general level is higher. I am sure certain gains are established and permanent.'(27)

'April 13th, 1908.

Joe has been getting on well with the assistance of an energetic doctor who comes himself every day to give him exercises; he is making progress again in walking. We went the other day to lunch at the casino, Joe and I, with the same energetic doctor, who is most insistent that he must move about more and do things.'(28)

In another of her letters, Mary writes to her mother, 'Joe is sitting in the drawing-room reading a French novel.'

While they were in England, Mary was greatly helped by the number of her husband's old friends and associates who came to see him. Balfour, Carson and Bonar Law each went to stay at Highbury. Another most welcome visitor both before and after Joseph became an invalid was Charles Gore, Bishop of Birmingham. Joseph Chamberlain had mellowed considerably in his old age and differences in point of view on religious matters did not affect the delight which he and Gore took in each other's company; and, in February 1908, his future biographer called on Joseph Chamberlain and Mary wrote, 'Yesterday, Mr. Garvin came to lunch and Joe was quite animated. It was delightful to see Mr. Garvin's pleasure in seeing him.'(29) Garvin was a perfervid admirer of Joseph Chamberlain, a fact which fully appears from his biography. Garvin had been a great help to Chamberlain in his Tariff Reform campaign, winning for himself the title of 'Chamberlain's first Lieutenant of the Press'.(30)

14

The People's Budget and the House of Lords

Meanwhile, on the domestic front, events were rapidly moving towards a constitutional crisis. This was due to the action of the House of Lords in either drastically amending or rejecting completely a number of Government Bills. During the election, Balfour had somewhat imprudently boasted that, whether as the Government or whether in Opposition, the Conservative Party would remain in control of the affairs of the country. When it came to the actual point of exercising the veto, however, Balfour and his co-advisers of the huge Conservative majority in the House of Lords acted with a good deal more circumspection. The policy now was to deal mercilessly with those measures which their Lordships did not consider to be particularly popular in the country, while letting through any which seemed to command a large measure of support, particularly among the large mass of uncommitted voters in the working class. Acting on this principle, they drastically amended the Education Bill, eradicating those provisions which they considered had been introduced solely in order to placate Noncomformist opinion, while letting through the Trades Disputes Bill, which was popular with organized labour.

To begin with, this policy seemed to pay quite good dividends and, during the latter part of 1906 and throughout 1907, there were definite signs that the tide was flowing in favour of the Opposition. The London County Council and other municipal elections showed a trend to the right, and the Government lost several important by-elections. Emboldened by this, the House of Lords became more and more drastic in its dealings with Government Bills. The Plural Voting Bill, the Scottish Small Holdings Bill and the Licensing Bill were all rejected *in toto*, the latter not as a result of a debate in the Upper House but of a resolution taken at a meeting of peers in Lord Lansdowne's house. The Government did not, however, feel itself to be on strong enough ground over any of these measures to face the country on that issue alone. Then, in the year 1909, the House of Lords committed the crowning blunder of rejecting the Finance Bill.

Judged by modern standards there was nothing very terrible about the Budget which Lloyd George, by then Chancellor of the Exchequer, introduced into the House of Commons in April 1909. A sum of sixteen million pounds was required in order to provide for Old Age Pensions, and to build more Dreadnoughts. The Chancellor proposed to raise this extra money by increasing income tax from one shilling to eighteenpence in the pound, by certain very complicated taxes on increases in land values, by additional duties on spirits and tobacco, by severe impositions on licensed premises, and by a new tax on motor-cars and petrol.

Lloyd George opened his Budget statement at 3 p.m. on April 29th and it went on until 8 p.m., though there was an adjournment for half an hour in the middle because Lloyd George needed a rest. He was tired out from the weeks and months of intense work which his proposals had involved, and the speech, certainly in the manner of delivery, was far below his normal standard. He read most of it from the manuscript and did not read it particularly well, for he frequently stumbled and ignored punctuation. Unusually for Lloyd George, there was only one touch of humour in the whole thing. This occurred when a Conservative M.P., who happened to be a millionaire, got up during the speech and left the chamber and Lloyd George managed to work in a remark about the man 'who went away sorrowful for he had great possessions'.

It fell to Austen's lot, as the ex-Chancellor, to reply. This was before the custom had been established whereby the ex-Chancellor merely offers a few perfunctory and congratulatory remarks. Austen was expected to develop, in broad outline, the attitude of the Opposition towards the Budget and that, without any advance notice of its provisions, was not, in dealing with proposals of this magnitude and complication, by any means easy. But he aquitted himself admirably, and earned warm congratulations from the other Opposition leaders. Neither he nor they had any objections either to Old Age Pensions or Dreadnoughts as such. As regards the former, Joseph Chamberlain had been in favour of them for years, and had been the first prominent politician to suggest them, and would certainly have secured them, had it not been for the high cost of the South African War. As for Dreadnoughts, the Conservatives had also been agitating for these to the accompaniment of the well-known jingle:

'We want eight and we won't wait'

It was in the proposed method of finding money that the Opposition found their principal objection to the Budget. They would have raised it by taxes on foreign imports which, accompanied by colonial preferences, would at one and the same time have 'made the foreigner pay' for Pensions and Dreadnoughts, stimulated British industry and cemented and developed the Empire. Austen's chief criticism of the taxation actually proposed was directed to the land taxes, not so much because they were unfair and unjust to the landed class, as because he regarded them as foolish and unworkable, and likely to cost the revenue far more to operate than they would actually bring in. In this he proved to be entirely right, and it is worth recording that it fell to his lot as Chancellor of the Exchequer in the first post-war Government (of which Lloyd George was Prime Minister) to recommend the repeal of these very taxes on the ground of their extreme unprofitability to the Revenue.

Whether or not Lloyd George deliberately planned the Budget with the idea that the peers should reject it, he certainly commended it to the electorate in terms which were not only such as to arouse the fury and apprehension of the 'backwoodsmen peers' but even to cause thoughtful and intelligent Unionists (Austen included) and high authorities on constitutional law to say that, in the circumstances, this was not just an ordinary money Bill, or an ordinary Budget, but the beginning of something far more sinister. This argument was largely based on the inflammatory speeches delivered by Lloyd George, the most famous being that at Limehouse in July 1909, which contained his attack on the Dukes of Northumberland and Westminster. (Oh these Dukes! how they harrass us!). And at Newcastle he spoke of issues being raised and questions being asked, 'which are now whispered in humble voices, and answers will then be demanded with authority'. He continued:

'The question will be asked, should 500 men, ordinary men, chosen by accident from among the unemployed, override the judgement – the deliberate judgement – of millions of people who are engaged in the industry which makes the wealth of the country? That is one question. Another will be: Who ordained that a few should have the land of Britain as a per-quisite, who made 10,000 people owners of the soil and the rest of us trespassers in the land of our birth? . . . Where did the table of the law come from? Whose finger inscribed it? These are the questions that will be asked. The answers will be charged with peril for the order of things that the peers repre-sent; but they are fraught with rare and refreshing fruit for the parched lips of the multitude who have been treading the dusty road along which the people have marched through the dark ages, which are now merging into the light.'(1)

The Budget was debated for seventy-two days and nights, including several all-night sittings. The committee stage alone lasted for forty-two days. There were 550 divisions. Except for a short period of about twelve days during which he was laid up by sciatica, Austen attended and spoke on nearly every day of the Budget discussions, his speeches occupying 526 columns of Hansard. Only those of Lloyd George and Balfour exceeded his in volume. The Finance Bill went through its third reading in the House of Commons on November 4th, 1909, being finally passed by 370 to 149. On November 30th, on its second reading in the House of Lords, it was rejected by 350 to 75. Asquith immediately decided to ask the King for a dissolution of Parliament. King Edward VII, while agreeing to this, made it clear that, even if the Liberals were successful at the Polls, he would not regard that as sufficient reason for any further exercise of the Prerogative than was necessary to carry through the Budget proposals. There must be a second election before any such exercise designed to alter the Constitution.

There followed an extremely keenly and bitterly contested General Election. Lloyd George had been delighted when the peers rejected his Budget and now went into the attack whole-heartedly and without any restraint whatsoever. At Carnarvon, for instance, early in December, almost immediately after the campaign had opened, he described a peer as one who 'has one man to fix his collar and tie in a morning, a couple of men to carry a boiled egg to him at breakfast, a fourth man to open the door for him, a fifth man to show him in and out of his carriage, and a sixth and seventh to drive him'.(2) And at Wolverhampton 'they [the Lords] have no qualifications, at least they *need* not have any. No testimonials are required . . . they only require a certificate of birth – just to prove they are the first of the litter. . . . You would not choose a spaniel on such principles.'(3) Nor did he confine himself to the 'blue-blooded' amongst the peers. He was equally hard on some of the later arrivals. 'We are not to have estate duties and a super-tax,' he said sarcastically at Wal-worth. 'Why? Because Lord Rothschild signed a protest on behalf of the bankers. . . . We must not put a tax on undeveloped land. Why? Because Lord Rothschild is chairman of an industrial dwellings company. . . . Are we to have all the ways of reform, financial and social, blocked simply by a notice board:

NO THOROUGHFARE
by order of Nathaniel Rothschild?'(4)

There was also some very hard hitting from the other side. F. E. Smith, for example, referred contemptuously to 'Mr. George's Limehouse vulgarity', and declared that Lloyd George's politics could be expressed 'in a simple formula "here is a duke; let us take his watch"'. And referring to the Liberal Government in general, Smith said, 'Let us for a moment drag these hypocrites into the light of day, and observe how closely they resemble the creeping things which are exposed to the sunshine, when a way-farer raises an ancient stone.'(5)

Austen was far more balanced and restrained in presenting the case against the Budget:

'We hear a great deal about the idle rich people; none of us here contend that there are not people of wealth with no particular sense of duty, no particular obligation to anyone but themselves, who live serving, perhaps, no very useful

175

purpose, but there is a great deal of rubbish talked about the idle rich. The great mass of those who will be hit by these taxes . . . are men who, in their own spheres, are discharging their full share of public duties, as well as carrying on, in the country and the town, the life and industry which is necessary to our national prosperity. In my opinion, the cumulative effect of all the taxes proposed in the Budget would be to work . . . a revolution in our country life, which will hit first and foremost, of course, the well-to-do but which will, glancing from their shoulders, fall with added weight upon those of the poor and labouring classes.'(6)

Dealing more specifically with the land taxes, he said, 'Look again at their taxes on land with a building value. Who is going to suffer most? Everybody is going to suffer who has any concern in or with land of that kind, but that which they are going to hit hardest is not an individual, not a class – it is an industry, one of the greatest industries of the country, the building industry, and it is a curious and significant fact that, in almost every case, and in each of these taxes, the worst weight of the burden falls upon an industry which is depressed at the moment that the tax is imposed'.(7)

In their fight over the Budget, the Liberal leaders once more found an invaluable ally in Arthur Chamberlain, who had by then become the President of the Birmingham Liberal Association and who took the chair for Asquith at a mass meeting in September 1909. This took place in the Bingley Hall, Birmingham, where, only a little over three years before, Joseph Chamberlain had made his last great public speech. In his opening remarks, describing himself as 'a business man first and a politician a long way second' Arthur referred to the Budget as 'so bold, so far-reaching and so evidently the landmark of a new age and of a nobler and more effective Liberalism that it might well secure the enthusiastic support of all true Liberals'. He declared that he supported the Budget because it was a Free Trade Budget, mainly based on direct taxation and fortified by many new proposals, which gave to it an elasticity which had been wanting in previous budgets of equal magnitude. . . . This Budget went with schemes for reproductive labour and social reform, and he

THE CHAMBERLAIN FAMILY
Neville   Austen   Joseph
Beatrice   Mary (Mrs. Joseph Chamberlain)

Norman Chamberlain by John A. M. Hay, 1920

[Arthur] felt that it was a business proposition of which he heartily approved. By the recovery of a portion of community value, and the taxation at its real value of undeveloped land, revenue would be obtained from sources that had hitherto escaped their fair share of the national burden. . . . The Budget would not injure a single legitimate interest, but it would remove obstacles to progress, and, for the first time in our history, it would provide an effective substitute for the workhouse and infirmary.

After these opening remarks, Arthur called on the Prime Minister to address the meeting, and Asquith, when the cheering had stopped, turned towards him and said: 'Let me first acknowledge the indebtedness of this vast gathering to you for your presence in the chair, and for the wise and encouraging words with which you have opened our proceedings. It is a great thing for us to have, as our President, one who has enriched the traditions of an illustrious name by such a record as is yours of civil and social service.' There were cheers at the mention of 'an illustrious name'.(8)

Addressing the annual meeting of the Birmingham Trust shortly before this, Arthur had said that:

'The Budget removed from labour something of its worst burdens and in doing that it rendered it more effective and labour, when more effective, added to the general wealth. There was nothing in the Budget which would do anything to depress any of our commercial and trading interests. The way in which it dealt with land would not injure our trade but would assist the process of going back to the land.'(9)

The result of the General Election was that the Liberals lost 104 seats, their majority over the Unionists being reduced to two. The final figures were: Liberals 275, Conservatives 273, Irish Nationalists 82, Labour 40. There was a pathetic scene at the opening of the new Parliament when Joseph Chamberlain was led to his seat by Austen; he was too weak to sign the Parliamentary roll.

The House of Lords accepted the verdict of the people, and duly passed the Finance Bill of 1909. Meanwhile, however, on April 14th, 1910, Asquith had moved the Parliament Bill in the

House of Commons. This provided firstly that the House of Lords should lose its power of veto over all Bills certified by the Speaker to be Money Bills, secondly that Bills passed through the House of Commons in three successive sessions should not require the consent of the House of Lords to become law, and thirdly that future Parliaments should be limited in duration to five years. The stage now seemed to be set for the final battle, when the whole situation was altered by the sudden and unexpected death of Edward VII.

15

Death Again Transforms the Scene

Austen was out of the country at the time of Edward VII's death; so was the Prime Minister. Both returned home immediately and, as the funeral did not take place until May 20th, both were in ample time for it. The vast company of mourners included the German Emperor and eight Kings and, at the request of President Taft, Theodore Roosevelt, who happened to be in England at the time, represented the United States.

By the leaders of the two main Parties, it was now felt that every effort should be made to avoid the new King, George V, becoming enmeshed in a constitutional crisis at the very beginning of his reign. An inter-Party Conference, to deal with future relations between the two Houses of Parliament, was, therefore, arranged. The Government's representatives were A. J. Balfour and Austen Chamberlain and Lords Lansdowne and Cawdor. The sessions lasted from June 17th until November 11th but no agreement was reached. It was during this Conference that Lloyd George made a suggestion which might well, had it been adopted, have altered for the better the whole future course of history. In an extremely important memorandum, addressed in the first instance to Asquith, he advocated a Coalition Government, which could alone, in his view, cope with some of the great dangers which threatened the country both at home and abroad. Lloyd George did from time to time, undoubtedly, have flashes of real genius and this was one of them. Intuitively, he was already coming to grasp something of the extent of the German menace, and the steps which were necessary, if that danger was to be dealt with and war avoided while there was still time. Most important of these steps was some form of compulsory military service, in favour of which both Cecil Spring Rice and Lord Roberts had been arguing for years. But Lloyd George knew that no one party by itself could ever be strong enough to secure this and (to his credit be it said) he pressed for a Coalition Government for all that he was worth.

Lloyd George's memorandum was dated August 17th and, at some time thereafter, though it is not clear when, it was seen by the other members of the Conference. Asquith was distinctly sceptical and probably more than a little apprehensive and distrustful of Lloyd George's ultimate designs in their repercussions on himself. Lord Crewe thought Lloyd George's Memorandum 'a clever document' and Grey expressed himself as being 'favourable' to it. Lloyd George's two strongest adherents in this matter were, however, F. E. Smith and Churchill, and Smith wrote to Austen asking him to contrast what was attainable under Lloyd George's plan with the results of defeat in January, when there would have to be another election if the Conference broke down. Amongst the benefits which would accrue from a Coalition, F. E. Smith said, were 'National Service and an adequate navy'. 'I am absolutely satisfied of Lloyd George's honesty and sincerity,' Smith added. 'He has been taught much by office and is sick of being wagged by a "Little England tail". But, if he proved, in a year or two, *difficile* or turbulent, where is he and where are we? He is done, and has sold the pass. We should still be a united Party. . . . I never in twenty years remember a time when so many men in England were sick of mere Party cries and faction. A great sigh of relief would go up over the whole of business England, if a strong and stable Government were formed.'(1) Austen replied that he was willing to give the matter 'attentive and friendly consideration,' and that 'if we can come to some agreement at the Conference on the points which we are there discussing' there was the possibility that 'a very much wider agreement and closer co-operation might be attainable'. He wrote later, 'I believe that I was the only Unionist member of the Conference who would have wished to pursue the matter further but in the absence of any other material I cannot speak confidently of my own attitude at the time.'(2) Balfour consulted his former Chief whip, Akers-Douglas, who told him that there would be most serious opposition from amongst the Conservative rank and file and that the result of falling in with Lloyd George's proposals would be to split the Conservative Party. In view of this advice, Balfour turned down the suggestion, though with a certain amount of reluctance. He declared later that he put Party unity before all else and was not willing to repeat the mistake of Peel. Lloyd George maintained, to the end of his life, that the rejection of his proposals was a colossal tragedy for the country and in his *War Memoirs* he wrote that if his proposals had materialized there would, by 1914, have been 'a body of trained young men aggregating between a million and one and a half million fit for incorporation into our armies' and 'what is still more important, rifles and other equipment for them', that if Germany had known of this she would have 'hesitated before plunging the world into the disaster of the Great War' and that, even if she had done so, the contribution made by such a force 'might well have been decisive and have shortened the term of the devastating struggle'.(3)

Lloyd George had even formulated suggestions as to the membership of the Coalition Cabinet, and these are said to have included Asquith as Prime Minister (though, perhaps with a seat in the Lords), Balfour – President of a National Defence Committee, Lansdowne – Foreign Secretary, and Austen – First Lord of the Admiralty.

The Inter-Party Conference finally broke down over Irish Home Rule. The Conservatives and Unionists, though quite willing that the House of Lords should be reformed, were unwilling to part with the Lords' veto in circumstances which would enable the Government to enact Home Rule without an election on thet specific issue. By November 1910, it was quite clear that agreement was impossible, and Asquith so informed the King on November 11th, at the same time asking for a dissolution. Further conversations followed as a result of which it was agreed that there should be a dissolution followed by a General Election, and, if the result of the latter was to return Asquith to power, and if the House of Commons then passed a Parliament Bill, which the House of Lords rejected, the King would, by the creation of further peers in exercise of the Royal Prerogative, enable the Bill to become law. The guarantee which Asquith had managed to extract about the exercise of the Royal Prerogative was not, however, to be disclosed until after the election.

Shortly after the Inter-Party Conference had broken down, Balfour, addressing a large meeting in the Albert Hall, gave a pledge that, if the Conservatives were returned to power, they would not introduce food taxes without the matter being submitted to the country by way of referendum. Balfour's so-called pledge was susceptible of more than one construction. One was that it was conditional on the Government giving a similar pledge in regard to Home Rule. Austen was greatly annoyed by the pledge which he regarded as completely unnecessary and likely to prejudice future negotiations within the Empire.

The election was fought with the utmost bitterness on both sides and resulted in the Liberals and Unionists each returning with 272 seats. The Irish Nationalists, however, received 84 and the Labour Party 42. With the support of these two latter Parties, therefore, Asquith was sure of a comfortable working majority but it was clear that, so far as the Irish were concerned, support would only be forthcoming provided that Bills were introduced to remove the House of Lords veto and grant Irish Home Rule. The latter could not, of course, be achieved without the former. The new Parliament was opened on February 5th, 1911, and on February 21st Asquith again introduced the Parliament Bill. This was passed by the House of Commons on May 15th. Now the great question was what the Lords would do. They and their advisers in the House of Commons were divided into two main groups which became known as the 'Hedgers' and 'Ditchers'. The 'Hedgers' favoured allowing the Bill to go through the House of Lords, either by voting for it or abstaining, rather than that the Upper House should be swamped by the creation of additional peers, for it ultimately became known that the King was pledged to an exercise of the Royal Prerogative. The 'Ditchers', on the other hand, favoured fighting it out to the bitter end, even at the risk of the creation of further peers. Austen Chamberlain was a 'Ditcher' so, curiously enough, in spite of his earlier tirades against Lords 'who toil not, neither do they spin' was Joseph. But neither Austen nor Joseph favoured the continuance of the House of Lords in its then form. Both felt that it should be reformed by the introduction of an elective element, but both felt, also, that a strong second chamber, with real powers, was essential, particularly in the circumstances of the time, with Home Rule in 'the offing'. The leader of the 'Ditchers' in the House of Lords was the veteran Ex-Lord Chancellor, Lord

Halsbury, and the two most outspoken 'Ditchers', in the House of Commons, were Carson and F. E. Smith.

On July 25th, 1911, the 'Ditchers' gave a dinner to Lord Halsbury at the Hotel Cecil. In the course of the evening, a telegram was read out from Joseph Chamberlain, urging 'no surrender'. Austen who replied to the toast of 'the House of Commons' spoke of 'this revolution, nurtured in lies, promoted by fraud, and only to be achieved by violence'. He argued that Asquith had 'tricked the Opposition, entrapped the Crown and deceived the people'.(4)

On the night of August 10th, the final division was taken in the House of Lords. It was one of the hottest evenings ever remembered, the thermometer having registered 100 degrees for most of the day. In this stifling atmosphere, in a packed House, the last stage of the drama was enacted. Down to the very last moment, the 'Ditchers' had maintained that Asquith was bluffing, and that there would not, in fact, be a creation of further peers. But, in the course of the debate, Lord Morley, speaking on behalf of the Government, read out a message which he had received from the King's secretary, Lord Stamfordham, that 'In the event of the Bill being defeated, the King would agree to a creation sufficient to guard against any possible combination of the Opposition by which the measure could again be defeated.' Then Morley added, 'Every vote given against my motion will be a vote for a large and prompt creation of peers.' The division was taken shortly after 10.30 and at 10.40 p.m. the final figures were announced, showing that the Government had won by seventeen votes. Thirteen bishops and thirty-seven Unionist peers voted for the Government. Lord Lansdowne and his supporters abstained.

During the remainder of the summer, and throughout the early autumn, dissatisfaction with the leadership was rampant in the Conservative Party. The 'Ditchers' were disgusted with what they regarded as a cowardly surrender over the House of Lords veto and futhermore no one seemed to know what Balfour had really meant by his Albert Hall pledge on food taxes. The longer he refused to commit himself, the greater the discontent with him grew and soon the letters B. M. G. (Balfour Must Go) appeared prominently in the Press and were whispered from mouth to mouth in the clubs. In the third week in August, Austen had gone abroad on a holiday to Switzerland and the Italian lakes. Neville, who had heard of the mounting discontent with Balfour and that a group of 'Ditchers' were banding themselves together with a view to stronger and more definite action, wrote advising Austen to come home as soon as possible because 'the critical point' of his career was at hand. Austen was not willing to take part in any underhand intrigues against Balfour for whom he had a high regard, which was fully reciprocated. But it was not long before Balfour himself decided that the moment had arrived for him to give up the leadership. He formally announced his retirement from it at a meeting of the City of London Conservative Association on November 8th. Austen had been informed that he would do so four days previously.

It is important to realize that the question which now had to be determined immediately was not who was to be the leader of the Conservative Party as a whole, and therefore the next Conservative Prime Minister, but who was to be its leader in the House of Commons. Lord Lansdowne remained the leader in the Lords and it *could* be he who would be the head of the next Conservative Government. It was clear, therefore, that the decision as to who should fill this particular vacancy lay with the Conservative and Unionist Members of the House of Commons. One other preliminary point which must be made is that the association between the two Unionist Parties was now so close that they were one party in all but name, and the Liberal Unionist M.P.s would therefore be entitled to, and in fact be given, their share in the making of the decision.

At the moment when Balfour announced his retirement, it was widely thought that there were only two possible candidates for the succession, namely Austen Chamberlain and Walter Long. Walter Long was a representative of an interest which had then and always had had a considerable, at one time an almost exclusive, influence in the Conservative Party, namely the landed interest. Now, however, with the rise of democracy, that influence was, on the whole, on the decline, but, in Conservative circles, it was still important, very important. Long was a country squire with a mansion and a fine estate in Wiltshire, for which county he was one of the members, and whither he repaired whenever he could get away from the House of Commons to pursue his favourite pastimes, including hunting. He was well liked in the county by farmers, labourers and gentry alike.

Long was not a man of great ability, but he was painstaking and sincere and generally popular in the House. Austen, who had described him as 'a typical country gentleman', had liked him in the past, and they would be friends again in the future, but, in the days of acute tension which immediately followed Balfour's retirement, they, and their supporters on both sides, were on the worst possible terms. Long himself had always been quick-tempered, and Lord Balcarres, the Conservative Chief Whip, was of the opinion that he was very jealous of Austen.(5) Austen had not served in the House for as many years as had Long.

Austen was a much abler man than Long, and this fact was generally recognized both in the House and in the country. Futhermore, there was genuine sympathy with Joseph Chamberlain throughout the Party, and a recognition of what they owed him for his immense services. Nevertheless, there were weighty considerations which militated against Austen's candidature. His background was quite different from that of the bulk of Conservative M.P.s. He was not, officially, a Conservative at all, but a Liberal Unionist, and had only recently joined the Carlton Club. Much more important, though not by nature an extremist, he had allied himself on two very important issues, food taxes and the House of Lords, with the extremist wing of the Party. Food taxes were particularly unpopular with an important section of the Unionists; Lord Derby, who wielded immense influence in Lancashire, felt particularly strongly about this. 'What the devil is the meaning of Austen's speech?' Derby had written in December 1910. 'I hold A. J. B. has bound his party to submit Tariff Reform to a referendum before it becomes law – that promise holds good for all time and not only, as Austen says, for *this* election. . . . Damn these Chamberlains – they are the curse of our Party and of the country.'(6) It may be added that, by the time Balfour retired, Salvidge had joined Derby in opposition to food taxes.

Long, on the other hand, had been careful to avoid committing himself too deeply on either of these issues. He was generally well liked by his fellow-squires, and was counting on them for support in his bid for the leadership. The landed gentry have, however, a strong and sure instinct for self-preservation and would not have voted for Long to become the leader, solely because he was one of themselves.

A meeting of the National Union of Conservative and Unionist Associations had been fixed to take place at the end of the week following that in which Balfour made his announcement, and it was considered most important to get the leadership settled before this meeting of the whole Party took place. Lord Balcarres, the Conservative Chief Whip, had therefore summoned a meeting of the Unionist members of the House of Commons, to be held at the Carlton Club on November 13th.

On the afternoon of Wednesday, November 8th, the day Balfour retired, Austen was driving with Henry Chaplin in a taxi to the House of Commons. Henry Chaplin was a squire on a very large scale, and had considerable influence with his fellow squires. As they stepped out of the taxi, Chaplin suddenly noticed Long. 'Ah, here is Walter,' he said. It soon became apparent that Long was annoyed at what he regarded as an attempt by Austen to ingratiate himself with the Squirearchy. Austen started to explain:

'Chaplin picked me up at the Tariff Conference,' he said. 'He was just telling me—'

At this stage Long interrupted. 'Oh,' he exclaimed, 'You don't think it is necessary to explain why you are in a taxi with a man, do you? You haven't come to that, have you?'

With great difficulty Austen managed to control himself, and entered the building with Chaplin. When they reached the top of the stairs, he turned round and said to Long:

'You interrupted me in the middle of a sentence. I was going to tell you that Chaplin was telling me of his conversation with you. Will you join us? We had better go into Balfour's room.'(7)

A rather acrimonious discussion followed, in the course of which the former Prime Minister tried to pour oil on troubled waters, but without a great deal of success. It was clear that neither Long nor Chamberlain was willing to withdraw, unless it became abundantly clear that the support for the other within the Party was overwhelming. Of this there was no likelihood at all. They did, however, both agree that, if a third candidate were to come forward with strong support within the Party, and

186

acceptable to their own particular supporters, then each would withdraw in favour of that third person. Such a candidate was at hand and he must now be introduced.

Andrew Bonar Law, like many others of his generation, on both sides of the Atlantic, who have attained high political eminence, was a child of the Manse. He was born in New Brunswick, soon to become part of Canada, the fourth child of a Presbyterian minister, who had himself been born in Northern Ireland. While still a boy, young Andrew had been sent to live with his mother's people near Glasgow, and it was they who became responsible for his education, and started him off in business in that city. He did well, and, in due course, made enough money to embark on a Parliamentary career, becoming M.P. for Gorbals in the year 1900.

Bonar Law and Austen had always been friends. Law was a great admirer of Joseph Chamberlain, and once confessed that he early decided to model himself on him. But he had not been long in the House of Commons before he came to have doubts as to whether he would ever make any real progress in that assembly. One day, Austen, finding him sitting alone in the smoking-room, a prey to depression, tried to cheer him up, but Bonar Law said: 'No, Austen, this is no place for me. It's all very well for men like you, who came into it young, but if I had known then what I know now I would never have stood for Parliament.' But he had a remarkable memory, and this, with his knowledge of business generally, and the iron and steel trades in particular, coupled with his debating skill, which was considerable, had, during the years that the Party had been in opposition, brought him to the front. Recently, however, he had lost his wife, to whom he was devoted, which had greatly increased his natural melancholiness of disposition. Austen had written to him on this occasion:

'I keep on thinking and thinking of you, and wishing that I could help you. If deepest, heartfelt sympathy could lessen your grief, you are assured of ours. . . . I hope you may find some little comfort in the sympathy of friends, and in the knowledge and regard which your wife inspired even in those who knew her as slightly as we did, for we could see all that

187

she was to you, and you to her, and how beautifully your lives were knit together. . . .

Time does heal our wounds, even in spite of ourselves, time and work. And when you are able to think about these things again you will find that there is much and great work for you to do. Your friends have need of you. You can help our cause, as none of us can. You bring peculiar qualities and a special knowledge to the work, and we shall claim your help again when the time comes, knowing indeed how hard and irksome it will be for you to resume it without *her* help, but knowing also that it is a duty from which you must not, and will not, shrink, and hoping that – hard as that duty is – it may help you to bear the heavier burden of your private grief, by occupying a part of your thoughts with public cares.'(8)

Bonar Law had made another friend who, as time went on, would become much closer to him than Austen. This was a young Canadian, also a son of the Manse, whose name was Max Aitken and who later became Lord Beaverbrook. Aitken had recently entered the House of Commons as member for Ashton-under-Lyne. It was he who persuaded Bonar Law to let his name go forward for the leadership and Aitken did all he could to win support for his friend's candidature. It is, however, possible to exaggerate the part played by Aitken in this affair, to see him in the role of one of the great masters of convention craft in the United States, playing the forces of Chamberlain and Long off against one another, and deliberately producing a deadlock. The fact is that the deadlock would have arisen anyway.

Meanwhile, Lord Balcarres had been 'sounding' the Unionist M.P.s. As a result, he had formed the conclusion that, if it came to a ballot, Long and Chamberlain would each get something over one hundred votes. Aitken had secured the pledges of some forty M.P.s for Bonar Law. On Friday, November 10th, Balcarres called to see Austen, and appraised him of the position as he saw it. Balcarres himself favoured Austen as did Balfour. He added that Carson would not allow his name to go forward but that Bonar Law was adamant that his own must. 'I am furious with him,' added Balcarres. 'Of course it injures your chances. Mind, I think that if the vote could be taken on Saturday you would win . . . but the lobbying is all on Long's side.'(9) He could not say what the position would be by Monday; either might be elected with a majority of between ten and twenty.

It was now clear to Austen that he could not hope for a really decisive and overwhelming victory, and he did not want to scrape his way into the leadership, because, under those circumstances, there would be no prospects of 'peace and loyalty' for him, but only constant intrigue against him. He therefore told Balcarres that he was willing to withdraw in favour of Bonar Law, provided that Long would do the same. Balcarres conveyed this proposal to Long, and he at once agreed. Bonar Law, however, on hearing the good news, insisted on seeing Austen before finally agreeing. He drove to Egerton Gardens, and opened the conversation by saying; 'Well, Austen, this is a very serious thing for me; I am not sure I can accept.'(10) To this, Austen replied, 'My dear Law, you must; you have no choice now. You allowed your name to go forward. Don't think that I blame or criticize you for it – long ago I said there should be no personal rivalry between you and me about offices – but you altered the situation by doing so; you cannot now shrink from the consequences.'(11) Then, after having been assured by Austen that it would make no difference to their friendship, Bonar Law agreed to accept.

The meeting at which the new leader would be elected took place at the Carlton Club on November 13th. It was actually the first time that Austen had been inside this, his new club. By arrangement between them, Walter Long proposed and Austen seconded that Bonar Law be elected leader. In their speeches both stressed the importance of Party unity and Austen asked the meeting to give Bonar Law this great opportunity in no grudging spirit and with no regrets, and no self-questionings left behind and for 'that whole-hearted support without which neither he nor any leader can do justice to himself, nor successfully conduct the affairs of the Party'.

Lloyd George's comment when he heard the name of the new leader was: 'The Tories have stumbled on their very best man, the only man. He is a very clever fellow I like him.' Joseph Chamberlain, though disappointed when he heard that Austen was not to be the new leader, said, when the circumstances had been explained, 'I don't see what else Austen could have done.'

On April 11th, 1912, Asquith introduced into the House of Commons the third Home Rule Bill. In Austen's opinion, it was even more unworkable than its two predecessors. He described it in a speech at West Bromwich as 'a measure more full of inconsistencies, more illogical, more contradictory than any that in my twenty years' experience I have seen presented to Parliament'. In actual fact, it came a good deal nearer to meeting Joseph Chamberlain's original objections than either of Gladstone's Bills. It was here that Austen differed from most other Unionists. To them, the important thing was 'The Orange Card' and they were resolved to play it vigorously. To Austen, however, the only solution to the Irish problem that would ever really commend itself was the particular one worked out by his father in 1886.

There was another of Lord Randolph Churchill's sayings which the Unionists invoked, 'Ulster will fight, and Ulster will be right', and it looked like coming true. On September 28th, 1912, in the City Hall at Belfast, at a table draped with the Union Jack, hundreds of thousands of Ulster Unionists followed their leader, Sir Edward Carson, in signing a solemn Covenant in which 'being convinced, in our consciences, that Home Rule would be . . . subversive of our civil and religious freedom, destructive of our citizenship and perilous to the Empire', they pledged themselves as 'loyal subjects of His Gracious Majesty King George V' to defeat by every means in their power, 'the present conspiracy to set up a Home Rule Parliament in Ireland' and to 'refuse to recognize its authority'. By the end of the year, more than half a million men and women had signed the Covenant.

It was shortly after this that Carson went with Austen Chamberlain to Birmingham where they were both to address a huge mass meeting. They spent the night at Highbury. Joseph Chamberlain by then was very weak and could only speak with great difficulty. But he was still mentally alert and he listened intently as Carson talked to him about the situation in Ireland. At last, he said slowly, 'Do you know what I would do?'

'I do not, sir,' answered Carson.

There was a long pause and then some of the old fire seemed to become kindled in Joseph and the light of battle came into his eyes as he thumped his stick on the floor and with great difficulty forced out of himself the words:

'If – I – were – you – I would – fight – it – out – to the – end.'

Carson was deeply moved and, addressing a big meeting in Belfast shortly afterwards, he referred to this incident. 'We will take his advice,' he said amidst loud cheering. 'We will fight it out. God give us men – a time like this demands great hearts, strong minds, true faith and willing hands:

> Men whom the lusts of office do not kill,
> Men whom the spoils of office do not buy,
> Men who posses opinions and will,
> Men who love honour, men who cannot lie.'(12)

It was about this time that Joseph Chamberlain announced that he would not seek re-election to Parliament. Austen was adopted by the West Birmingham Unionist Association as their candidate and held the seat from 1914 (the year in which his father died) until his own death in 1937.

Meanwhile, Joseph Chamberlain and his wife had continued every year to go to the South of France. They generally left England towards the end of March and returned to Highbury some time in May. Their establishment on the Riviera included a butler and at least one other man-servant (taken out from Highbury), a nurse for Joseph, and at least nine indoor servants. For the first two years after Joseph's illness, they took a villa at Valescure, set amongst pine trees in the foothills of the mountains about two miles away from St. Raphael. Since then they had taken the Villa Victoria at Cannes. In the spring of 1913, Mary was suddenly taken seriously ill, and peritonitis developed. An immediate operation was necessary, and, for several days, her condition was critical. She faced her ordeal with great courage, being fortified by her deep religious convictions. 'The happiness which no turmoil can reach is within us, if we but follow the paths marked for us,' she was to write to her mother a few years later, 'and the more we yield to the leading hand the more we are enfolded by it.'(13) Just before the operation which, in fact, was completely successful, she said to one of the Chamberlain relations, 'I must get better because of Joe. What will become of him, if anything happens to me?'(14)

The previous November, Mary had written to her mother:

'Few women can be so blessed as I have been, in my husband, and grateful indeed am I for these years of close friendship and companionship and sympathy we have passed together, bound by love and devotion to one another. I should be more than human if I could altogether suppress a pang that we must now lead such a restricted life but, in spite of it, we manage to find much to interest us, and I know I ought to be thankful that we have so many blessings – and I am thankful. I try not to wish for things which may not be, and he is so wonderful, in his patient endurance, that I am ashamed when I find myself in rebellious mood.'(15)

To Mrs. Herbert Chamberlain, a short time before her illness, Mary had said, 'You have no idea of the gentleness and tenderness that can be shown you by a very strong man.'(16)

The northern Irish continued to give concrete evidence of their will to resist Home Rule. An Ulster Volunteer Force was formed and large numbers of Ulstermen were recruited and, joined by Carson and F. E. Smith, they started to drill. By September of 1913 about fifty-six thousand men had been enrolled.

F. E. Smith described this Parliament as the 'Mad Parliament' which, like the 'Mad Hatter' in *Alice in Wonderland* kept on repeating, 'What I say three times is law.' Under the Parliament Act, the Irish Home Rule Bill would become law in the summer of 1914. During the intervening period the dreary process of repetition continued in an atmosphere of mounting tension. It was the contention of the Unionists that the Constitution was now in a state of 'suspension' pending legislation to reform the House of Lords in accordance with Asquith's promises, and that, in default of such legislation, the Government had no moral right to force Home Rule through under the present Parliament Act, without a General Election. When Asquith said that he hoped to introduce a Bill to reform the House of Lords, 'during the present session if time permits', Smith commented sarcastically, 'Surely it is time to revise our ethical category. Formerly we could classify men as (1) honourable men and (2) dishonourable men. Now we must admit a third category – honourable men if time permits.' Scenes of disorder which were almost unparalleled prevailed in the House. Asquith was howled down by the Unionists amidst cries of 'Who killed the King', 'Traitor', 'Rats, and 'Go back to your Irish bosses'. One enraged Conservative picked up a book from the Speaker's table and hurled it at Winston Churchill, hitting him hard on the head. There is no evidence that Austen ever joined in all this rowdyism, but F. E. Smith did so, swaying backwards and forwards and leading the chorus of yells and catcalls with great exuberance.

To the King, the whole matter was a source of great anxiety, and this was increased when Bonar Law argued with him that the only way to prevent civil war might be the exercise of the Royal veto over the Home Rule Bill. 'I think I have given the King the worst five minutes he has had for a long time,' Bonar Law told Austen. For months George V strove to bring the two sides to the conference table. To begin with, however, he made no head-way with the Prime Minister, who, during the early part of the controversy, was of the opinion that Ulster was bluffing. But, in the spring of 1914, events occurred which caused him to alter both his ideas and his tactics. There was an ugly incident at the Curragh, when a number of officers resigned their commissions, because they thought they were liable to be ordered to fire on the inhabitants of Ulster. Then one night, a few weeks later, the Ulster volunteers mobilized secretly and managed to land, at Larne, 25,000 rifles and three million rounds of ammunition. It was clear that civil war of considerable magnitude would follow any attempt to put Ulster under the dominion of a Dublin Parliament and Government. Asquith therefore was now disposed to fall in with the King's suggestion of a Conference. He decided, however, to explore the ground carefully first and to define the issues and it was not until July that, after an opening address by the King, the Buckingham Palace Conference started under the chairmanship of the Speaker on July 21st. By this time, death had entered and transformed the scene.

Joseph and Mary Chamberlain had returned from Cannes about the middle of May 1914. Joseph had stood the journey well and seemed to be in quite good health. They settled down in their London house in Princes' Gardens. Joseph liked to spend a certain portion of the year there because he retained a keen interest in political affairs and wished to keep in as close touch as possible with Austen. On the morning of July 2nd, Austen called and they talked about the political situation. Joseph agreed fully when Austen told him of the course he had taken in a recent debate and said just as his son was leaving the room, 'Quite right, someone has got to give way but I don't see why it should always be us.' Those were the last words that Austen heard his father utter. The same day, Joseph fell seriously ill. Neville was summoned from Birmingham, but, by the time he arrived, his father had lost consciousness. At eight minutes past ten that night, he died.

An Abbey funeral was offered by the Government, but both Austen and Neville felt strongly that it would have been their father's wish to be buried amongst his own people. So the coffin was taken to Birmingham and there, in brilliant sunshine, followed by Mary, his widow, and by Austen and Neville, the last remains of Joseph Chamberlain were taken from Highbury to the Key Hill Cemetery where the interment took place. All along the route, and at the cemetery itself, there were crowds of ordinary, humble people, who had come out to pay their last tribute to 'Our Joe'. The flags over the Town Hall and the Council House building flew at half mast.

Moving the adjournment of the House of Commons, the Prime Minister said:

'It is fitting that within these walls, where the echoes of his voice seem to linger, we should suspend for a few hours the clash of controversy while we all join in acknowledging our common debt for the life and example of a great Englishman.'

And Bonar Law said:

'At the time when I first entered this House, I was still young enough, and indeed I hope I still am, to be a hero worshipper, and for me the essence of my political faith was belief in Mr. Chamberlain ... He, almost alone, has changed the whole spirit of the relationship of the different parts of the Empire towards each other and has thus laid strongly the foundation on which other men may build. I think there is no instance in our history of any statesman who has not filled the highest post whose name has become, like his, a household word.'

Death Again Transforms the Scene

Four days before that of Joseph Chamberlain, another death occurred, which was destined to have even wider repercussions. On June 28th the Archduke Franz Ferdinand was shot by an assassin at Serajevo. Sir Winston Churchill has described in immortal language(17) how the Buckingham Palace Conference was toiling around the muddy by-ways of Fermanagh and Tyrone, when Sir Edward Grey read out to them the terms of the Austrian ultimatum to Serbia. The Buckingham Palace Conference broke down, and the international situation seemed to deteriorate. Austen had gone to spend the August Bank Holiday week-end, with his family, at Westgate-on-Sea. Scarcely had he got there, however, when he was asked by friends in the Party to come back to London because of the worsening of the situation abroad. He did not arrive in London until 1 a.m. on Sunday, August 1st, and there he met George Lloyd who had been in touch with the French Ambassador, M. Cambon.

Cambon had told Lloyd that the situation was extremely serious and he had been very critical of the inactivity and general tendency to drift of the British Government. He reminded Lloyd that, in pursuance of the general policy of the *Entente*, conversations had been going on between the military staffs of Britain and France, in consequence of which the entire French fleet had been moved to the Mediterranean, and the Normandy and Brittany coasts were therefore unguarded. *'Vous nous avez livré'* he said. He admitted that there was no written agreement, but pointed out that 'everything, every act of the last few years gave us the assurance of your support . . .' Then he added bitterly, *'Et l'honneur? Est ce que l'Angleterre comprend ce que c'est l'honneur?'*(18

Austen, who declared later that he loved France 'like a woman', was stung to the quick when he heard those words. There was nothing more he could do that night, but the following morning he called early at Lansdowne House. While he was waiting for Lord Lansdowne (Foreign Secretary in the last Conservative Government) to come down, Austen made out a rough draft of a communication from the Unionist leaders to the Prime Minister. This draft was as follows:

'We feel it our duty to declare that, in our opinion, any hesitation in now supporting France and Russia, our intimate

195

friends (with one of whom, at least, we have, for years past, concerted naval and military measures affecting gravely her own naval and military dispositions at this moment) would be fatal to the future security of the United Kingdom; and we offer His Majesty's Government the assurance of the united support of the Opposition, in all measures required by England's intervention in the war.'(19)

After Lord Lansdowne had had breakfast, they both went round to see Bonar Law and Austen managed, with some difficulty, to persuade them to agree to a message on these lines being sent to Asquith, though Austen's draft was altered somewhat, particularly by the omission of the words between brackets. Exactly what effect (if any) it had, is not certain. It may be that to some extent the wiser elements in the Cabinet were strengthened by it. That body itself was utterly divided. For the last few weeks, their minds had been entirely on Irish Home Rule and domestic issues, and the first time they had even discussed the international situation was a week before war was declared. At the time when the Unionist message was despatched, the majority of the Cabinet were almost certainly against intervention. It was only when Belgium was invaded, and her King made his appeal to George V, that the tide of public opinion swept the country and the Government into war.

16

Arthur junior, Neville and Norman

The outbreak of war was soon to change the face of England. In Birmingham in particular its impact on industry, on municipal affairs and on the lives of individuals was very great.

Arthur Chamberlain had died in the year 1913. His health had been poor for the last few years of his life, but he kept complete control of Kynochs and retained a keen interest in the other businesses with which he was connected, being regularly wheeled round the Witton works in an invalid carriage until the very end. It was largely due to his untiring efforts and perseverance in the face of conditions which, at times during the last ten years, had been extremely adverse, that the company was now in a position to make the tremendous contribution which it did make to the war effort, and thereby to the future of the country and the world.

Arthur was succeeded as chairman by his son, Arthur junior. He had inherited a great deal of his father's dynamism and receptivity to new ideas. Fortunately for the country he immediately decided on a vigorous policy of expansion. Within a month of taking office, he had persuaded the board to invest £10,000 in additional rolling plant. This and other expansive moves on the part of Arthur junior resulted in a considerable increase in the company's overdraft but, rather than curtail them, he suggested that payment of directors' fees should be deferred until such time as the overdraft had been reduced. At the same time he was responsible for raising the minimum wage for unskilled workers from twenty-two shillings to twenty-three shillings a week 'in view of the increased cost of living'. He was as intolerant as his father of outside interference but he was determined to look after the staff to the best of his ability. One of the first actions of the board after the declaration of war was to vote £10,000 'to be expended on war charities and in bonuses and increased salaries to officials engaged at high pressure in consequence of the war effort'. The directors immediately agreed to make up the wages of employees who joined His Majesty's forces with the consent of the company, granted an immediate all-round increase in pay, instituted bonuses, and made arrangements for a reserve fund out of which further bonuses would become payable at the end of the war.(1)

In October 1914, Kynoch Limited signed their first wartime contract with the War Office. Under it, the company agreed to make an additional three million cartridges a week and to increase their capacity progressively to $7\frac{1}{2}$ million a week. Arthur let it be known that when this latter figure was reached there would be a special bonus and, when it happened, he sent out the following letter to all employees:

'Well done all,

It is with the greatest pleasure that I enclose your cheque as promised. I shall be even more pleased to have to do the same thing again in a month's time – or shall it be less than a month? – when we reach the delivery of 9 millions.

There are not many companies which could do what we have done, and while we are proud of the company, your directors proud of you who have taken such a part in this achievement.

Let us now do the 9'(2)

Arthur Chamberlain attached great importance to maintaining at the highest possible level not only the pay and living conditions but also the prestige of munition workers. It was, therefore, arranged that every foreman should be given, amongst other documents, a card, contained in a leather case, and engraved in gold, containing the words:

'The bearer is employed by Kynoch Limited on work for the supply of munitions of war for H.M. Government and is therefore unable to serve his country in any other manner. Lord Kitchener has stated in a letter to the firm that men so engaged are doing their duty to their King and country equally with those who have joined the army for active service in the field. God save the King.'(3)

It was Arthur's great grievance that he was not allowed to join the army and go to France. He made repeated attempts to enlist but always his applications were refused on the ground of his indispensability at Kynochs. (4) His only brother went and was killed.

At the outbreak of the war, Neville Chamberlain was in his forty-sixth year and it was seventeen years since he had left the Bahamas for good and settled down in Birmingham. For the first of those years he had lived at Highbury. He was alone there for large parts of the year for Joseph Chamberlain, right down to the time of his death, invariably spent the spring in the South of France. But it was far from being a dull life. When the family were at home Neville had the great advantage of his father's company and Joseph Chamberlain was once described as 'the best talker in Europe'. Nearly all the great political figures of the day and many men of high eminence in other spheres came to Highbury at one time or another.

Another place where Neville was always welcome was the home of his uncle and godfather, George Kenrick, who lived in a large house at the end of Farquhar Road, Edgbaston. 'Uncle George' was a bachelor but he had an excellent housekeeper and maintained a most comfortable establishment. He was a delightful character, exuding the milk of human kindness, and did fine public work as chairman for a long time of the Birmingham Education Committee. For years he used to ride every day on horseback to and from his business. Every year he gave a large tennis party for the benefit of all his nephews and nieces. Neville, was, perhaps, his favourite nephew and George it was who taught Neville to shoot and fish, taking him with him for an annual holiday in Inverness-shire where ample facilities for both pastimes existed. Neville in time became good at both. When George Kenrick died, he left Neville a substantial legacy.

During all this time, Hoskins & Company had been Neville's main business interest. Every weekday, he cycled the two miles from Highbury to the works in Trinity Street, hanging up his bicycle on the wall of the loading bay when he got there, arriving never later than 9 a.m. and leaving between 5.30 and 6 p.m. As a business man, he was never in the first class and one reason for this was that his business was never his chief interest nor was his heart ever in it to the extent that the hearts of the two Arthurs (his uncle and cousin) were in theirs. No more than to his father did money for its own sake ever make much appeal. The fact is that Neville, though having inherited all his father's obstinacy and a good deal of his toughness, had not inherited his ruthlessness. His was an essentially gentle and kindly nature – perhaps a trifle too kindly and trusting for the hard competitive ways of modern business. By his workpeople, in Birmingham as in the Bahamas, he was adored. 'A true gentleman' was the verdict of more than one of them on him. Like his cousin Arthur he was a great believer in bonuses and he introduced a 5 per cent bonus on output and a pensions scheme at Hoskins.(5) And at Elliots' he was responsible for the introduction of a surgery, welfare supervisors, and, subsequently, war benefits for injured men and their dependants. 'He was a real man in all his doings,' wrote one old pensioner after his death. 'I do hope and pray I shall meet him in the next life.'(6)

But it was almost certainly outside business, in various forms of public and charitable work, that his main interest lay even at this stage. From the moment that he returned from the West Indies he threw himself enthusiastically into work for the new University, becoming an original member of the council and canvassing hard for funds. From the start he had clear and definite ideas about the lines on which he wanted it to progress. 'We do not despise any branch of learning,' he said, 'but the essential point of the University must always be science – pure and applied.'(7)

He was also extremely active, during these early years, in hospital work. He became in turn a visitor, member of the board of management and finally chairman of the Birmingham General Hospital. He was extremely painstaking and conscientious over this, paying frequent visits to the great London hospitals to get ideas, and often he would go straight from Hoskins to the hospital and then go round the wards or record some suggestions in the visitors' book.

During this period, though still not particularly anxious to enter the House of Commons, he took a keen interest in politics. Following in his father's footsteps he became a member of the Birmingham and Edgbaston Debating Society and there he got good practice and soon became an excellent debater. Ultimately he became president of the society.

In the spring of 1910, Joseph and Mary Chamberlain went as usual to the South of France. This time they had taken Beatrice with them and it so happened that Mrs. Lilian Cole, the widow of Joseph's brother Herbert, was staying in Cannes at the same time as they. Mrs. Cole's niece, Anne, had gone out to stay with her aunt.

Lilian's second husband was a certain Alfred Clayton Cole. He owned a fine country house in Berkshire called West Woodhay and a considerable estate over which there was excellent shooting. West Woodhay had at one time been the home of the well-known nineteenth-century writer, the Rev. Augustus Hare, and his book *Memorials of a Quiet Life* contains a description of the place as it was in the year 1829 when the Hares first went there. It is described as having been 'the very perfection of an old manor house with the three drawing-room windows down to the ground opening on a long lawn running up to the hills with trees on each side and roses clustering in at the windows. . . .' Since then it had been consistently enlarged.

It was at West Woodhay that most of Anne's youth had been spent. Cole was a wealthy man, who had at one time been governor of the Bank of England, and Lilian had a considerable income of her own derived from Herbert Chamberlain's estate so that between them they could afford to and did keep the place up extremely well. Anne's brother was the celebrated practical joker Horace de Vere Cole. A gay and colourful atmosphere prevailed at West Woodhay – very different from that of Highbury.

Anne's background, though not identical with that of Ivy, was much nearer to it than either background was to that of the Chamberlains. For many generations the Cole family had been squires in Norfolk, though the land which they owned and had from time to time farmed themselves had never been very extensive in area. Anne's grandfather, however, had migrated from Norfolk to London, becoming a merchant in the city, in which capacity in due course he had prospered. Her father, who had gone into the army and become a major in the Third Dragoon Guards, had died in India when Anne was nine years old. Her mother, whose maiden name had been De Vere, came of an old Irish family.

Anne was twenty-nine years old when she first met the

Chamberlains. She made an immediate impression on them and particularly on Beatrice, who had seen the great happiness which Austen's marriage had brought him. When they all got back to England she arranged a party to which Neville and Anne Cole were both invited. It is possible, however, that Neville and Anne had already met at West Woodhay, where Neville used to go to shoot. They soon fell in love. Anne was invited to stay at Highbury and then the engagement was announced. They were married at St. Paul's, Knightsbridge, in January 1911. Like Austen's, Neville's proved to be a very happy marriage. Neville was never perhaps quite as demonstrative as Austen but he was, through life, equally devoted to his wife and he had every reason to be so. Again and again he paid her well-deserved tributes for the way she had helped and sustained him. 'I'd never have done it without Annie,' he said over and over again. The two brothers and their wives all got on very well together. 'You have a warm admirer in your sister-in-law,' Neville wrote to Austen rather over a year after his marriage.

In November 1911, Neville became a member of the Birmingham City Council. He had been elected to represent the All Saints Ward, then part of his father's old constituency of West Birmingham. He had been drawn into local government by his keen interest in town planning and this in turn had been largely due to the extension of the boundaries of Birmingham, the city having recently taken in a number of outlying districts. Neville almost immediately became the chairman of the Town Planning Committee. He did not feel himself by any means a stranger on this Council, to which so many of his relations had given, down the years, so much loyal and conscientious service and on which so many of them had held high office. Still serving on it were his uncles, William and George Kenrick and C. G. Beale, and his cousin, Ernest Martineau. And, in November 1911, there had been elected another relation who was actually fifteen years Neville's junior. This was Norman, the son of Joseph's younger brother, Herbert.

Norman's father had died in the year 1904. Like all the brothers, Herbert Chamberlain had had considerable business ability. He had become first a director and then the chairman of the Birmingham Small Arms Company. He also became a director of a number of other Birmingham companies and was a pioneer in industrial and accident insurance, a field opened up by the Workmen's Compensation Act, which his brother Joseph had done so much to bring into being. Herbert was one of several prominent Birmingham businessmen who founded the Midland Employers' Mutual Insurance Company. Most of the leading insurance companies had had exaggerated ideas of the liabilities to which the new legislation would expose employers and they demanded correspondingly high premiums. It was Herbert's idea that the Midland Mutual, of which he became the chairman, should charge reasonable rates and this policy proved extremely successful. This led on to Herbert becoming chairman of another insurance company, the Central, which specialized in fire insurance. Herbert was never a member of the Birmingham Council. He was elected to it but refused to take office. He was a magistrate and a member of the Licensing Bench during part of the time that his brother Arthur was the chairman. Furthermore, he subscribed generously to hospitals and other philanthropic institutions and was associated with the management of many of them.

Herbert's health was not good and he was compelled to retire early from business. His wife liked London and, in due course, they moved there, taking a house in Ennismore Gardens. Throughout his life Walter, the nearest to him in age, was the one of his brothers that was the closest to him in every way. They were both keen on shooting and fishing and from time to time shared in renting and running a country house where they could join in enjoying these pastimes. Herbert had four children; Norman and his twin brother Walter were born in August 1884, but Walter died nine months later. There were also two daughters – younger than Norman.

Few people had a more decisive influence on Neville than did Norman. It was Norman's death in action in 1917, which, more than anything else, produced in Neville that deep loathing for war which so characterized him during the 'thirties – with momentous consequences. Norman was educated at Eton and Magdalen College, Oxford. He early showed signs of his two most striking attributes – great intellectual ability and a deep religious conviction which reflected itself in constant unselfishness and the doing of good works. He won a scholarship to Eton but refused to take the money so that it could go to some boy who needed it more. He joined the Eton Volunteers and marched with them to Windsor Castle immediately after Mafeking was relieved and again to take part in Queen Victoria's funeral. When he left Eton, his tutor wrote that 'I shall never forget his moral courage', adding that 'he has more than I have ever known in a boy'. He was a passionate admirer of 'Uncle Joe', whose speeches he devoured avidly and he organized a Tariff Reform League at Oxford and was rewarded by his uncle coming there in December 1905 to speak on its behalf. While at Oxford, he spent a long vacation in Germany as the guest of a Prussian officer who had stayed with the Herbert Chamberlains in England. Norman wrote home:

> 'What awfully nice people these German officers are. They are all so awfully clever and know what they are talking about. At the same time they have lovely manners and are so smart and so awfully kind. I don't wonder the German army is such a good one. What surprises me is the number that speak English, some of them beautifully.'(8)

In his biography of Norman, the only book he ever wrote, Neville commented 'Fourteen years later he was killed fighting against these same Prussian Guards, of whose officers he had spoken so warmly.'(9)

Herbert Chamberlain had left a substantial though by no means an enormous fortune. It is an odd circumstance that the Chamberlain brothers, though their lives had been so utterly different, died worth very much the same amount of money. Joseph, Arthur and Herbert each left between £100,000 and £150,000. Austen got a much larger share of his father's estate than did Neville.

Norman became entitled to a small income under the terms of his father's will immediately after the latter's death and, after leaving Oxford, he travelled extensively in both Eastern and Western hemispheres with his friend, John Murray.(10)

Norman's great ambition was to go into politics but he was not quite sure how to set about it. His mother consulted Austen and he wrote to her:

My Dear Lilian,

I appreciate your kindness in sending me Norman's letter which I return to you. You are right to be proud of him and he is worth taking trouble for. He has character, brains and a loving heart as this letter shows and he must now be a great comfort to you and will become ever more so. I hope he will also treat me as a friend to whom he can speak freely all his hopes and fears and I will do my best to help him as I would my own brother. That is how we ought to regard our relationship and if he will look on me as such that will give me the best chance of being a useful friend to him . . .'(11)

Norman decided that he needed outside experience before trying for the House and thought that it would be a good idea if he served for a time on the Birmingham Council. Lilian was not at all keen on him settling down in Birmingham when London and West Woodhay seemed to have so much to offer him. A year or two later, she again consulted Austen who wrote in reply:

'I share your anxiety about him [Norman] . . . He is so good a fellow that I deeply sympathize with him and am greatly interested in him but he is terribly unpractical and visionary. The crucial difficulty is that he wants beyond all things to go into politics but that he really has not the means to do so. Add to this that his views are very boyish and I agree with you that honestly he is not fit at the moment. Yet if he had the means to take an average constituency with a fighting chance that might be the best for him. But how can I advise him to go into a Parliamentary life on £1,000 a year or less? And he himself will look at nothing less and wants not an ordinary chance but the pick of all our seats. I was obliged to tell him that Birmingham seats were few and much sought after; that others with greater claims were seeking them; that I myself could not afford to refuse one if it were offered to me, for my present seat costs more in time and money that I can afford, and I am richer than he is. . . . I have told him that the first thing he ought to do is to seek to make himself an income. But I fear I produced no effect on his mind and certainly none on his actions. . . .'(12)

It seems fairly clear that, at this particular juncture, Norman's mind was in a state of confusion. While still abroad, he had written:

'I'm having an awful time trying to find out my real intentions and duty as to future movements. I must settle down after I get home. Of course what I want to do, what would interest me most, and what I know most about is politics . . . but there always comes the thought . . . oughtn't I to try to make money, go into business in fact? But I can only think of that as a preface to my real ambition – a few years and then of course that is not enough to make any money in. . . . I want to be useful and I feel sure I could be most useful where I am most eager and keen on my work and after all politics in its wide sense is the only thing I know anything of – I know a certain amount about it and have a certain advantage in it.'(13)

It so happened that, in the year 1907, the Rector of St. Philip's, Birmingham, the Rev. W. H. Carnegie, who later married Joseph Chamberlain's widow, was trying to get together a group of Oxford men to come to Birmingham and undertake social work among the more unfortunate of the working class. Norman was attracted by this idea because he thought it would increase his knowledge of industrial conditions and give him experience which would prove invaluable in politics later on. In July 1907, he settled down with two other young men at Calthorpe Cottage in Edgbaston, Birmingham.

The next three years were devoted entirely to running boys' clubs and to general welfare work on behalf of the youth of Birmingham. And, though politics may have been his original spur, he soon became intensely interested in and devoted to this work for its own sake. He was appalled by the wastage of human material which he found to be taking place and by the fact that no one seemed to be trying to cure it, whereas he was convinced that something could and should be done. From the first, his particular care were the newspaper boys and 'station loungers', aged generally between sixteen and twenty-one, who, after a year or two in some 'blind alley' occupation, had found themselves superfluities on the labour market and had drifted into selling newspapers or lounging around the station looking for odd jobs.

By society in general these boys were looked on as 'good for nothings' but to Norman each was an individual with infinite potentialities. He made it his business to get to know many of them personally and his sympathies were soon aroused as is shown by the following extremely perceptive letter which he wrote to a friend:

'As soon as they [the boys] appear round the station they are done for absolutely unless external aid is forthcoming. Every day that is spent round the station makes it harder to get away and start afresh. All the boy's old friends, his family even, all the connecting links between him and the regular work at the factory break off one by one; his clothes become shabby, his boots unfit for working in; if he goes to a lodging-house he could not keep himself for the first week of work even if he gets a job. Further, the demoralizing effect of unemployment on a grown man cannot compare with the havoc it wreaks on the character of a youth who finds himself cut adrift from all his old friends and in the continual company of out of works. Lastly it is hard to overestimate the effect on the character and stamina of a growing youth of the cold and wet of a Birmingham winter and of continuous ill-nutrition. An average weekly budget shows 3s. 2d. out of 8s. spent on food – the rest going towards lodgings, cigarettes and gambling.'(14)

Two of Norman's special characteristics soon became widely noticed. One was his genius for organization and leadership, a gift possessed by nearly all the Chamberlains, but pre-eminent in Neville and Norman, who soon established a boys' club of his own. He arranged its activities himself including a summer camp. He also applied himself diligently to the children's courts then being established for juvenile offenders and served on the Borstal committee of the local prison. His other outstanding characteristic was his intense humanity, his sympathy with and desire to help the less fortunate amongst his fellow human beings. To him the 'station loungers' were not just an amorphous mass of 'flotsam and jetsam', or 'riff-raff' but intensely interesting human beings, with whom he could and did make friends without any element of patronage or condescension in the friendship. He was utterly unsparing in the trouble he would take to find the kind of work that he thought would suit each particular boy. He sent several of them to Canada at his own expense, not only fitting them up with suitable clothes and equipment and paying for their passages but giving them money with which to start a new and healthier life overseas. In due course he himself spent a summer holiday in Canada, visiting the boys he had sent out and being delighted to find how well they were doing.

He became completely absorbed in this work. 'One thing I feel sure of now,' he wrote, 'nothing will make me give up the study of the social and industrial questions that Brum has introduced me to, or working to put them right. The personal knowledge we've got there has burned into me a definite wish to do my best in that way and nothing – much less the advice of people in London – will stop me doing it. . . . I have got a burning sort of enthusiasm and indignation which nothing seems able to put out – I've tried time after time to go to London – but I can't do it; now I don't want to. . . I hope it won't go out. It's a much greater spur to work my hardest and make the best of myself than mere interest in politics or desire to get on or to "follow Joe", great as these are.'(15)

But political ambition had by no means died in him and, at the end of the year 1909, he was adopted as the Unionist candidate for the Camborne Division of Cornwall at the next Parliamentary Election. It was a safe Liberal seat and he was beaten, but his character and personality impressed everyone and after the fight was over the Chairman of the Liberal Association wrote to him;

> '. . . I can with all sincerity congratulate you on having made a plucky fight and with clean hands. You have won the esteem and respect of very many who have voted for the Party who have opposed you. You have shown such a serious interest in life and the questions that affect the country that I very much hope that the time is not far distant when you will have a place in the House of Commons and when you are there I feel sure you will fill that place worthily.'(16)

Returning to Birmingham after this campaign, Norman once more threw himself vigorously into welfare work on behalf of the youth of the city. It was then that he started to work out the plan which became known as the 'After Care Scheme'. This was

designed to secure that boys and girls should receive guidance as
to a suitable occupation when they left school and generally that
every possible good influence should be brought to bear on them
instead of their being left to fend for themselves at this important
stage of their lives. Each school district was to have its own 'care
committee', which would include teachers, parents and social
workers. By the middle of 1914, largely as a result of Norman's
untiring efforts, about one hundred committees had been
organized, controlling well over two thousand voluntary workers.
As Neville wrote later:

'With a vision and grasp almost uncanny in one so young,
he [Norman] seems to have gathered in all the scattered threads
and given them their place in his completed fabric, so that
according to his view every individual boy or girl should be
subject to the guidance and sympathetic aid of some qualified
helper from the time of leaving school until the day when they
should be fairly launched on a career, fit in body and mind,
trained to their craft, and yet provided with interests sufficient
to occupy their leisure. Nothing which had any bearing on
this subject escaped his attention. Not only the Education Committee but every organization working for the betterment of
young life in the city found in him an active and untiring
helper.

Boys' and girls' clubs, the Street Children's Union, the
Children's Courts, the Workers' Educational Association and
the Women's Settlement are among those in which he was
prominent and his work as a member and afterwards chairman
of the Parks Committee of the City Council was undertaken and
carried on primarily because of its possibilities in providing
means of recreation for young people.'(17)

In 1911, Norman moved into a house of his own at 44 Russell
Road. Here he collected a lot of books and a few other treasured
possessions around him and here too he entertained his friends
including boys from his clubs with whom he spent many
an evening singing songs, playing games and talking about
their troubles and their futures. At week-ends he would go for
long walks round the city boundaries, looking for new sites
for playing-fields. In time, he became chairman of the Parks

Committee. He joined the army very soon after the outbreak of war and by 1915 had become a captain.

Meanwhile, Neville, after less than three years on the Council, had become an alderman and a year later Lord Mayor. This, at that time, was a most responsible position, for the importance of Birmingham to the war effort was very great.

No less than ten of Neville's relations (including his father) had held the office of Mayor, the last of them to do so having been Ernest Martineau who held it from 1912 to 1914 but resigned in the latter year in order to go and fight in France. Like the Chamberlains and the Kenricks, the Martineaus were Non-conformists and like them they had given fine service to Birmingham down the years, five Martineaus having already served on the Town Council – others would do so later. The original Martineau, Robert, first came to Birmingham early in the nineteenth century. His son, Thomas, married Emily Kenrick, younger sister of Florence, the second wife of Joseph Chamberlain. Thomas, who was father of Ernest, served on the Birmingham Council from 1876 to 1893 and was thrice Lord Mayor. It is an interesting and significant fact that, for a period of fifty years from 1903 to 1953, with only two short breaks, the chairmanship of the Education Committee of the Birmingham City Council was held by a member of the Kenrick and Martineau families. Neville was thus impregnated through and through with the spirit of public service by way of local government in his native city.

Since the turn of the century, the scope of the Corporation's activities had been widely extended. It now owned farms in Wales and sanatoria in the Cotswolds. It had become responsible for activities as widely diversified as inspecting ice cream, dipping sheep, the licensing and insurance of motor-cars, shop hours, tuberculosis and the feeding of children. After the outbreak of war, these responsibilites were greatly added to. The Gas Department, for example, co-operated at once with local industry and a number of highly valuable inventions were developed.

It was not with an eye to this kind of activity or responsibility that Neville had first entered the Council. His great hope had been, as he explained when he took office, 'the transference of the working classes from their hideous and depressing surroundings to cleaner, brighter and more wholesome dwellings in the still uncontaminated country which lay within our boundaries'. All this had been halted by the 'wicked ambitions' of 'the German Emperor and his advisers'. Neville now applied himself conscientiously to playing his full part in the thwarting of those ambitions. There was nothing very dramatic or glamorous about the war work of a Lord Mayor but it was vitally important, and Neville dealt most thoroughly with such matters as recruitment, securing food and coal supplies, the running of the hospitals, and arranging civic receptions for the men who had won distinction on the battlefield. It was his belief that the monotony of war work and the drabness which war had inevitably brought to a great industrial city must be relieved as far as possible by recreation and refreshment of the spirit. He inaugurated a Civic Recreation League to promote all forms of healthful and refreshing activity for the workers' scanty leisure. Music was his own great passion; he was one of the greatest living authorities on Beethoven. To his great delight a Hallé concert was arranged in Birmingham in March 1916 and he made this the occasion for suggesting a municipal orchestra to be supported by the rates. This idea was ultimately realized, though not until after the war. But his greatest single achievement as Lord Mayor, the one of which he himself was always proudest, was the Birmingham Savings Bank. He accomplished this in the teeth of considerable difficulty and opposition and it required all his skill to do so. During his time as Lord Mayor, Neville was greatly helped by his wife who did really wonderful work as Lady Mayoress and was greatly admired by all. She was particularly active in arranging for comforts for the troops and in welfare work generally for soldiers, sailors and airmen and their families.

In September 1916, the annual meeting of the Trades Union Congress was held in Birmingham. It fell to Neville's lot as Lord Mayor to welcome the delegates and the speech which he made on that occasion attracted attention far beyond the confines of his native city. The *Morning Post* declared that, 'He broke all precedents in the way of civic welcomes and seized the opportunity to make a most valuable and statesmanlike contribution to the problem of national reconstruction after the war. As he stood addressing the congress from the Town Hall, many who in years gone by had been privileged to hear his father speak from the same place could almost imagine that the great Imperialist was with us again. . . . Here were proposals for a coming together of capital and labour that will be discussed a long way beyond Birmingham for a long time.'

In the course of his speech, Neville said that he 'desired to express pleasure at the presence of the overseas delegates. Their presence was symbolic of the hope that when this war was over our dominions across the seas together with our allies and the great part of the powerful neutrals might combine to make a recurrence of such a catastrophe impossible.' Then he added that 'recognizing the dangers to be faced after the war he believed employers and workmen should come together to see whether they could not make arrangements to enable them to take the place to which they believed they were entitled. Workers who now formed the bulk of our army would now want a good many things. First they would want a greater share in the wealth they had helped to produce. Then they would want a wage which would give them a reasonable margin over the cost of living so that it might be worth while to live in the country they had done so much to preserve.' He thought that 'if trade union leaders were occasionally admitted to the councils of employers and allowed to see a little bit more of the game from the inside they would be of assistance in preventing a recurrence of periods of unemployment'. The third thing that the workers would want, he said, was 'improved external conditions both in factories and homes' so that they 'might be able to bring up their children in cheerful and healthy surroundings'.(18)

Meanwhile, on the formation of the first Coalition Government, Austen had become Secretary of State for India. He retained this office when, in December 1916, Lloyd George succeeded Asquith as Prime Minister. In the political manoeuvrings which resulted in this important change and which have been very fully chronicled Austen was not one of the chief actors. His main importance was as a witness and he left his own account of what happened in a letter written at the time to Lord Chelmsford, the Viceroy of India. This account he later reproduced, with certain explanatory comments, in *Down the Years*. Nobody has ever seriously challenged his version of the story which remains the most reliable account of that part of it which was within his own knowledge.

Perhaps the most acute problem with which the new Prime Minister was confronted was the vexed question of manpower. Compulsory military service had been instituted earlier in the year but the army was still clamouring for more men. Furthermore, there were numerous exemptions – munition workers in particular. The power of compulsion applied only to the armed forces; there was no such power in regard to industry and its extension in this direction was bitterly resisted by the trade unions. In order to deal with this complicated problem, Lloyd George decided to create a new Department of National Service. The position of Director was originally offered to a prominent Liberal, E. S. Montagu, but he declined it. It was then that Austen, who had been appointed the chairman of the manpower board the previous September, recommended to Lords Milner and Curzon that Neville should be invited to fill the new post. Milner had read Neville's speech to the Trades Union Congress and had thoroughly approved of it, and he warmly supported Austen's suggestion in discussing the matter with Lloyd George, who then agreed that the position should be offered to Neville but said it was imperative that a decision should be obtained right away. The War Cabinet confirmed the decision at 1 p.m. on December 19th, and Austen was asked to communicate the offer to Neville immediately. On telephoning to Birmingham, however, Austen was told that his brother had gone to London that morning for a conference at the Local Government Board. By the time that Austen had ascertained this fact, the conference was over and Neville was on his way back to Paddington, whither Austen dispatched an official from the India Office in hot pursuit. Neville was hauled out of the train just as it was about to leave and taken to Austen's room. Thence the two proceeded to the House of Commons where they saw Lloyd George, who told Neville that it was the unanimous wish of the War Cabinet that he should undertake this work, which was vital in the national interest and that Labour was particularly enthusiastic about him. Neville then mentioned his work in Birmingham and its great importance to the nation.

'*This* is national work,' said Lloyd George, '*Imperial* work. . . .'

He was about to develop this theme when the telephone bell rang. The Prime Minister picked up the receiver. 'Hullo,' he said. 'What? My questions? Yes, I will come in.' Then, turning to Neville, he said, 'Well, talk it over with your brother. If you can, give me an answer in time for me to make the announcement today – it is *so* important, it is *everything* to announce the name at the same time as the creation of the post.' After these hurried remarks, the Prime Minister darted out of the room.

'Knowing my Neville,' Austen continued in the letter to his sisters on which this account of the day's proceedings is based, 'I did not offer to talk but sat silent and waited for his decision. He sat looking very unhappy and thinking hard for some five or ten minutes and then said: "Well, if it is put like that, there is only one answer that one can give – YES, but I don't like it. I know I can do my present work. I don't know about this. It will all be new to me, but I suppose I have no right to refuse."

'And so I rushed into the House, caught Lloyd George almost on the hop, said "he accepts" and rushed out again to pick up Neville's things at the India Office . . . and speed him off to Birmingham by the 4.20 train.'(19)

The *Birmingham Post* made the following interesting comments:

'No one in Birmingham will be very much surprised at Alderman Neville Chamberlain's new appointment. Ever since he became actively associated with the public life of Birmingham he has been regarded as a coming man – as a man bound to make his mark. His conduct of affairs in the highest office capable of being bestowed on him by his fellow citizens has abundantly confirmed that impression. One has only to recall the energy with which he has thrown himself into such movements as the establishment of a municipal savings bank, the granting of increased allowances to men broken in the war, the better protection of the Midlands against Zeppelin raids, the preservation of child life, the utilization of available land to increase our food supply, civic recreation and his efforts to elevate the musical life of Birmingham by the formation of a permanent orchestra, to realize the scope of his energies and the breadth of his sympathies. There is also his work as a former member of the Central Control Board to aid the supply of munitions by reducing facilities for obtaining alcoholic drinks.'(20)

The article also referred to some of Neville's earlier work, both on the Council and outside it, in connection with Town Planning and development of inland waterways, and then added, 'Alderman Neville Chamberlain has a clear intellect and combined with the keenness of the successful business man . . . he has a strong element of idealism in his character.'(21)

Neville's severance from Birmingham itself would prove to be only temporary but there were other severances of Chamberlain links with the city which were of a more permanent character. In the late summer of 1916, Mrs. Joseph Chamberlain had announced her engagement to Canon Carnegie who had by then become a Canon of Westminster and the Chaplain to the Speaker of the House of Commons. She never returned to Birmingham. By his will Joseph Chamberlain had left Highbury to Austen. He disposed of the house itself to the Corporation, selling the surrounding land for £15,000.

Neville worked hard and conscientiously in his new post but his efforts were not crowned with success – at least so far as he himself was concerned. This was certainly not wholly or even mainly his own fault. But he laboured under great difficulties. He was not a member of the War Cabinet or even of the House of Commons. Therefore, the heads of other departments were able easily to get their claims preferred to his. Much more important than this, however, was the fact that he never enjoyed the confidence of the Prime Minister. Lloyd George was extremely interested in phrenology and it is said that, in the course of one of Neville's early interviews with him, the Prime Minister was heard to murmur aside, 'The wrong shaped head.' After that Neville could do nothing right in Lloyd George's eyes. It was Neville's conviction that the only solution to the manpower problem was the removal of the exemption in the case of male munition workers of under 25. The War Cabinet turned down this suggestion, greatly to Neville's disappointment. Throughout, Lloyd George treated Neville with scant consideration and considerable tactlessness. For instance he made important appointments to the Department without consulting Neville.

Initially, however, it had been Neville himself who had chosen his chief subordinates and this had to some extent proved his own undoing. Coming from outside London to a newly created Department it was essential for him to have at his right hand a top civil servant who understood the ways of Whitehall. Instead of this he insisted on appointing the ex-town clerk of Birmingham (whose name was Hiley) to the chief position under himself.

It is clear from a letter which Neville wrote to Norman in May 1917 that he himself soon realized that he had made a mistake in transporting Hiley to Whitehall.

His new appointment had involved Neville in the necessity of finding a house in or near London. Temporarily, he had solved the problem of where to live by sharing a house both in the country and in London with Austen. The country place was called 'Rowfant' and was near Crawley in Sussex. It was from here that Neville wrote to Norman:

'. . . It is only in the last 2 or 3 weeks that we have been able to appreciate the flowers for the season has been so cold and late as to throw everything very much behind time but when the change came it seemed to bring the spring with a rush and I have never seen more splendid masses of primroses, dog violets, cowslips and oxslips. There are a lot of fine old trees, too, near the house and they are always full of birds – tits, finches, wagtails and nuthatches, besides all the family of warblers, while the cuckoos sing all day in the neighbouring woods. The house itself is a delightful Elizabethan building with big open fireplaces and exposed beams and rafters that harmonize so well with the old oak panelling. . . .'

Then he went on to tell Norman something about his problems in the new Department, explaining that – 'Northcliffe who wanted compulsion and didn't get it' had been 'doing his best to make everything impossible', and that 'I do not think the Prime Minister is any more friendly to me than he was, but owing to the terrific congestion . . . he has largely left Cabinet business to Milner and Henderson', and finally that 'Hiley is still with me but quite between ourselves he has been a great disappointment to me'.(22)

In August 1917, realizing that he could accomplish nothing

worth while as Director of National Service in view of Lloyd George's attitude towards him, Neville resigned. There is no doubt that he felt bitter about his experience and particularly about Lloyd George, under whom he was resolved never in any circumstances to serve again. What particularly disappointed him was that he had been forced to give up his work as Lord Mayor of Birmingham in which he rightly felt that he had been serving his country honourably and well. It infuriated him to think that if it hadn't been for 'my damned well-meaning brother' he would still have been Lord Mayor 'practically in control of the town' and about to enter his third year of office. He never forgave Lloyd George and when, some months later, the ex-Premier came to Birmingham to receive the freedom of the City, Neville arranged to be away. And, years later Austen was to write: 'I think Lloyd George behaved shamefully to Neville and showed in his relations with him all the worst traits in his character. . . . I have seen another side of Neville – a better one.'(23)

Throughout the autumn of 1917, Neville was feeling depressed but, in December, a far worse blow than the mere loss of a political appointment befell him. The news came that Norman had been killed in action; it was not, however, until the following February that Norman's body was found in no-man's-land, and his belongings included a number of sheets of paper, sodden and discoloured by rain, which contained Norman's views on education. Like every other soldier, he had had before him constantly the chance that he might be killed and he had written out a letter to be circulated in the event of his death amongst the boys who had been members of his clubs. It was in the following terms:

'My Dear Boys,

You won't get this unless I'm knocked out, and I'm writing it not because I think I will be, but because if I did go under I should hate to feel I'd gone without saying good-bye to you all and wishing you a happy life and one as worth living as mine. We've been a very happy family, and all our rows and failures and disappointments have only made it all the more worthwhile because we've generally speaking been able to put things right and learn from experience – both you and I.

I don't know anything except my love for my mother and

sisters which has made life so pleasant to me as your friendship
and companionship and seeing all the pluck and cheerfulness
and unselfishness and real uphill struggling to keep your end
up and make headway which I've seen in all of you one time
or another. And don't forget that nothing worth doing is done
without failures for the time being, without misunderstandings,
and without a damned lot of unpleasantness.

We've all been able to help each other a lot; go on doing
that amongst your own families. And I think somehow you'll
feel that I can still sympathize with your bad luck and all the
unfairness and difficulties that surround one when one is trying
to make good – even if I'm not there to tell you and keep you
at it.

Anyway, keep pegging away, don't be downhearted, and
don't forget.

Your old pal,
Norman Chamberlain'(24)

Norman's death affected Neville as no single event up to now
had affected him. Another Chamberlain cousin, John Chamberlain,
had already been killed but he had not been as close to Neville as
Norman had been. The strange thing is that until the time when
they served together on the Council Norman and Neville had
not been particularly intimate. But a strong affection and admiration had grown up during their joint years of municipal service
and it was quite mutual. Norman wrote of Neville that he was
'one of the very few people who roused in me all the sensations
of a willing and enthusiastic follower'. And Neville, after attending the memorial service to Norman at West Woodhay, wrote of
him:

> 'Strange that we do not fully realize men's characters while
> they are alive. Only now do I begin to see the full beauty of
> his. His life was devoted to others and I feel a despicable thing
> beside him.'(25)

To Norman's mother, Neville wrote:

> 'Somehow, perhaps half unconsciously, Norman was associ-
> ated in the back of my mind with everything that I thought I
> might or could do in the future. I always fancied him helping

and suggesting, criticizing perhaps but invariably sympathizing and supporting. Now he has gone I feel as if the hope and the future had gone too. One could only feel like this about a man with very rare gifts. I wish I had the power of analysing them and putting them into words so that others could understand and appreciate him. He was to me always a delightful companion with his quick sense of humour and his extraordinarily intelligent, suggestive brain. . . . He used his leisure to think and his thought was fertile in practical ideas. He had a constructive mind, the most valuable of all, and he devoted it to helping other people . . . When I think about Norman I see that his moral character was as nearly perfect as a man's could be. He was just as free from the small vices as the big. There was never a trace of jealousy or insincerity about him . . . some good men are too conscious of their own virtue but Norman was absolutely free of anything like priggishness and indeed he had too keen a sense of humour to be capable of it.

He said to me once that he was physically a coward. It showed a high moral courage even to say such a thing but as I told him it was not true and the manner of his death proved it. Of course I knew what he meant and it is true that he had not the sort of animal courage that many men are born with. That was not his fault but the courage that he had was of a far higher order and it did not fail him at the last.

It is horrible and ghastly that a life with such infinite possibilities should have been wasted in this futile way. . . . It is the desperate tragedy of war that it makes this useless sacrifice inevitable and what we are suffering from is only what thousands of others have passed through . . .

Dear Lilian, my whole heart goes out to you in misery. You were so proud of him and so justly proud. Only time can soften this blow and make it possible for us to think of him without that dreadful, stabbing pain. . . . I have some letters from him that I shall always keep, full of the most generous confidence and affection. I am very proud to think that I had it. He has only lived half his life but he has left a great name behind him, not only for his outstanding ability but as a clean, honourable, unselfish and public spirited man and that is something for his family to rejoice in.

It is nearly one, and I must go to bed. Good night, Lilian, and may you find strength to bear this trouble.

Yours very affectionately,

Neville Chamberlain.'(25)

By his will, Norman had bequeathed a portion of his estate to Birmingham City Council, directing that the interest should accumulate until there was a sufficient amount to provide playing-fields and recreational facilities for the working classes of the city and other members of the public. By January 1957, the original bequest together with accumulated interest, amounted to about £31,700 and the City Council decided to use this fund for the provision of playing-fields (to be known as 'The Norman Chamberlain Playing Fields') on land owned by them which is part of their Shard End Estate.

The Norman Chamberlain Playing Fields were officially opened on July 28th, 1964, by Sir John Hunt, C.B.E., D.S.O.(27), in the presence of the Lord Mayor of Birmingham, Ald. Barrow, the Chairman (Ald. E. W. Horton) and the members of the Parks Committee, and of Norman's sister, Enid.

The example of Norman was a most potent influence in determining Neville to contemplate something which hitherto he had regarded with unutterable abhorrence, namely a Parliamentary career. 'When I think of Johnnie and Norman,' he wrote to his sister, 'I cannot back out of public work of some kind.' He was still conscious of what he described as 'the humiliation, the meanness and pettiness of that (political) life' but, as he wrote in a later letter, 'I can't be satisfied with a purely selfish attention to business for the rest of my life.'(28) Accordingly, he allowed his name to go forward as a possible Conservative candidate for the Ladywood Division of Birmingham. The local Conservatives jumped at him and he was duly adopted. It was a poor district and, in normal times, anything but a safe seat. But in the 'Khaki Election' Neville was returned, with a clear majority over his Labour and Liberal opponents combined of more than five thousand.

A few years later, Austen, after a visit to Birmingham, wrote to his sisters:

'The future of Birmingham gives me great anxiety and Neville's position in particular. I heard much this time that I had not heard before. . . . Boiled down it all comes to this. . . . Neville's manner freezes people. His workers think that he does not appreciate what they do for him. Everybody respects him but he makes no friends.'(29)

It is undoubtedly a fact that the first impression of himself which Neville gave was often one of coldness and aloofness. It was the opinion of many of his contemporaries and associates and indeed of some of his relations who were genuinely fond of him that he was not at all an easy man to know. Like nearly all human characteristics, this was due to a mixture of heredity and environment. The former can, we know, play strange tricks and people sometimes owe their most prominent characteristics to a remote ancestor. But all the evidence goes to show that Neville was pure, undiluted Chamberlain and Kenrick through and through and futhermore that of the two strains it was the Kenrick which predominated.

As to environment, most of Neville's youth and early manhood (apart from the years in the Bahamas when he was thrown almost entirely on his own resources) had been spent at Highbury, the atmosphere of which was described by one of Neville's cousins (not of Kenrick descent), but accustomed on the contrary to the gaiety and fun of West Woodhay as 'distinctly awe-inspiring'.(30) It is hard to analyse this but more than one observer noticed a certain critical attitude which united the 'Chamberlain-Kenrick clique' among themselves but sometimes set up a barrier between them and the outside world.

All this does not mean that Neville was fundamentally either cold, pompous or priggish. Innumerable acts of kindness bear witness to the fact that he had an essentially sympathetic and generous nature. And, contrary to the general impression, he had a strong and excellent sense of humour which, however, was seldom displayed except in his family circle and to his few intimate friends. After his shooting and fishing holidays, particularly, he would bring back amusing and excellent imitations of ghillies and Welsh peasants. And when, later, he became a member of the Government and was invited by George V to shooting parties at Sandringham, he used to do an excellent impersonation of His Majesty's inquisition at the end of the day into the contribution to the bag of each of his sons. 'How many did you shoot?' the King would ask each in turn and Neville could assume the voice and the expression of both father and son when one of their Royal Highnesses was forced to confess, 'None, father.'(31) Neville could tell and enjoy a good story, but there was never anything unkind or sarcastic in his sense of humour – at least in its private manifestations. He reserved his sarcasms for the House of Commons and the political platform. A good example of his sense of humour is afforded by a certain visit which he and Baldwin paid to the Aquarium at the London Zoo, when they both became convulsed with laughter as they identified various fishes as they swam past with different members of the House of Commons.(32) Like his father, Neville was an excellent mimic and to his family he could do extremely good imitations of some of his political associates and opponents.

In London, Neville liked to go now and again to a variety show and there was at least one clown whose antics made him laugh until his sides ached. And in Paris he thoroughly enjoyed an evening at the Folies Bergères.(33) But it was his wife who, of all people, brought out his sense of humour most strongly, often unconsciously. There was a 'wild irish' side to her and, when this side was uppermost, he would throw his head back and roar with laughter. 'Oh, Annie you're marvellous,' he would exclaim.(34) To children and young people generally he was often surprisingly attractive. Thus the young son of Arthur junior (Arthur the third) used to look forward keenly to Neville's visits because of the delightful walks he would take him, made so fascinating by Neville's seeing eye and ability to point out natural objects of every kind, whether birds, flowers, butterflies, animals or the beauties of the countryside.(35) Still it remains the fact that the outside world generally got an impression of reserve and aloofness.

His wife and family saw a very different side of Neville. To them he was devoted and by them he was adored. He was the most loving and considerate of fathers. The fact that he ruled out an applicant for the position of governess to his children on the ground of 'lack of tenderness' may be given as one example out of many of his continual solicitude for their welfare.(36) He entered into their fun and games and would get down on his hands and knees and help them to build castles with toy bricks and generally to play with their toys and animals. He read aloud to them constantly, his favourite books for this purpose being the novels of Scott, Dickens and Marryat and *Treasure Island* by Robert Louis Stevenson, and a book on natural history by Richard Jeffries.(37) And he was no mean story-teller himself. One serial, a tale of excitement and adventure, which he invented for the benefit of his children, lasted for several years and there were parts of it which used to make his son's (Frank's) hair stand on end.

Every year at the festive season he dressed up as 'Father Christmas' and would emerge from the shrubbery at Westbourne, his Edgbaston home, and would come plodding across the garden with a sack of presents on his back, watched from the nursery by his two children, Dorothy and Frank, who would rush down to let him in when he reached the door.(38) After Neville's death, the costume passed to Frank who kept it and used it later for the benefit of *his* children. Frank died in October 1965 and the following Christmas, his son, young Neville (aged 5½) used it for the benefit of his little sister.

One of Neville senior's letters contains a description of a play in which he was to act with his children at Christmas, himself taking the part of a 'fool giant'.(39) Amateur theatricals at the festive season had always been a tradition with the Chamberlains and the Kenricks and there was generally a performance at one or other of the 'clan' houses, in which, in the days of his youth, Neville had often taken part. *The Rose and the Ring* and *Pickwick* were favourite subjects and, in the latter, Neville once took the parts both of Mr. Winkle and the red-nosed man.(40)

17

The Coalition and the Carlton Club Meeting

Almost immediately after the armistice was signed on November 11th, 1918, Lloyd George and Bonar Law decided to go to the country as a Coalition Party. Accordingly, Parliament was dissolved at the end of November, and polling took place on December 14th. It is important, in view of what happened afterwards, to appreciate the circumstances and conditions of this election.

In May 1918, a certain General Sir Frederick Maurice had criticized statements made by Lloyd George as to the strength of our armed forces in France. Maurice had written to Asquith about this and the latter, still resentful of the manner in which Lloyd George had succeeded in supplanting him as Prime Minister, moved in the House of Commons for a Select Committee to investigate the matter. Lloyd George made it clear that he would regard this vote as one of confidence and when the House divided he won the day easily. In the 1918 General Election the voting in the 'Maurice Debate' was made the test of who was and who was not a Coalition candidate. It was for this reason that Asquith dubbed it 'the coupon election'. Only those who had voted for the Government in that debate received the 'coupon', i.e. a letter of support signed by Lloyd George and Bonar Law. Asquith and the 106 Liberals who had followed him into the Opposition lobby did not receive it and in consequence most of them, including Asquith himself, lost their seats. They and their supporters bitterly resented Lloyd George's treatment of them and this was undoubtedly a major factor in the disintegration of the Liberal Party which followed. The immediate result of the election was a sweeping triumph for the Government which returned with a total of 534 seats against Labour's 61 and the Asquithian Liberals' 29.

In the new Government, Austen became Chancellor of the Exchequer. He had not been pleased with the manner in which the appointment had been offered to him, because it had looked at first as though he would not be in the Cabinet and he took this as a not inconsiderable affront. He was also annoyed at what he considered the unduly curt and hurried manner in which the offer was made to him, which he described as rather like 'a bone being flung to a dog'. Austen did not consider that Lloyd George was giving him the consideration he deserved and was particularly irritated by the apparent likelihood that he might not be allowed to inhabit No. 11 Downing Street, the official residence of the Chancellor. However, in the end, all these difficulties were eradicated or smoothed over and Austen accepted the office.

Austen's second period as Chancellor of the Exchequer, during which he introduced three Budgets, took place under very different conditions from his first. A short but very lively post-war boom, during which prices soared and employment was easy to find, was succeeded by one of the worst depressions ever to be known in British history. There was widespread unemployment and by June 1921 the total number of men registered as out of work was 2,580,000. Industry started to stagnate, exports grew less, the demand for industrial capital diminished with the growing lack of confidence on the part of businessmen, agricultural prices fell acutely; there were numerous strikes and industrial disputes. It was against this background that Austen had to budget in the year 1919–20 for an expenditure of £1,600,000,000. At one time the Government, dependent though it was on Conservative support, seriously considered a capital levy and Austen's papers contain an interesting account of the arguments for and against this proposal which were brought forward both by the Treasury and within the Cabinet. In the end, however, this particular proposal was turned down and, instead, Austen raised Excess Profits Tax from 40 to 60 per cent. The other measure for which his Chancellorship will be chiefly memorable was the repeal of Lloyd George's famous land taxes. They had proved unremunerative, having been too costly to administer.

In March 1921, Bonar Law, whose health had been deteriorating for some time, resigned both from the Government and from the leadership of the Conservative Party. At a meeting which took place at the Carlton Club on March 21st Austen was unanimously and with considerable enthusiasm elected to the leadership of the whole party. The ball was now at his feet and he had every chance of becoming Prime Minister within a few years or even months. His failure to achieve this high office provides perhaps the most striking example of the truth of Churchill's description of him as 'the man who always played the game and always lost it'. In order to see how this came about, we must now give some account of the relations between Austen and Lloyd George and between each of them and the bulk of the Conservative Party.

Austen had every reason both to dislike and distrust Lloyd George, who had been the leading spirit in the attacks on himself and his father in the matter of Kynochs and Hoskins during the South African War. He had, however, admired the great qualities which the Prime Minister had shown in leading the nation to victory but this had been tempered by resentment at his treatment of Neville and the rather 'off-hand' manner in which he (Austen) had been offered the Chancellorship of the Exchequer by Lloyd George. What were the Prime Minister's feelings towards Austen? Perhaps the best indication of them is to be found in certain recently published extracts from the diary of Miss Stevenson, then the secretary to and later the wife of Lloyd George. 'Since Bonar left,' she wrote 'he [Lloyd George] has lost an ideal companion with whom he could laugh and joke and enjoy himself. He cannot do that with Chamberlain, who is pompous to the last degree, and has become increasingly so since he took Bonar's place. He is a vain man.'(1) It must be remembered that these views were based on a rather superficial observation and slight acquaintance by Miss Stevenson, but it is the fact that first impressions of Austen were not always very favourable and that, sometimes, even to people who became later his devoted friends, he gave the appearance of aloofness.

But, he was not fundamentally a pompous man, as is clear from the fact that he could enjoy a joke against himself. An excellent illustration of this occurred at a dinner-party given by a well-known society hostess, the Hon. Mrs. Ronald Greville. Unfortunately, the butler was drunk and, noticing this, Mrs. Greville hastily scribbled a note on a piece of paper and handed it to him.

The butler walked solemnly but unsteadily round the table to where Austen was sitting and handed him the piece of paper on which, after adjusting his eyeglass, Austen found the words 'You are drunk. Leave the room instantly'. Far from being offended, Austen was genuinely amused.

A few weeks after making the entry in her diary which we have already quoted, Miss Stevenson wrote:

> 'There is no doubt that he [Lloyd George] has a lot of enemies in the Government who will leave him if they think they can better themselves. Austen he thinks will stick to him. He certainly gets on much better with him than he expected to. Austen plays the game and he sees that he can trust the P.M. who conceals nothing from him.'(2)

The House of Commons, which was returned in December 1918, was unlike any to which Austen had been accustomed. This is scarcely surprising because more than eight years had elapsed since there had been a General Election and, in the interval, the face of England had changed utterly. When Austen looked round the House or walked with his followers into the division lobbies he cannot have failed to be impressed by the contrast with pre-war years. In those days the Conservative benches had been composed mainly of country gentlemen, scions of noble houses and a fair sprinkling of the learned professions. Culture and intellect were well represented on both sides of the House and this had created an atmosphere which was thoroughly congenial. Now the atmosphere was quite different. More than one observer spoke of the new House as consisting largely of 'hard-faced men' who had 'done well out of the war' and contrasted the old-fashioned country gentleman who had gone into the House from a sense of duty or from family pride, because he believed it was the right thing to do, with these 'modern, unscrupulous characters' who were mostly 'on the make'.

Bonar Law, himself a businessman, was far more qualified than was Austen to cope with this new element and he appealed far more to them. But it was vital to Austen's future that he should do what he could to consolidate his position as the leader of the Party by making himself agreeable to his followers, losing no opportunity of talking to them in the smoking-room and getting to know their views. But Austen, though he had one or two staunch supporters among the 'back benchers' was not in general 'hail-fellow-will-met' with the Party as a whole.

As time went on, the Coalition became increasingly unpopular with the rank and file of the Conservative Party and particularly with its representatives in the House of Commons. Coalitions are, of course, always unpopular with the rank and file because they mean that the spoils of victory have to be shared with another party. This particular Coalition was especially unpopular with the Conservative 'back benchers' because they felt that the Coalition Liberals were getting an unduly large share of those spoils and would make less and less contribution to victory as time went on. A powerful element in the Conservative Party had made a very shrewd appraisal of the weakness of Lloyd George's position. This was that he was a Prime Minister without a party of his own. The so-called Coalition Liberal Party was, these Conservatives felt, largely an illusion. Its 124 members of the House were there only because, by reason of the 'coupon', they had received Conservatives' votes. Most of the Liberals in the constituencies regarded Asquith as their leader and would tend, as time went on, to turn more and more towards him and away from Lloyd George.

It is probable that even if Lloyd George's political acts had commended themselves to them, a large section of the Conservative Party would for these reasons have striven to end the Coalition at the earliest possible moment. They did not, however, so commend themselves. On the contrary his policies both in the domestic and in the foreign field tended more and more to widen the gap between himself and the Conservatives. The appointment of Dr. Addison as Minister without Portfolio at a salary of £5,000 per annum after he had been (in the view of the Conservatives) a failure as Minister of Health and at a time when the need for economy was being preached by the Government and was urgently called for, the removal from his command of General Dyer for taking strong action in India, the Honours scandal, Lloyd George's incursions into foreign politics which (in the view of the Conservatives) brought Russia and Germany together unnecessarily and by favouring the Greeks against the Turks brought the country to the brink of war at Chanak – these were only a few of the matters in respect of which Lloyd George had increased the unpopularity of both himself and the Coalition with the Conservatives. But for the one single cause which of all others precipitated the fall of the Coalition we must look to the Emerald Isle. In a speech made early in 1922, Churchill described the way in which this old sore had once more arisen to plague British politicians. 'The mode and thought of men, the whole outlook on affairs, the grouping of parties, all have encountered violent and tremendous changes in the deluge of the world but, as the deluge subsides and the waters fall, we see the dreary steeples of Fermanagh and Tyrone emerging once again.'(3)

The truce arranged at the outbreak of the European war had not brought internal tranquillity to Ireland for very long. There had been rebellious activities in Southern Ireland during the war, particularly when conscription was introduced, but these were crushed with a stern hand by the British Government. After the war, trouble broke out again. Then, in the summer of 1921, Lloyd George, prompted and encouraged by Austen(4), decided on the bold step of agreeing to a conference at Downing Street with the Irish representatives. Austen Chamberlain was one of the delegates who attended this conference on behalf of the British Government. It was successful and, in December 1921, the Irish Treaty was signed.

The idea of a conference with the 'Irish rebels' had never been popular with the right wing of the Conservative Party. On October 31st, 1921, what amounted to a vote of censure on the Government for entering into negotiations with the 'rebels' was moved by Colonel Gretton and supported by some forty other Conservative M.P.s whose general attitude towards Austen when he spoke in justification of the Government's policy was one of hostility. Even the fact that the rights of Ulster were fully safeguarded did not satisfy the 'Diehards'. Carson delivered a particularly bitter attack on Austen in the House of Lords. 'The other evening,' he said 'I saw with disgust that Mr. Austen Chamberlain, the son of Mr. Joseph Chamberlain, having agreed to put Ulster into these terms, then said he made an appeal to the comradeship of his old friend Sir James Craig to come in and submit to the domination of Sinn Fein. I could not help thinking that it was rather like after having shot a man in the back going over to him and patting him on the shoulder and saying "Old man, die as quickly as you can, and do not make any noise."'(5)

But before the annual meeting of the National Union at Liverpool, Austen had won the day, defending the Government's Irish policy with great vigour in a speech of considerable eloquence. 'Now and again in the affairs of men,' he said in conclusion, 'there comes a moment when courage is safer than prudence, when some great act of faith touching the hearts and stirring the emotions of men achieves the miracle that no arts of statesmanship can compass. Such a moment may be passing before our eyes now as we meet here. I pray to God with all my heart and soul that to each of us to whom responsibility is brought there may be given vision to see, faith to act and courage to persevere.'

Lloyd George was pleased with and proud of the Irish Treaty and he was inclined to think that it presented him with a good opportunity to go to the country. He consulted the Coalition Chief Whip who, after having instituted a preliminary canvass in the constituencies, reported favourably. He also discussed the matter with Austen, who, in his turn, consulted both the Conservative Chief Whip and the Chairman of the Party (Sir George Younger). Having obtained their views, Austen wrote to Lloyd George, who was at that time at Cannes, that he was not in favour of an immediate election. Younger, meanwhile, had given a number of interviews to the Press in which he broadcast both the proposal for an early election and his own reasons for opposing it. Lloyd George was furious with Younger and annoyed with Austen when he heard of this. He wrote to Austen in February 1922, saying that, in his view, Younger had 'behaved disgracefully' by making public revelation of matters about which he had been consulted 'confidentially'. Austen wired back:

'I don't think you realize immense difficulties created for us by premature revelations of our discussions. These breaches of confidence almost make me despair. . . . Dissolution talk produced great reaction in Unionist Party against Coalition and I feel my effort to secure ultimate union has received an immense set-back.'(6)

'Ultimate union' referred to the idea of fusing the more moderate and responsible sections of the Conservative and Coalition

Liberal Parties into a new National Party. Birkenhead and Churchill were keen protagonists of this idea and Austen himself had been favourably disposed towards it.

It so happened that at that time Bonar Law was also staying in Cannes. Lloyd George was now anxious to bring him back into politics and into the Government. He offered him the Foreign Secretaryship but there is no evidence that he consulted or even considered the effect this would have on Austen before doing so. Lord Curzon, the incumbent at the time of the office which Lloyd George proposed to confer on Bonar Law, was also, needless to say, not consulted.

In February, Younger again expressed himself forcibly on the subject of the Coalition. After letting it be known that he intended shortly to retire from the chairmanship, he described the Coalition to a meeting of the women's branch of the National Union as 'a matrimonial alliance that I want to get rid of'. Then he added 'A Bill of divorcement would be the best means of accomplishing that end. It would be a divorcement but, as our American friends say, it would leave the parties concerned friendly.'

The following day, Birkenhead replied to this at the Junior Carlton Club in characteristic fashion. 'When the tempest rages, and when the Captain would naturally be on the bridge,' he said, 'I would not give any particular encouragement to the cabin boy to seize the helm. And I am more than ever of that opinion when the cabin boy has announced that he does not intend to make another voyage'.(7) All this greatly increased the rift in the Conservative Party and strengthened the hand of those who wanted to end the Coalition.

At the end of February 1922 Lloyd George wrote a very important letter to Austen in which he offered to resign so as to allow Austen to form a 'homogeneous government'.(8) Austen, however, greatly to his own detriment as well as to that of his country and even of Lloyd George himself, immediately went round to Downing Street and begged Lloyd George not to resign.

Why Austen should have made such a colossal mistake it is hard to understand. He owed nothing to Lloyd George, who had constantly maligned his father as well as having made base insinuations against both Joseph and Austen at the time of the

South African War. Furthermore (though Austen was unaware of this) Lloyd George had, only a few weeks previously, been trying to intrigue with Bonar Law behind Austen's back. There is of course no doubt that Lloyd George could, when he chose, exert extraordinary charm. Many men had fallen under his spell but none so completely and so disastrously as Austen who now, out of a mistaken sense of loyalty, threw away the chance, indeed the certainty, of becoming Prime Minister.

All that spring and summer the Coalition continued to become more and more unpopular with the rank and file of the Conservative Party. One of the main reasons for this was the deteriorating situation in Ireland. There were many Conservatives who had never liked the Irish Treaty and they now felt that their worst fears were confirmed.

It soon became clear that the Provisional Government for Southern Ireland, set up under the terms of the Treaty, was utterly incapable of preserving order. On April 13th, a group of terrorists, led by one Rory O'Connor, seized the four courts in Dublin and proclaimed themselves 'The Republican Government of Ireland'. Emanating from them, armed bands of terrorists spread rapine and murder throughout the land and a campaign of organized violence and terror was launched against Ulster with the object, it was thought and feared at the time, of coercing the newly formed Government of Northern Ireland. But the culmination of Tory anger was reached when Field Marshal Sir Henry Wilson, a native and champion of Ulster, was shot dead by two Southern Irish fanatics as he was about to enter his house in Eaton Place. No single event which had taken place up to now did more to strengthen the Anti-Coalitionists than this, for a considerable section of the Conservative Party attributed this and other Irish outrages, perhaps rather unjustly, to the Irish Treaty with which, of course, Austen was prominently identified. When he called on Lady Wilson to offer his condolences, she greeted him with one word – 'Murderer'.(9)

All through that summer the signs and portents increased that the Coalition could not possibly endure with Lloyd George at the head of it. At the end of July, a group of Conservative junior Ministers sought an interview with Austen in order to put forward the arguments for ending the Coalition. He, however, made the mistake of asking Birkenhead to deal with them and the latter proceeded to lecture and storm at them in such a rude and arrogant manner that, in the words of one of them, they departed 'spluttering with indignation'.(10) None of these protests had the least effect on Austen, however. He was determined to adhere to Lloyd George at all costs and had even addressed a letter to him begging him 'as a friend speaking in your own interests, as a colleague speaking on behalf of your colleagues, and as the leader of one of the parties whose fortunes are inseparably bound up at the present time with your decision, to take the earliest opportunity of definitely declaring your resolution to continue as Prime Minister the leadership of the Coalition. . . .'(11) And shortly before this he had said to Lord Riddell, an intimate friend of Lloyd George, 'Things are better. We shall pull through all right. I am getting letters from the great industrial centres urging us to remain united. They realize that disintegration means Labour victories. Tell the Prime Minister that. He will get his health back again. He is a great man and great men have a way of pulling themselves together.'(12)

There was no shrewder observer of the political situation in the whole Conservative Party than Lord Derby. He had enormous influence and his views carried very great weight, particularly in Lancashire. In September 1922, he wrote to Austen telling him that in his view the Coalition as then constituted could not possibly go on. Lord Salisbury had recently suggested that if the present Coalition went to the country independent Conservatives should stand against them and Lord Derby now said that 'the vast sentiment of the electors favours Salisbury and his new party'. The only solution was for Lloyd George to resign 'in a friendly spirit'. Then 'a Coalition with a Conservative at its head would succeed'. 'Your letter,' Austen replied 'is a great shock to me. . . . It seems to me that Salisbury has manufactured differences where none ought to exist. The electoral results of the split must be bad and may easily be disastrous.'(13) In a later letter, Derby told Austen that he had been talking to the Manchester Conservatives and that they had confirmed his own view that 'there is no feeling against the Liberal Coalitionists but there is intensely bitter feeling against Lloyd George and unless there is some distinct under-standing that, in the event of our being returned with a big majority, the new Prime Minister will be a Conservative, there will be a complete break away.'(14)

The annual meeting of the Conservative Party as a whole was due to take place in the middle of November and it seemed likely that there would be a large number of resolutions condemning the Coalition. In order to forestall this, the Cabinet decided on an early election which should take place before the National Union had had an opportunity to make its condemnation. This really amounted, as Lord Beaverbrook has rightly said, to 'a piece of sharp practice so far as the Tory rank and file were concerned'.(15) It seems incredible that Austen should have so far fallen under the spell of Lloyd George as to agree to it. When the Conservative Party managers heard of the decision they were aghast. Sir George Younger wrote, 'I have received from Fraser an account of your decision at Chequers last Sunday and I am frankly appalled at the results it must entail. . . .'(16) And Sir Leslie Wilson, the Chief Whip, wrote:

> 'I must ask you to consider the advisability of not making public your decision without consulting the Party first, and without informing all your colleagues in the Government (Junior Ministers, etc.) of your decision. . . . I know the feeling in the Party well and you will have very little support in the proposed continuation of the Coalition as it is with Lloyd George at its head. . . .'(17)

A day or two later, Wilson told Austen that already no fewer than 184 constituencies had decided to run independent candidates if the Coalition went to the country under Lloyd George.

On October 10th, there was a meeting of the Conservative Cabinet Ministers to discuss the election. They decided to go to the country as soon as possible and in any event before the meeting of the National Union. The only Minister to dissent was Baldwin. Sir Leslie Wilson attended this meeting and he was also strongly against this proposal but he was over-ruled. The next day, he and Younger both told Austen that they would be left with no alternative but to repudiate his leadership if he persisted in his present disastrous course. In this connection it is important to notice that Austen was not the leader of the Party as a whole but only of the Party in the House of Commons. No leader of the Party as a whole had been elected since the resignation of Balfour.

Austen, however, had his full share of the Chamberlain obstinacy. There is no doubt that he greatly underestimated the strength of the Anti-Coalition feeling amongst the Conservative rank and file and overestimated both the electoral advantages of Lloyd George and his own indispensability. On October 12th, he wrote to Birkenhead:

'I am not sure that it may not now be necessary to call a party meeting and to tell them bluntly that they must either follow our advice or do without us, in which case they must find their own Chief and find a Government *at once*. They would be in a d—d fix. . . . I am not willing to step into Lloyd George's shoes and to take any part in a Government formed on personal opposition to him. The malcontents assume they can reject our advice and use us for their own purposes. They make a mistake and it may be well to prove it to them.'(18)

Down to the very last moment nobody knew what Bonar Law would do – probably he had not made up his mind himself. It is known, however, that he tried hard to persuade Lloyd George to retire – at least temporarily, but he was met with a refusal, the reason given being that it would not be fair to the Coalition Liberals. Curzon had originally agreed to stand by the Coalition but, at the last moment, he changed his mind.

Ultimately, as a result of a good deal of pressure, Austen agreed to summon a meeting of Conservative M.P.s to the Carlton Club for October 19th. This was to be the 'party meeting' referred to in his letter to Birkenhead and it was to forestall the meeting of the National Union. It was, however, to be confined to Conservative Ministers and members of the House of Commons. In fixing the date Austen had in mind the fact that there would be an important by-election at Newport where a Coalition Liberal was being opposed by an Independent and a Labour candidate. Austen was confident that either the Coalition candidate would win easily or the Labour man would get in on a split vote. In either case, the result which would be declared on the morning of the meeting, would provide a salutary rebuff for the recalcitrants and would draw the waverers into his own camp.

The afternoon before the meeting, Austen went to see Bonar Law, who spoke sympathetically of the position in which Austen now found himself, but apparently he himself was still undecided as to what to do. His was, he said, a hateful situation and he felt inclined to plead ill-health and keep away from the meeting altogether. In that case he would have, he explained, to leave Parliament and give up public life but if he came he would have to speak against Austen. Austen said that in that case his speech would be decisive, the Government would have to resign and he (Law) would have to form another. 'Well,' said Bonar Law finally, 'it's a hateful position; I expect if I had remained in your place I should have acted like you.'(19)

That same evening, Sir Archibald Salvidge called on Bonar Law, who, by this time, had definitely made up his mind that he would speak against the Coalition at the meeting and Salvidge knew that this would be decisive and told him so. He also reminded him of an occasion during the war when he had said (referring to Lloyd George) – 'We must never let the little man go.' Bonar Law flushed at this and then said that the whole position had changed. As Salvidge was leaving, Bonar Law called him back. 'Tell Austen and F.E. to be moderate,' he said. 'Do you think I or Curzon imagine we can rule the country with the sort of people that will be left to make up a Cabinet after the break tomorrow? I must have Austen and F.E. back at the first possible opportunity.'(20)

The Carlton Club meeting began at 1 p.m. on October 19th. Some 275 M.P.s and ministers were present. All of them had read in their morning newspapers the result of the Newport by-election, in which the Independent Conservative candidate had been returned with a majority of more than 2,000 votes.

Austen could not possibly have chosen a worse moment at which to appeal to the Conservative M.P.s to continue the Coalition. Their faces were wreathed in smiles at this wonderful portent and the idea of sharing the great Conservative victory, which now seemed clearly in sight, with the Coalition Liberal made no appeal at all.

Austen was, on the whole, received rather coldly when he walked into the room where the meeting was to be held. He was cheered, but nothing like as loudly as Bonar Law, who was received with vociferous applause. This was the more significant in that the cheering on both occasions was quite unorganized. Nor was Austen's speech received with great enthusiasm. He relied almost entirely on the dangers of socialism, dwelling particularly on the Labour Party's programme and especially on their proposals for nationalization and a capital levy. Austen was followed by Baldwin, who described Lloyd George as a 'dynamic force'. And, said Stanley Baldwin, 'a dynamic force is a very terrible thing'. It was the measure of this particular 'dynamic force' that it had induced himself to risk the wilderness rather than continue the Coalition and Austen to risk it rather than break it up. Baldwin's was undoubtedly an effective speech and he was warmly applauded when he resumed his seat. After this Ernest Pretyman moved and Lane Fox seconded a motion that the Conservatives should fight the next election as an independent party. Before this could be put to the vote there were cries from all over the room for Bonar Law. Looking pale, he rose slowly and as though with reluctance, and at first he spoke with some hesitation. It soon became clear, however, where his sympathies lay. 'The feeling against the Coalition is so strong,' he said, 'that if we follow Austen Chamberlain's advice our Party will be broken and a new Party will be formed. . . . It will be a repetition of what happened after Peel passed the Corn Bill. The body that is cast off will slowly become the Conservative Party, but it will take a generation before it gets back to the influence which it ought to have.'(21) He concluded by saying that he would vote against the continuance of the Coalition and this announcement was greeted with enormous enthusiasm. The vote was then taken on Pretyman's motion which was carried by 187 votes to 87.

Immediately after the meeting, Austen went round to No. 10 Downing Street and said to the Prime Minister, 'We are beaten. We must resign.' A number of other Ministers were there and, on hearing of Curzon's defection, one of them remarked, 'So our punctilious pro-consul has ratted.' That same afternoon Lloyd George drove to Buckingham Palace and tendered his resignation and the King sent for Bonar Law, who, however, made it clear that he was not willing to form a Government until there had been a full Party meeting. Meanwhile Austen and his fellow Coalitionists amongst the former Conservative Ministers drew up a manifesto in which they said that they dissented from the course proposed by the majority at the meeting and were not willing to 'serve notice of dismissal' on the Prime Minister in a message telling him, in spite of his 'incalculable service to the country during the war' that 'your value to us is much less than it was even a few months ago' and 'we propose . . . that you should relieve us of your embarrassing co-operation'. The manifesto also said:

> 'We advised the Unionist Party not to take a course which must repel powerful allies in the anxious campaigns which lie in front of it. The meeting today rejected that advice. Other men who have given other counsels must inherit our burden and discharge its consequent responsibility.'(22)

The Party meeting was duly held and Bonar Law was unanimously elected leader. He then accepted the King's commission to form a Government and kissed hands on his appointment as Prime Minister. Baldwin became Chancellor of the Exchequer and Curzon remained Foreign Secretary. To Neville, who had only just got back from Canada, Bonar Law offered the position of Postmaster General.

Neville was anxious to accept but he feared at first that to do so would cause trouble with Austen. He told Austen that, if he wanted him to, he would refuse, but that, having thus refused to serve under both Bonar Law and Lloyd George, he would not feel that he had any future in politics and so would get out as soon as he could in fairness to his consituents do so. 'What more could affection offer?' Austen wrote to his sisters, 'and equally I could not accept such a sacrifice, so I changed my attitude and said "Accept". . . . So I have learned the depth of his affection.'(23)

18

The Rise of Baldwin

Almost immediately after becoming Prime Minister, Bonar Law asked for and obtained a dissolution and the ensuing General Election was from his point of view extremely satisfactory. It resulted in a Conservative majority over all other parties of seventy-seven seats. Austen was returned with a handsome majority in West Birmingham and Neville was also victorious in the far less safe Ladywood Division, though with a smaller majority than his brother. In March 1923, Neville became Minister of Health.

Bonar Law did not last long as Prime Minister. His health once more deteriorated under the strain and trouble developed in his throat and this was later diagnosed as cancer. On his doctor's advice he left England on April 27th, 1923, for a short sea cruise but this did not result in any improvement in his condition. He returned on May 11th, very weak and hardly able to speak. Lord Curzon had expected to be sent for by the King but it was Stanley Baldwin who became Prime Minister.

At the critical time of Bonar Law's resignation, Austen was out of the country. He had gone with his wife for a holiday in the Pyrenees. It so happened that on May 21st there was a fête at Verney les Bains, the little place where they were staying, and it was not until the following day (22nd) that he got an important telegram advising him to return and suggesting that he should call at the Hotel Crillon in Paris on the way back. Here he was met by Lord Birkenhead and they discussed the situation in some detail and decided to stay in Paris until the position had become clearer. It was not until the evening of Friday, May 25th, that Austen arrived in London, and he had not been back very long before he got a telephone message asking him to come to Chequers the next day, Saturday.

Baldwin met him when he arrived and Austen gave the following account of their interview in a letter to his sisters:

'I spent one and a half hours with Baldwin, very friendly but making no change in the situation of any kind whatever. He told me the whole story – how he wished to invite me to join, how two or three (actually I think three) colleagues said that they would resign if I joined, how he felt that he could not throw over men who joined when the boat was very rickety, how he wired Horne and failing him turned to McKenna and how Worthy was still uncertain. Then he tried the Washington proposal (Curzon had left him ignorant of the fact that I had already refused), in terms so simple and sincere that I could only say that I had been outraged when told of his intention but could only answer quite calmly now, and then said, "If you wanted unity why didn't you send for me – even if it was only to say what you have said today so frankly, that you wished to include me but could not but that you still wished to heal old wounds – and ask my help with my friends – why, why didn't you send for me?" Answer: "I'm very sorry I never thought of it. I'm very sorry."'(1)

Baldwin *had* sent for Austen but what apparently annoyed the latter was that he had not done so until he had decided on the composition of his Cabinet and then had only sent a telephone message, whereas Austen considered that Baldwin should have written him a personal letter. Austen made it clear to his brother that he considered he had been treated with discourtesy, but Neville, while agreeing that Baldwin had shown lack of tact, assured Austen that the Prime Minister had meant no offence. Neville was determined to bring the two together if he possibly could. There is little doubt that Baldwin himself was genuinely anxious to bring Austen into the Government at the earliest possible moment. The difficulty was Birkenhead; he was particularly unpopular with some of the Junior Ministers who had not forgotten his rude behaviour to them. He had made it clear to Austen, between whom and himself feelings of great regard and affection had grown up, that Austen must on no account allow their friendship to interfere with his career. But Austen was the most loyal of men and he insisted that in no circumstances would he join a Government from which his friend was excluded and furthermore that Birkenhead must be given a position at least equal in prestige and status to that which he had held in the Coalition, namely the Lord Chancellorship.

In August 1923, Neville became Chancellor of the Exchequer, thereby stepping into the position which Baldwin himself had occupied until he became Prime Minister. He received a rather pathetic letter from Austen. . . . 'I must send you my hearty congratulations and affectionate good wishes. I am sorry that fate has separated us instead of, as I once hoped, uniting us in the same Cabinet, but you are making a fine career, and I am proud of your success. How it would have rejoiced father's heart. . . .'

And two days later, he wrote again to Neville:

'It is an immense regret to me that you and I do not see eye to eye and are no longer acting together. I do and say as little as I can, for politics are hateful to me since we two parted. I shall see this Parliament out, but my position is very difficult, and I think it not unlikely that I shall not stand again. The fact that you and I both sit for Birmingham makes my position more and more difficult, for whilst I will not argue with you anywhere, Birmingham is the last place I would choose for the theatre of our differences – and without Birmingham I am nothing.

Well fate has so willed it, and its no use kicking against the pricks, but it's d—d hard that fate should separate the fortunes of two brothers who are to one another as you and I.'(2)

Baldwin had not been Prime Minister for very long, before, faced with mounting unemployment and dwindling trade, he decided that the best way to deal with these evils was to institute a measure of Tariff Reform. But Bonar Law had given a pledge that there should be no major change in fiscal policy during the present Parliament and Baldwin felt therefore that he ought to obtain a fresh mandate from the country before introducing the Protective legislation which he had in mind. Accordingly, on November 12th, 1923, he asked for and obtained a dissolution.

The results of the General Election were declared on December 8th. They showed that the Conservatives had lost a total of 88 seats and would not have a majority in the new Parliament. They did, however, return the strongest individual party with 258 seats against 191 for Labour and 158 for the Liberals.

There was now considerable speculation as to what would happen. One rumour was that Austen would be called on to form a Government with Liberal support, it being suggested that Asquith had said that he would not lift a little finger to maintain in power such a stupid man as Baldwin but that he would 'look with benevolence' on a Government in which Austen and Balfour were the chief figures. Almost certainly, however, there was nothing in this; there was considerable feeling against Austen amongst the rank and file of the Conservative Party and, though many of them blamed Baldwin for the loss of the election, they would never have 'killed him to make Austen King'. Nor is there any reason to suppose that Asquith ever seriously contemplated any other course than that which he, in fact, adopted, namely to turn the Conservatives out and put Labour in.

The process of re-uniting the Conservative Party, which had proved impossible while they were the Government, was accomplished in Opposition. Neville claimed and was entitled to a good deal of the credit for this. He invited Baldwin and Austen to dinner at his new home in Eaton Square. Austen, according to Neville, was 'a bit stiff just at first' but 'gradually thawed'. Then, to quote Neville again, 'as soon as Annie had left us I started in and called on Stanley Baldwin, who then suggested that Austen should join the rest of them on the Opposition front bench and that he and Birkenhead should forthwith become members of the Shadow Cabinet. Austen accepted the invitation and soon they were addressing one another as "my dear Stanley" and "my dear Austen".'(3)

The *entente* thus newly formed nearly perished still-born. Soon after the dinner-party at Neville's house, there was a by-election in the Abbey Division of Westminster and Winston Churchill decided to stand as an 'Independent Constitutionalist' against the official Conservative. Birkenhead and Austen both announced their intention of supporting Churchill and a breach in the newly closed ranks was only avoided by Baldwin promising that none of the Conservative leaders would speak for the official candidate and, in return, Austen and Birkenhead promised not to speak for Churchill who only just missed getting in.

The first Labour Government lasted little more than eight months. It came to an end in October 1924, in the rather squalid circumstances of the Campbell prosecution. There had now been three General Elections within two years and the country was sick of them. Above all it wanted a period of stability when it could go about its own business in its own way. It gave vent to these feelings in the usual way – by swinging heavily to the Conservatives, who returned with a majority of more than two hundred over Labour and Liberals combined. When the names of the new Ministers were announced everyone was surprised. Austen was Foreign Secretary, Winston Churchill Chancellor of the Exchequer and Neville, greatly to his delight, Minister of Health. In forming his Government Baldwin had shown both magnanimity and wisdom.

There is no doubt that Austen was very pleased with his new appointment but at the same time he approached it with a keen realization of the great responsibility involved. 'I am Secretary of State for Foreign Affairs. My garden will go to ruins and you need not expect to get a letter from me for the next four years if I survive so long,' he wrote to his sisters.(4) He was also pleased with most of the other appointments, particularly those of Churchill and Birkenhead. 'All the ministries are well filled,' he said, 'and some of them exceptionally well filled.' He added that Baldwin 'has shown the greatest consideration for me personally, especially by naming me Deputy Leader of the House. I can only accept it as a compliment and not as a duty to be filled. But the motive is obvious and I have thanked him in the spirit of his kindness.'(5) And a few days later:

'I seem to fall naturally into the business and though I entered on this new chapter as indeed on each fresh episode of my life with great diffidence and some misgiving I rapidly found my feet and began to acquire confidence with the first important telegram that I re-drafted and with the effect of my re-draft on my advisers. And it is an immense pleasure to think that the opportunities Father gave me in my young days are my qualification for my present post. I shall make my mistakes (I have indeed made some) but I hope not more or worse than another man.'(6)

One of the first things that Austen did as soon as he had become Foreign Secretary was to summon to his room a conference of all the senior and some of the more important junior members of the Foreign Office staff. He asked them to draw up a memorandum which would include a list of Britain's commitments. Upon the threshold of their inquiry one stark and formidable fact confronted Austen and his advisers. This was the failure of the United States Senate to ratify either the Treaty of Versailles or the French Security Treaty which President Wilson had provisionally agreed to while in Paris. The French felt particularly worried and aggrieved about this because it had been in reliance upon Wilson's promises that they had abandoned their claim to the left bank of the Rhine.

At this time the British Ambassador in Germany was Lord D'Abernon, formerly Sir Edgar Vincent. He was not a professional diplomat. His youth and early middle age had been spent in banking and finance, mainly in the Middle East, where he had acquired a substantial fortune, and he had been Governor of the Imperial Ottoman Bank. After this he was for seven years a Conservative member of Parliament, and, in 1920, he was appointed by Lloyd George the first post-war Ambassador in Berlin. He had married Lady Helen Duncombe, reputedly the most beautiful woman of her day.

D'Abernon had been extremely popular in Germany and he had worked hard to bring that country back into the community of nations. It had been his suggestion that the Germans should of their own volition put forward proposals which would provide for French security. The result of this was that he received from the German Foreign Office, on January 20th, 1925, a definite proposal for a new pact of non-aggression between France and Germany, which would also include provisions for the demilitarization in perpetuity of the Rhineland. This was the germ from which the Locarno Treaty sprang and, though the idea originated in Germany, Austen is entitled to the fullest credit for the way in which he encouraged and developed it. In a letter to Lord Stamfordham, Secretary to the King, Austen set out his ideas on this subject:

'I regard it as the first task of statesmanship to set to work to make the new position of Germany tolerable to the German people in the hope that, as they regain prosperity under it, they may in time become reconciled to it and be unwilling to put their fortunes again to the desperate hazard of war. I am working not for today or tomorrow but for some date like 1950 or 1960 when German strength will have returned and when the prospect of war will again cloud the horizon, unless the risks of war are still too great to be rashly incurred and the actual conditions too tolerable to be jeopardized on a gambler's throw. It is on the realization of this double factor that the hope of permanent peace depends. I believe the key to the solution to it is to be found in allaying French fears and that unless we find means to do this we may be confronted with a complete breakdown of our friendly relations with France and an exacerbation of her attitude towards Germany.'(7)

Between the time when the idea was first mooted and the actual signature of the Treaty, important changes took place in the Governments of France and Germany. The two statesmen with whom Austen actually worked out the details of the famous agreement at Locarno were M. Briand and Herr Stresemann. To Briand, Austen was attracted from the first. 'Geneva was extraordinarily interesting,' he wrote to his wife in March 1925. 'Briand was as charming as ever. I delight in his company and in his wit and humour.'(8) And much later he wrote that, as he listened to Briand speaking, 'I felt my love for France justified, for in Briand's words I heard the voice of all that is noblest and most generous in the soul of the French nation'. Briand had a vivid imagination and flashes of real genius. His idea of a United States of Europe was derided at the time but we can now see that there was a great deal to be said for it. There is no doubt that he fully reciprocated Austen's feelings, for he it was who charmed everyone by arranging a special trip down the lake of Locarno in the steamer *Orange Blossom* to celebrate Ivy's birthday, and who, coming out of the conference room after the final session, seeing her waiting outside, seized her by the hand and said referring to Austen, '*Ah sans lui je ne l'aurais jamais tenté*'. 'Is it strange that I loved him?' Austen wrote long afterwards.(9)

As to Stresemann opinions differ. Austen, though never feeling the same affection for him that he did for Briand, undoubtedly

liked, admired and trusted him. He wrote of his 'great qualities
of foresight, insight, courage, loyalty and patience, by which so
much was achieved', adding that he was 'a man for whom I
had come to feel not only a profound admiration but a sincere
personal affection'.(10) Against this must be set the opinion of
Lord Norwich (formerly A. Duff Cooper) that 'people believed
that it (the Treaty of Locarno) had brought Germany back into
the comity of nations and that it would serve as the basis of her
future relations with France and England. But the Germans saw
it merely as a step towards recovering the strength they needed
to wage a war of revenge, and they broke its terms as soon
as it suited them to do so. Their true intentions were made
perfectly plain to the German ex-Crown Prince at the time by
Stresemann.' (11) Lord Norwich based his opinion of Stresemann largely on information supplied by Count Grandi who, he
said:

'Told me that during the Hague Conference he had seen a
great deal of Stresemann and would often go back with him
to his hotel. . . . Stresemann would always drink a bottle of
champagne before going to bed and in the course of one of
their late conversations he said to Grandi with unusual solem-
nity, "I am an old man and I am dying but you are young and
you will live to see the second Punic War."'(12) And Lord
Vansittart was of the opinion that it was the fate of each of the
political Chamberlains to be deceived by a German – Joseph by
Von Bülow, Austen by Stresemann and Neville by Hitler.(13)
The truth probably is that the agreement reached at Locarno
was an excellent achievement provided that it was intended to
enforce it and it certainly was not Austen's fault that it was not
enforced.

There were in all seven Locarno Treaties but the most important was that to which Germany, Belgium, France, Great Britain
and Italy were all parties. This was formally signed in London
on December 1st, 1925. It guaranteed the inviolability of the
Franco–German and Belgo–German frontiers and the demilitarization of the Rhine Zone. After the Treaty had been signed
Germany was admitted to membership of the League of Nations;
furthermore, the British and French Governments agreed to
vacate certain occupied areas along the Rhine five years earlier

than the time stipulated for in the Treaty of Versailles. For his work in connection with the Treaty Austen became a Knight of the Garter and, what pleased him even more, Ivy was made a D.B.E. As he said later, her grace and charm had contributed in no small measure to the result.

19

Austen's *Nunc Dimittis*: Neville's Ascent

While Austen was thus covering himself with glory as Foreign Secretary, Neville was achieving a less spectacular but very solid and enduring success as Minister of Health. The period of rather over four years which he spent at that Ministry was probably, in spite of the intensely hard work which it involved, the part of his political life he enjoyed most. For here he was dealing with those subjects – hospitals and slum clearance in particular – which had always been nearest to his heart. Furthermore, as Minister, he was brought into direct contact with some of his own favourite projects in Birmingham, and was consulted by those responsible for them, in a manner in which he would not have been at any other Ministry.

The volume of legislation for which he made himself responsible is most impressive. Within a fortnight of taking office, he had placed before the Cabinet a list of twenty-five measures which he wished to see passed into law. No less than twenty-one were dealt with by him during this period. The subjects covered ranged from Widows and Old Age Pensions, Housing, Slum Clearance, Reform of Rating, Local Government, and National Health Insurance to Maternity, Midwifery, and Food and Drugs including Milk. Housing occupied a great deal of his time and, while he was the Minister and largely as a result of his administrative skill, a record number of houses was built annually, while at the same time the cost of subsidies was continually diminished. In one year, 1926–27, the phenomenal total (for those days) of 273,000 houses was reached.

There was one particular aspect of the work of his new department which his own family experience made particularly dear to his heart – Maternity. His own mother and Austen's had both died in childbirth; this was something that he never forgot. Throughout his time as Minister of Health he worked tirelessly to reduce the incidence of maternal mortality. He was responsible for the Midwives and Maternity Homes Act of 1926 and for a very considerable increase in the expenditure on the Maternity and Child Welfare services. In these ways in time a considerable reduction in the rate of maternal mortality was made.

During his time as Lord Mayor of Birmingham and in his early days in the House of Commons, Neville's relations with the leaders of organized labour, including M.P.s, had been excellent. Unfortunately, a situation now arose which altered this. This was Neville's introduction into Parliament of the Guardians (Default) Act, and the steps which he subsequently took under the powers thereby conferred on him. This statute enabled him in certain circumstances to replace the elected Guardians by his own nominees. What lay behind all this was the profligacy of certain Socialist-controlled Councils and Boards of Guardians in the dispensation of outdoor relief. He acted under these powers in the case of West Ham, Bedwelty and Chester-le-Street. The Labour Party were furious and, in revenge, attacked him in the House because, perhaps a little unwisely, he had, after becoming a Minister, still remained a director of Hoskins. The old story of the 'Admiralty contracts' (still insignificant) once more reared its ugly head and an extremely acrimonious debate ensued. Neville did not mince his words and this was the beginning of that hostility towards him on the part of the leaders of the Labour Party which persisted for the whole of his time in politics. There is no doubt that Neville's manner in addressing and referring to members of that Party was at times unfortunate. Baldwin had occasion to reprove him for it; he said he gave the impression that he 'looked on the Labour Party as dirt'. But Neville's answer to this was that 'their gross exaggerations, their dishonesty in slurring over facts that tell against them and their utter inability to appreciate a reasonable argument do embitter my soul sometimes and if I seem hard and unsympathetic to them it is the reaction brought about by their own attitude'.(1)

In the spring of 1929, Baldwin decided to submit his Government's record to the verdict of the country. Accordingly a General Election took place and there appeared throughout the land posters containing the slogan 'Safety First' under a huge picture of Stanley Baldwin looking the very reverse of a 'Dynamic Force'.

Neither the slogan nor the picture proved sufficiently alluring, however, and the result of the polling which took place on May 31st was a severe reverse for the Conservative Party. Labour for the first time in history returned the strongest individual Party, though not with an 'over-all' majority, having 287 seats against the Conservatives' 261 and the Liberals' 59. On this occasion, Baldwin decided not to face Parliament but resigned immediately and, on June 5th, Ramsay MacDonald went by car to Windsor and kissed hands on his appointment as Prime Minister.

The second Labour Government lasted rather over two years, during which period an economic blizzard of great severity swept across the Western world. The Socialists were unable to cope with the financial problems with which they found themselves confronted and the result was that, in August 1931, a National Government was formed with Ramsay MacDonald as Prime Minister, the Conservative and Liberal leaders, Baldwin and Samuel, having agreed to serve under him. Baldwin became Lord President of the Council, Samuel Home Secretary and Austen First Lord of the Admiralty. Philip Snowden remained Chancellor of the Exchequer and Neville once more became Minister of Health.

Snowden was not one of those Socialists who either irritated or disliked Neville. On the contrary between these two feelings of mutual esteem soon developed. Snowden had been impressed, as had all those present, by the extraordinarily clear grasp which Neville had shown of the financial situation and the problems involved during the discussions which had preceded the formation of the National Government.

One of the first acts of the new Government was the introduction of an emergency Budget and there was a dramatic scene and wild enthusiasm when Snowden concluded his speech with Swinburne's well-known lines:

'All our past acclaims our future: Shakespeare's voice and
   Nelson's hand,
Milton's faith and Wordsworth's trust in this our chosen and
   chainless land,
Bear us witness: come the world against her, England yet shall
   stand.'(2)

It was the cuts in the pay of the armed forces which provoked the Invergordon riots with which Austen had to deal almost immediately after he became First Lord.

In November 1931, Ramsay MacDonald decided to appeal to the country for what he called a 'Doctor's Mandate' to deal with the country's immediate financial problems. Unfortunately the different 'Doctors' in the Government did not agree about the proper treatment. 'Dr. Neville Chamberlain' thought that what the patient needed was a dose of Tariff Reform whereas 'Dr. Snowden' remained a rabid Free Trader. It says much for the great tact with which Neville handled Snowden that, for the time being, they agreed to differ. The result of the election was the greatest landslide in history. The supporters of the National Government returned 558 strong. The Opposition was reduced to a total of 56 members – 52 Labour and 4 'Lloyd George Liberals'.

In the second National Government, Neville went to the Treasury and Snowden, who had been made a Viscount, became Lord Privy Seal. Austen had expressed his willingness to renounce all claim to office in order as he put it that 'younger men, who must bear the burden of responsibility in the future, should gain experience for their tasks'. This unselfish action on his part evoked universal admiration and respect but what pleased Austen most was a letter which he received from the King who had been very deeply moved by Austen's action:

> 'You may be assured that, after your devoted service during the last 36 years in Conservative and National Administrations, I feel that I am parting from, though not losing, an old and valued friend. Today, as you say, circumstances are wholly abnormal and I know that your present action in voluntarily withdrawing in order to make way for younger men, in order to further the best interests of your country and your colleagues, is in harmony with the public spirit and self-sacrifice which have always characterized your career. You have set a fine example and I trust that you may be given health and strength for many years to continue to help your Sovereign and your country.'(3)

There was a consolation for Austen, and indeed for the whole

Chamberlain family, when, a few weeks later, Neville had his day of triumph. Austen was in his place and his sisters were in the gallery, as well as Mrs. Carnegie, Joseph's widow, to hear Neville, at what was probably the proudest moment of his life, achieve that for which his father had striven so long and so ardently, and introduce, on February 4th, 1932, a Bill providing for a measure of Tariff Reform. He spoke, as always, calmly and with great lucidity but his final words give some indication of the strength of his feelings:

> 'Nearly twenty-nine years have passed since Joseph Chamberlain entered upon his great campaign of Imperial preference and Tariff Reform. More than seventeen years have gone by since he died without having seen the fulfilment of his aims and yet convinced that, if not exactly in his way, yet in some modified form, his vision would eventually take shape. His work was not in vain. Time and the misfortunes of the country have brought conviction to many who did not feel that they could agree with them. I believe he would have found consolation for the bitterness of his disappointment if he could have foreseen that these proposals which are the direct and legitimate descendants of his own conception would be laid before the House of Commons which he loved in the presence of one, and by the lips of the other, of the two immediate successors to his name and blood.'

When Neville sat down, Austen got up and walked over to the Treasury Bench and silently shook hands with Neville while the House cheered them both to the echo. No doubt to both brothers, as they stood there in silence, there came the memory of the scene in the Bingley Hall nearly a quarter of a century previously and of the well-loved voice uttering the words:

> 'Others it may be if not we
> the issue of our toil shall see.'

The next day, describing this scene to his sisters, Austen wrote: 'I can say my *nunc dimittis* now with a full and grateful heart. How proud father would have been of Neville, and how it would have moved him that Neville should complete his work.'(4)

20

Hitler and Mussolini

In due course, the economic climate improved and, under Neville's wise administration of its finances, the country's trading position got gradually better. Unfortunately, however, as the economic clouds lifted, so those on the international horizon got lower and blacker. On January 30th, 1933, Adolf Hitler became the Chancellor of the German Reich.

Amongst the first British statesmen to appreciate the importance of this event was Austen. As early as April 13th, 1933, he addressed the House of Commons in significant language. 'What is this new spirit of German nationalism?' he asked. 'The worst of the old Prussian Imperialism, with an added savagery, a racial pride, an exclusiveness which cannot allow to any subject not of "pure Nordic birth" equality of rights and citizenship within the nation to which he belongs. Are you going to discuss revision with a Government like that? Are you going to discuss with such a Government the Polish Corridor? The Polish Corridor is inhabited by Poles; do you dare to put another Pole under the heel of such a Government? After all we stand for something in this country. Our traditions count for our own people, for Europe and for the world. Europe is menaced and Germany is afflicted by this narrow, exclusive, aggressive spirit by which it is a crime to be in favour of peace and a crime to be a Jew. That is not a Germany to which we can afford to make concessions. That is not a Germany to which Europe can afford to give equality.'(1)

And on May 26th, 1933, he had this to say in the House of Commons:

'When we last discussed the foreign situation many of us were filled with deep anxieties. I cannot say that they are altogether dispelled today. The new movement in Germany with its domestic manifestations shocked the House and shocked our people and I do not know that those manifestations have been much qualified since that time. I still feel that the spirit which manifests itself in the proscription of a whole race within the boundaries of Germany is a spirit which if allowed to prevail in foreign affairs will be a menace to the whole world. We have had since then some profoundly disquieting utterances from men in high authority in Germany. . . . The German Foreign Minister's written threat that if certain things do not happen as Germany wished she would re-arm in spite of her Treaty obligations . . . the terrible speech of Vice-Chancellor Papen in which he said that warfare was to a man what child-bearing was to woman, something without which their lives were not complete . . . I think we ought to insist that . . . equality can only come by stages and that Germany must show by acts, by the whole conduct of her policy, that, as we go to meet her in disarmament, in physical disarmament, so she comes to meet us and others in moral disarmament.'(2)

He uttered another warning in July. 'Whether you read the story of the twenty or thirty years which preceded the war or whether you read the story of the post-war years,' he told the House, 'you will find the same thing. While something is refused to Germany it is vital. If you say, "Well, we will give it to you and now our relations will, of course, be on a satisfactory footing", it loses all value from the moment that she obtains it and it is used by her merely as a stepping-off place for a further demand. Until Germany shows that there is a moderate, reasonable and acceptable readjustment of the Peace Treaties which would be final and would be treated as final by her, no man serves the interests of peace if he allows the Germans to suppose for one moment that revision is possible.'(3) And in August he asked, 'Have we in fact a policy, and is the Cabinet behind it and do our representatives abroad know what it is if it indeed exists?'(4)

It was not long before the fullest possible justification was forthcoming for Austen's forebodings. In the autumn, Germany withdrew from the Disarmament Conference and from the League of Nations. At the same time, the British Labour Party was accompanying the darkening international situation with a vigorous campaign in favour of disarmament by Britain which made great headway throughout the country. George Lansbury said – 'I would close every recruiting station, disband the Army and dismiss the Air Force. I would abolish the whole dreadful equipment of war and say to the world, "Do your worst."'(5)

Churchill might dismiss these and similar utterances as 'the visionary vaticinations of a kindly hearted old soul who would get us into the worst of troubles from the best of motives,' but these were not the words of an irresponsible 'back bencher'. They were the words of the elected leader of the Labour Party. In the event of an immediate election, and should the Labour Party win it, Lansbury would become Prime Minister.

Unfortunately signs and portents were soon forthcoming that in the event of an immediate election on the issue of re-armament Labour *would* win it. In October 1933 a by-election took place in East Fulham. The Labour candidate conducted his campaign purely on the issue of armaments, claiming that he stood for 'peace and disarmament' whereas the Government's policy was 'armaments and preparations for war'. The result of the polling was to turn a Conservative majority of 14,521 into a minority of 4,840. It has frequently been said that the result of this by-election greatly influenced Stanley Baldwin in his political calculations. This is probably true. It has also been suggested that Baldwin in particular and the Conservative Party in general should at this stage have ignored public opinion and pushed on with a vigorous policy of re-armament. This assumes that they had the power to do so. Of course, they had not. Baldwin was not the Prime Minister at that moment. Ramsay MacDonald was the Prime Minister.

It is, on the whole, unlikely that Ramsay MacDonald, even if pressed by Baldwin, would have shown a great deal more enthusiasm for re-armament than did his former Labour colleagues. His whole record was one of Pacifism and objection to war in any circumstances whatsoever. Churchill had described him as 'The Boneless Wonder', comparing him to a certain spectacle at Olympia in the days of his youth which was considered to be too horrible for his (Churchill's) young eyes to gaze upon. What Baldwin could have done was to withdraw or threaten to withdraw the support of the Conservative Party from MacDonald on the ground that he was neglecting the defences of the country.

The Chamberlains

There would then probably have been a General Election in which the issue would have been re-armament and, as Baldwin himself, 'with appalling frankness', said later, 'nothing is politically more certain than that I should have lost the Election'. Lansbury would then have been in a position to implement his policy of 'closing every recruiting station and disbanding the Army and dismissing the Air Force'. To have to choose between the 'Boneless Wonder' and the 'Kindly Hearted Old Soul' was, no doubt, hard but this was Baldwin's dilemma.

Neville, meanwhile, along with other members of the Government, soon came to see the importance of some measure of re-armament. 'Common prudence,' he wrote to his sisters in October 1933, 'would seem to indicate some strengthening of our defences.' (6) And a little later, 'For the old aphorism "force is no remedy" I would substitute "The fear of force is the only remedy".'(7) And his speeches conveyed the same message. 'We shall not make peace certain by leaving ourselves so weak that we become a temptation to other nations to bully us.' And, in the spring of 1934, he wrote, 'We shall be more likely to deter Germany from mad dogging if we have an Air Force which in case of need could bomb the Ruhr from Belgium.'(8)

Neville was probably aware of, and in agreement with, Clemenceau's dictum that 'politics is the art of the possible'. He was also at all times anxious not to dislocate trade and not to undo the slow but steady improvement in the country's economic position which was gradually taking place. He was also, no doubt, unwilling to run undue risks, through being too blatant over re-armament, of the disbandment of the Army and the dismissal of the Air Force by a Labour Government. For it must here be stated that Lansbury's foolish remarks were not repudiated by his colleagues and supporters. On the contrary, in October 1933, the Labour Party Conference supported a resolution of the Miners' Federation by undertaking:

'To pledge itself to take no part in war and to resist it with the whole force of the Labour Movement and to seek consultation forthwith with the Trade Union and Co-operative Movements with a view to deciding and announcing to the country what steps, including a general strike, are to be taken to

Austen Chamberlain and his fiancée driving in Joseph Chamberlain's
70th birthday celebrations, Birmingham, 1906
Sir Austen and Lady Chamberlain making a tour of the Birmingham
constituency, polling day, May 1929

Sir Austen Chamberlain

organize the opposition of the organized working-class movement in the event of war or threat of war. . . .'(6)

The Labour Party voted against all the Service estimates in
1934 (as did the Liberals) and continued to do so in subsequent
years. A picture of a baby in a gas mask figured prominently on
Labour hoardings. The Labour majority on the L.C.C. withdrew
the grant from the Schools' Cadet Corps.

As time went on, Neville became more and more convinced of
the need for re-armament and, within the limits of the practical,
politically and economically, he was determined to do his utmost
to bring it about. Futhermore, he had the shrewdness to see the
direction which re-armament should take. He it was who, from
the beginning, put the emphasis on the Air Force. In July 1934,
the Government, largely at his instigation, announced its intention
of increasing the R.A.F. by forty-one squadrons. For this decision,
Ministers were severely castigated by the Socialists. In the course
of the debate on this matter which took place in the House of
Commons on July 30th, 1934, Attlee said:

'They [the Government] may do lip-service to the League
of Nations and to collective security but at the back of their
minds there is always the belief in reliance on the old, anarchic
principle of self-defence. We deny the need for increased air
armaments. . . . We deny the proposition that an increased
British Air Force will make for the peace of the world, and we
reject altogether the claim to parity. We think that parity is an
out-of-date pre-war conception of the balance of power. . . . We
believe that you have got to have the absolute abolition of
national fighting forces. . . . Sooner or later there will be a
Government which will have to take the responsibility of telling
people that there is no such thing as national defence in an
armed world and they will have to work for a world organization for peace and collective security, and tell people to put
aside their old idea of defending this little country by their own
little force because it is entirely out of date.'(10)

And again, a few months later; he said:

'We stand for the reduction of armaments and pooled
security. Our policy is not one of seeking security through

rearmament but through disarmament. Our aim is the reduction or armaments and then the complete abolition of all national armaments. . . . The Government want unity on defence questions. If they want that they must first agree on policy. . . . They will only get agreement in this country on policy . . . if they work for disarmament and not re-armament . . .'(11)

Neville, along with other Conservative Ministers, was described by the Labour leaders as a 'warmonger' and a 'militarist' who was 'ready and willing to spend millions of pounds on machines of destruction' but 'had no money for the unemployed, the depressed areas and the social services. He would spend on the means of death but not on the means of life.'(12) The author of this latter remark Mr. Herbert (later Lord) Morrison added that 'that was the kind of fellow he looked'.(13)

Meanwhile, the international outlook continued to deteriorate. In March 1935 Hitler, in breach of the Treaty of Versailles, introduced conscription into Germany and admitted the possession of an air force which he had every intention of increasing. These announcements were made just as the Foreign Secretary, Sir John Simon, was about to pay him a visit. On Simon's return, there was an important debate in the House and one of the most trenchant speeches was made by Austen. 'I think it is of vital consequence that this House should be told . . . what is the impression gathered by the Foreign Secretary in his conversations in Berlin,' he said. 'Is it a Germany that is ready and willing to come to an agreement? Or is it a Germany that is pushing here, seizing there, drilling her own people daily, building up the greatest army of Europe, building this immense air fleet, building a new navy? Is it a nation which . . . instead of being a partner in a collective system intends to present Europe with a power so strong that Europe will be at its mercy and that we shall have nothing to do but obey her commands? That is the question we have got to settle. . . .'(14)

On June 7th, 1935, Ramsay MacDonald resigned and Baldwin became Prime Minister in his place. Sir Samuel Hoare succeeded Sir John Simon as Foreign Secretary. Four months later, Mussolini invaded Abyssinia. The League of Nations declared Italy to be an aggressor and proceeded to impose sanctions which, while they thoroughly irritated Mussolini, did not seriously interfere with his conduct of the war. It was at this stage that Baldwin decided to appeal to the country and a General Election took place. His appeal was based mainly on the need for a strong British Government to support the League of Nations, but Neville, who had drafted the Manifesto, had also stressed the necessity to 'repair the gaps in our defences'. Baldwin's tactics were extremely successful and the National Government returned with a clear majority of 245. Austen and Neville both got in by comfortable margins. Describing his campaign, Austen, whose last it was to be, wrote:

'It is wonderful how father's memory is still cherished – "I saw your dad; I carried a torch in the procession; we've always voted Chamberlain; my dad thought everything of Joe", and so on and so on in every variety of expression. And yet it's a regular slum constituency, good, wide streets but courts and back-to-back houses, many still to be condemned, over 3,000 voters fewer than four years ago. Really one's heart is warmed by their kindness, and one's admiration roused by their courage, but thank God there were none of those idle youths leaning against doorposts and railings of whom I saw so many last time. They are all now in work.'(15)

On December 10th, just under a month after the election, Sir Samuel Hoare, stopping at Paris on his way to a holiday in Switzerland, met M. Laval. Between them they came to a provisional arrangement for a proposal to be put to the League as a basis for the cessation of hostilities in Abyssinia. This involved the handing over of large parts of that country to Italy. Unfortunately for Sir Samuel, there was a leakage to certain French newspapers of the broad terms of this arrangement and when these became known in England there was a violent political storm, the ultimate result of which was that Hoare was forced to resign. In the debate on this affair, in which Hoare made his resignation speech, Austen took a prominent part. His prestige was now very high and the 'back benchers' had been flocking to him. In the end, he supported Baldwin though he wrote to his sisters afterwards that, 'Had I thought it compatible with the public interest I believe that after Stanley Baldwin's miserably inadequate speech and the initial blunder I could have so reduced his majority as to force his resignation'.(16) There can be little doubt, however, that an important contributory factor in inducing a spirit of caution in Austen was intense loyalty to Neville. Austen knew that Neville was 'heir apparent' to Baldwin and he was most reluctant to do or say anything which would jeopardize his brother's chance of the succession.

The following day, Baldwin asked Austen to call, and when he arrived told him that he would much have liked to offer him the Foreign Office but he felt that his health would not stand the strain. The Prime Minister then asked him what he thought of the idea of appointing Eden. Austen was pleased with this suggestion for Eden had been his Parliamentary Private Secretary when he himself (Austen) had been at the Foreign Office and they had formed very strong feelings of mutual regard. Later, Lord Avon, as Eden had by then become, wrote:

> 'Austen Chamberlain, in appearance and sometimes in speech, could be stiff and forbidding. This had nothing to do with the real man who was warm-hearted, considerate and generous. He was incapable of a mean action and conscientious to a fault. Sir Austen's international policies were based on a traditional Foreign Office pattern. They were none the worse for that. . . .' (17)

After Austen had given his warm approval to the idea of Eden as Foreign Secretary he went to see Baldwin again at the latter's request. Baldwin then asked him whether he would be willing to join the Cabinet as 'Minister of State' without a Department but with the particular duty of giving advice to the Government on foreign affairs. Austen asked for time to consider the offer, but wrote later declining it. In a letter to his sisters, he said:

> 'I have no doubt that my situation if I had accepted would have been most unsatisfactory. Neither in foreign affairs nor in defence should I have had any defined position or authority. . . . I could perceive no prospect of public usefulness in the acceptance of such an offer so conveyed, and I came to the conclusion that what he wanted was not my advice or experience, but the

use of my name to help patch up the damaged prestige of his Government.'(18)

The New Year of 1936 brought great changes both in the domestic and the foreign scene. On January 20th, George V died and was succeeded by his eldest son who abdicated less than a year later in favour of his younger brother who then became George VI. By February, it was known that the Government had decided to appoint a Minister for Co-ordination of Defence. Of this proposed appointment, Austen wrote, 'In my view there is only one man who by his studies and his special abilities and aptitudes is marked out for it, and that man is Winston Churchill. I don't suppose that Stanley Baldwin will offer it to him and I don't think that Neville would wish to have him back, but they are both wrong. He is the right man for that post, and in such dangerous times that consideration ought to be decisive.' (19) Austen was quite right about the views of Neville, who wrote on March 11th, 1936:

'I summed up my opinion (as to the proposed appointment) as follows. Every name involved risks and I should play for safety. The events of the week-end afforded an excellent reason for discarding both Winston and Sam since both had European reputations which might make it dangerous to add them to the Cabinet at a critical moment. Inskip would create no jealousies. He would excite no enthusiasm but he would involve us in no fresh perplexities.'(20)

It was Inskip (later Lord Caldecote) who was appointed.

The chief of the 'events of the week-end' to which Neville referred was, characteristically, a fresh breach of international law and obligations by Hitler. On March 7th, his troops entered the demilitarized zone of the Rhineland in breach of the provisions not only of the Treaty of Versailles but also of that of Locarno, which latter had been freely negotiated by Germany and whose provisions Hitler had himself promised to respect.

Austen, who saw the Treaty which had been his great pride thus torn into shreds, was deeply distressed. 'That has happened,' he wrote to his sisters, 'against which we guaranteed France, and Press and Public seek excuses for evading our pledges. The

Government which asked (and received) promises of support from France when it thought us in danger now hesitates to keep its solemn engagement. Hitler against the advice of the more moderate elements in his Government, Schacht and the chiefs of the army, etc., has marched into the Rhineland to escape from an internal crisis, urged on by Goering and Goebbels. The economic crisis will recur but when it does the army will be much stronger, the army chiefs will not again seek to hold him back, every country in Europe will feel that England is a broken reed and the end can only be the complete triumph of Germany and I fear our own ultimate ruin. And our Government has no policy. As far as I can make out it is as much divided as Asquith's Cabinet on the eve of the Great War. My confidence is rudely shaken.

On the top of this, Baldwin chooses Inskip, a man with no experience in administration, who has never given a thought to problems of defence, as the new Minister.'(21)

The French Government had had ample warning that Hitler would probably attempt a military *coup* in the Rhineland but, in spite of this fact, they were entirely without a plan for dealing with the situation and M. Sarraut's Cabinet was hopelessly split. The French General Staff were consulted and they advised that, if it was proposed to oppose Hitler's latest move by force, general mobilization would be necessary. It has since been computed by French military authorities that the Germans had at their disposal at that particular moment 26 infantry divisions, 2 cavalry divisions, 3 armoured divisions and 99 squadrons of aircraft, while the French had 28 infantry divisions, 8 mixed brigades, 3 cavalry divisions, 2 light armoured divisions, 14 tank battalions and 134 air force squadrons.(22) It is therefore doubtful whether the ejectment of the Germans from the Rhine provinces would have been quite as simple and easy as is sometimes suggested. The mere mention of general mobilization within a few weeks of an election was quite enough, however, to deter most of the French Cabinet from a show of force. Whether their attitude would have been any different if they had received promises of support from the British Government cannot be regarded as certain. In any event, no such promises were forthcoming. M. Flandin, the French Foreign Minister, came to London and saw both Neville and Baldwin. Flandin and Neville lunched together at the French Embassy and Neville wrote afterwards:

'His [Flandin's] view is that if a firm front is maintained by France and England, Germany will yield without war. We cannot, however, accept this as a mad dictator's reactions.'(23)

Austen also dealt with Hitler's re-occupation of the Rhineland when, a day or two after it had taken place, he addressed the annual meeting of the Cambridge University Conservative Association. He referred to the Treaty of Versailles and then said, 'Do you think there would have been a less rigorous peace to the beaten party if Germany had won the war? Have you ever looked at the terms imposed on Rumania when Germany was victorious? Have you ever asked what our fate would have been, what British colonies would still be in our hands, what kind of life we should be living in this country or what ransom we should have had to pay if Germany had won? It has been said that the peace imposed by the Treaty of Versailles was dictated but I know of no peace except the peace of exhaustion which was not a dictated peace. Locarno was not a dictated peace. It was a treaty the proposals for which came from Germany itself and the particular provision for the guarantee of the *status quo* and for the observance of conditions in the demilitarized zone was in the original German offer.'(24) He declared that his 'memory was quivering at the moment with the events which led up to the Great War' and that he was 'impressed by the similarity of Germany's policy today to the policy which rendered the Great War inevitable'. 'All the world and most of all the little states are looking to Great Britain today,' he concluded.(25) On March 19th, he was the guest of the Jewellers Association at Birmingham. With him on that occasion was Winston Churchill and Austen returned to the same theme. 'Was there any international morality or law,' he asked, 'or had we returned to the rule of force in which the strongest did what he liked and the weakest went to the wall.' Then, turning towards his fellow guest, he said: 'Mr. Churchill has great courage and intense energy and great and wide experience on matters of defence and there will be many in the House of Commons who regret that Mr. Baldwin has not thought fit to call him to that new office for which he has greater qualifications than any living politician.'(26)

Austen had always liked and admired Churchill, though he had frequently differed from him on political matters. Churchill himself had disagreed with the official Conservative policy on India and, in consequence, had withdrawn from the Conservative hierarchy after the 1929 election. Austen, though he never identified himself with Churchill's Indian views, had been, on the whole, sympathetic towards his attitude.

During the ensuing months, Austen found himself drawn more and more towards Churchill. He went to stay at Chartwell, which he described as 'a wonderfully pretty place and a very comfortable house'.(27) From Chartwell, he wrote to his sisters: 'We were a merry party last night and the talk was good. There were almost as many opinions as men but on one thing we were all agreed – that Germany was a danger, the one danger that might be fatal to us and that dealing with that danger had been too long delayed.'(28) As to his host, Austen repeated his view that 'My own choice [for the new Ministry of Defence] would be Winston Churchill whom I consider marked out by study, genius, power, drive and imagination for this particular post.'(29)

Austen was also worried about the future of Austria. In the House of Commons on April 1st, 1936, he gave vent to his feelings of anxiety. 'What attitude shall we take if Austrian independence is threatened or destroyed whether by an attack from outside or by a revolution fostered and supported from outside like that which caused the death of Dolfuss?' he asked. 'If we mean anything by the declarations that our policy is founded on the League and that we shall fulfil our obligations, founded on the League, possibilities of this sort must give food for thought to every British citizen. For we may have to intervene at any moment. The independence of Austria is a key position. If Austria perishes, Czechoslovakia becomes indefensible. Then the whole of the Balkans will be submitted to a gigantic new influence. Then the old German dream of a Central Europe ruled by and subject to Berlin will become a reality from the Baltic to the Mediterranean and the Black Sea, with incalculable consequences not only for our country but for our whole Empire.'(30)

He himself spent his Easter holiday in Austria and what he saw there fully confirmed his fears.

There was another Chamberlain who, at that time, had clear and definite views on foreign affairs which he could express in forceful language. Arthur junior had ceased to be the chairman of Kynochs when the company amalgamated with Nobel Industries, later to become part of a still larger combination – Imperial Chemical Industries. But Arthur had remained the chairman of Tube Investments. In his annual address to the shareholders of this latter company he advocated 'an old world League of Nations comprising all the European states and China, pledged to resist aggression with all their forces automatically not permissively'. 'Can you dream for a moment that anyone would dare to attack it?' he asked. Then he added, 'It is just because they all leave themselves the right to withdraw or do only what they think fit that there is no real belief in the security afforded by the League of Nations and therefore no real certainty that aggression won't take place and take place successfully. If we took the lead in suggesting such a League I verily believe that all the others would come in, not excepting Germany and Italy, for who would dare to stop out? . . . Until we rebuild the League on these lines, the contributions we here have all made to English and to world happiness by creating and expanding this business to its present dimensions . . . are all at the mercy of any madman or group of lunatics who may plunge the world into war to attain the impossible or to cloak their own failure to have won happiness for their own people.'(31)

Shortly after the end of the First World War, his main link with Birmingham, Kynochs, having been severed, Arthur left the city and acquired a London house and an estate in Devonshire. He was a man of considerable business ability and he became a director of the General Electric Company, Stewart & Lloyds, Churchill Machine Tools and many other companies and a Governor of the Midland Bank. He was very keen on and good at shooting and, being much wealthier than Neville, was able to indulge his taste for this sport on a considerably greater scale. He died in August 1941.

In July 1936, the centenary of Joseph Chamberlain's birth was celebrated both in London and Birmingham. In London, Austen was one of the speakers at a big meeting at the Royal Albert Hall. Mrs. Carnegie, Joseph's widow, was there, as were also his two daughters, Hilda and Ida Chamberlain. Supporting Austen on the platform were Amery, Geoffrey Lloyd, Lennox Boyd and Page Croft. Austen was obviously filled with deep emotion and in the course of his speech he said:

'I think of the love with which he [Joseph] surrounded my childhood, of the friendship which grew between us. I think of him as the centre of a happy and united family, sharing his thoughts with us, taking an interest in our interests, ever ready to help with counsel if we sought it. He never attempted to dictate our course, trusting to the atmosphere of the home which he had made for us. He was the first to see, more than a generation after Disraeli, that "the great domestic question of the day was not the franchise but the condition of the people".' (32)

And, in Birmingham, Neville represented the family at a great gathering at the Town Hall. In the course of his speech, he said:

'The greatest service of Joseph Chamberlain to local government was the setting it on a new pedestal of dignity and honour. Joseph Chamberlain always upheld municipal work as one of the most honourable and useful avocations that any man or woman could follow. In honouring him today, Birmingham is honouring herself and falsifying the saying that a prophet is not without honour except in his own country.'(33)

In November 1936 Austen went to Lyons to receive an honorary degree upon the invitation of M. Herriot and, in January 1937, he and his wife paid their last visit to Paris. He met M. Blum, the French Prime Minister, but what he enjoyed perhaps most of all was a visit to the École des Sciences Politiques, which he had last visited some fifty years before, and the tremendous reception which he was given by the students. On March 16th, while taking a book down from one of his shelves, he suddenly dropped dead.

The news of his death came as a great shock to everyone, including his family. He had not shown any signs of being seriously ill but had been dining out and going to the House of Commons in the usual way right up to the day of his death. On

March 18th, Neville stood behind the Speaker's chair while the tributes to his brother were being paid. He did not feel equal to sitting on the Treasury Bench. As he was leaving, three Labour Members came up to him, held out their hands and said something to him about their respect and admiration for Austen. He was deeply touched and for a moment the barrier between himself and the Labour Party came down and these three got a glimpse of the real man. In his diary he wrote: 'This afternoon we have been to the St. Marylebone Cemetery beyond Hampstead . . . the spot looks over a wide view, the birds were singing, and I felt it was a wonderful place.'(34) Messages of condolence poured in on him. In reply to one of these (from the Archbishop of Canterbury) he wrote: 'From my earliest days I have looked up to Austen with perhaps much more deference as well as affection than is usually the case where the difference of years was so small. He was a good brother to me and the only one I had.'(35)

Like his father and like Neville, Austen would probably have described himself as a 'reverent agnostic'. The Chamberlains as a whole did not wear their hearts on their sleeves and Austen was no exception. But included in his papers there is a letter which he wrote to his wife about their son's confirmation and the following extract is, perhaps, worth quoting.

'If you agree I think it would be well to postpone his confirmation till he is older . . . I daresay that you will like to talk about it a little with Joe. If you do . . . say something about my position – merely that I was brought up to honour God in another church, so that he may understand why I do not go to Communion with you both as I should wish to, but that I want him to join with you and hope that it may be to him all the comfort and strength that it is to you. You will naturally think of this and the other things that I should like to say. The form of our faith is not always within our own control and we ourselves may change our views on the great mysteries of the here and the hereafter as we grow older but none will go very far wrong if he is reverent and truthful and clean and honest with himself and others and the mercy of God is infinite and our love for our boy inexhaustible.'(36)

Few families can ever have been so united as the Chamberlain family and in few can there have been such devotion to one another and such complete absence of envy of each other's successes. To Ivy the heartfelt sympathy of the whole family went out. Like Neville's wife and Joseph's widow she had greatly endeared herself to them all. From the start she had made herself part of the family, entering into all their joys and sorrows and anxious at all times to help in any way she could. An illustration of this occurred at the time of Joseph's paralysis, when she happened to be away and she wrote immediately to Austen:

'I cannot tell you how much I feel for and with you all. I pray God that your dear father may soon get well. God will give you strength, darling, and I know you will always be a help to Mary and the girls. If I could only do something for you. . . . I feel so impotent and I want to do so much. I can only pray and that I do from the bottom of my heart. God bless and comfort you.'(37)

Now she longed again to do something not only for the family but for the causes to which her loved one had dedicated his life. And soon she believed that she saw her opportunity.

On May 28th, 1937, Neville succeeded Baldwin as Prime Minister. For Neville Ivy had always had considerable admiration and respect. She knew that he was anxious to reach an understanding with Mussolini and, in this, she felt that she could help.

Ivy knew Italy well. She spoke the language and had travelled widely in the country. In 1929, she had played a prominent part in the running of the Italian art exhibition in London. She was on good terms with Mussolini as well as with several important members of his administration, including Ciano and Grandi. Mussolini had been or had professed to be a great admirer of Austen. They had met one another on a number of occasions, both before and during the time that Austen was Foreign Secretary, and had got on well together.

Mussolini's feelings of esteem for Austen had been returned by the latter who, shortly after Locarno, had described Mussolini in a letter to his sisters as 'a strong man of singular charm and, I suspected, of not a little tenderness and loneliness of heart'.

'Meeting me but seldom and quite alone and finding me

sympathetic, I suspect that he showed me a side of his character which the public is never allowed to see and even his most intimate friends but seldom if ever. I believed him to be accused of crimes in which he had no share and I suspect him to have connived unwillingly at other outrages which he would have prevented if he could. But I am confident that he is a patriot and a sincere man; I trust his word when given and I think we might easily go far before finding an Italian with whom it would be as easy for the British Government to work,' the letter concluded.(38)

Ivy had decided to live in Italy during the winter months following Austen's death. Before leaving, she had been to see Eden (then Foreign Secretary) and had told him of her forthcoming visit. While in Rome, Ivy saw both Mussolini and Ciano. She wrote to Neville about her conversations with them and received replies from him, at least one of which she showed to Ciano. Early in February, after seeing Mussolini, she wrote to Neville informing him that the Italian Dictator was anxious to reach an agreement on all matters in issue. Neville was extremely anxious to get talks going with the Italian Government but Eden felt that Mussolini should give concrete proof of his good intentions by withdrawing some of the Italian volunteers from Spain before the talks started. Eden was also annoyed and disappointed that Neville, without consulting him, should have poured cold water on Roosevelt's plan of an international conference, because, apparently, he thought it might prejudice his chances of reaching a speedy agreement with Mussolini. By what Eden called her 'unofficial diplomacy' Ivy played a part, though perhaps not a very important part, in the events which led up to Eden's resignation towards the end of February 1938. It need hardly be added that her motives throughout were of the best.

On March 12th, 1938, German troops entered Austria and that evening Hitler proclaimed from the Rathaus in Vienna the incorporation of that country in the Reich. He accompanied this by sending a message to the Czechs assuring them of his good intentions and that their relations with the Reich were unaffected. This meant that they were, in fact, the next on the list.

Meanwhile, members of the Labour Party had continued to

oppose the Defence estimates and to introduce into the House of Commons resolutions calling for the reduction of armaments and the diminution of the armed forces of the Crown. Furthermore, important members of that Party were doing their best to sabotage the Government's re-armament programme. Sir Stafford Cripps, for example, had addressed a working-class audience as follows:

'The capitalists are in your hands. Refuse to make armaments; refuse to use them. That is the only way you can keep this country out of war and obtain power for the working class. Refuse to make armaments and the capitalists are powerless.'(39)

It was well for Neville that, faced with the immense strain of the Premiership, he had the faculty of being able to divorce his mind completely from affairs of state during his rare moments of leisure. To bird watching, music and the beauties of nature he could turn his mind at a moment's notice and become completely absorbed. And he was by now a very competent shot and was often invited to shooting parties for which he stayed at some of the great country houses, including Sandringham, where he was more than once the guest of George VI as he had been of his father and where he aquitted himself well. To Chequers Neville became increasingly devoted; the spaciousness of the place, with its lovely, finely wooded park made a great appeal to him, and he planted some trees there himself. Until he became Prime Minister, he had had no idea of the delight which a country house could afford. It was something entirely new to him.

Meanwhile, Neville's son Frank had been living for a time in Germany. Born in January 1914, Frank had been educated at Winchester and Trinity College, Cambridge. After leaving the University he had studied in France, Spain and Germany, becoming an excellent linguist. While in Germany he had lived in Munich with a Jewish family, and had had the feeling that he was being watched and followed about by the Gestapo.(40) He had been greatly worried by the rise of the Nazis to power and by their subsequent behaviour, particularly their treatment of the Jews and had, in his own words, 'reported' to Neville (then Chancellor of the Exchequer) 'very unfavourably about the Nazi regime' and Neville had 'listened closely and with concern to what I had to say'.(41)

21

Two Ladies in Hampshire

The Misses Hilda and Ida Chamberlain are certainly entitled to their place in history. Few sisters can ever have received the number of regular letters from their brothers that these two did and fewer still can have been regaled so constantly with such a first-hand picture of political life at the highest level. From about 1916 onwards, Neville and Austen both wrote to them regularly once a week, though there is a gap in Austen's letters during the time that he was Foreign Secretary.

It had been these two sisters who had encouraged Neville to go into Parliament when, after his unfortunate experience at the Ministry of National Service, with its interruption of his municipal work, he was wondering how best to shape the future course of his life.

Ida had written to him in August 1917:

'The more one thinks of it the more one feels that it must be public work of some kind and that the only avenue to it is to go into Parliament. I gather from Mary(1) that this is her view too and that she has told you so, and as the family has a great tendency to think alike on these matters I think it probable that by this time you have come to the same conclusion. I can't say that the immediate prospect is particularly inviting, but your experience shows you what a handicap it is to be out of Parliament and consequently out of the political swim . . . of course then there is the question of a seat, and if you decide to go into Parliament it *must* be a Birmingham seat, but surely, if it were known that you wanted to go in, someone would make room for you.'(2)

And the following week Hilda wrote:

'Your letter makes me feel even more strongly, if that were possible, that Parliament is the next step for you. I don't suppose that A [Austen] ever will be in a position to form a Government, because one knows how often such things are anticipated and how constantly things turn out otherwise, but, if you have already made up your mind that in those circumstances you could not become a member of it without having been in Parliament, why, the sooner you are in the better. However, I need not labour this point for I feel pretty sure that almost from the first you have seen this as a necessity and at bottom you have known that it must be, much as you dislike the idea of it. . . . You *are* a natural born leader of men . . . and I believe you will shortly be recognized as such. I don't mean that you will be P.M. for many things bar the way to such a post, but that you will be a leader with a devoted following before long I am sure. . . . However, as I say, I feel pretty sure that you *do* mean to go into Parliament in your inner mind, and have known it for some time, however much the outward man protesteth. You could never sit down to make a fortune for yourself and the children, and Annie is not the woman to accept such a decision. You are neither of you extravagant people, and certainly would not be happy leading aimless lives, however rich you might be. Even the amelioration of the lot of your own particular workpeople is not nearly a big enough field for you. No, public service claims you and you recognize its claims.'(3)

Neville had replied to Hilda:

'Your letter was abominably clear-sighted and brutal in pulling off the clothes under which I had crawled. I suppose I have had a sort of uncomfortable feeling all along as to how things would turn out, but I have tried to avoid coming to a decision, even in my own mind. But the fact is, as you say, I could not settle down to make money, much as I should like to be rich . . . I suppose therefore that really and truly I have what you may call made up my mind to go into the House, and last week I wrote to Vince about it.'(4)

Hilda and Ida had moved to Hampshire not long after Highbury was sold in 1916. They wanted to be near their brothers in whom they were completely wrapped up, the only competing

Neville Chamberlain, Ottawa, 1932

Mrs. Neville Chamberlain

interests being their home, their garden and their public work. Ida had become a member of the Hampshire County Council. She was made a County Alderman in 1931, and remained one until her death on April 1st, 1943. On joining the Council she became a member of the Public Health and Housing Committee and was chairman of that Committee from 1931 to 1943. She was also a member of the Education Committee from 1928 to 1943, of the Public Assistance Committee from 1931 to 1943 and of the Finance Committee from 1937 to 1943. She became a great authority on rural housing and gave Neville detailed advice, plying him with dozens of questions in regard to his intentions when he was preparing his Housing Legislation as Minister of Health. She was extremely intelligent, and Neville relied a great deal on her advice; she was a great help to him. Hilda was a governor of the Odiham Grammar School from 1923 to 1947.

Both Austen and Neville visited their sisters as often as they could. After one of his visits, Austen wrote to his wife:

> 'The aunts [Hilda and Ida] are very pleased because with the aid of Neville's rural housing Act they are gradually getting all the bad cottages in the district put into good repair and made weatherproof and decent sanitary arrangements made. What with impoverished and careless landlords and speculators, the cottage property in the neighbourhood was in a really shocking condition and it delights them to see in their walks now this cottage, now that taken in hand and made decent for the poor old folks to live in.'(5)

On September 19th, 1938, Ida received the greatest news letter of all. It came from the Prime Minister of England and it told her how he had flown out to see Hitler and had driven on to the Brown House in the mountains, how he had been greeted by the Fuehrer who was standing waiting for him half-way up the steps and how Hitler led him inside and then they sat down to have tea together and then they talked. Neville told his sisters, 'I got the impression that he [Hitler] was a man who could be relied upon when he had given his word.'(6) There were more flights and more talks with Hitler after this. There was the meeting on the Rhine when Neville stayed at Petersburg with its wonderful views over the river and Hitler was at Godesburg on the other side of the Rhine. After this, it looked as though war was extremely likely, if not inevitable, and, on the night of September 27th, 1938, Neville delivered a broadcast address to the nation in the course of which he said:

'How horrible, fantastic, incredible it is that we should be digging trenches and trying on gas masks here because of a quarrel in a far away country between people of whom we know nothing. It seems still more impossible that a quarrel which has already been settled in principle should be the subject of war. . . . After my visits to Germany, I have realized vividly how Herr Hitler feels that he must champion other Germans and his indignation that grievances have not been met before this. He told me privately, and last night he repeated publicly, that, after this Sudeten German question is settled, that is the end of Germany's territorial claims in Europe . . . I am myself a man of peace to the depths of my soul. Armed conflict between nations is a nightmare to me; but, if I were convinced that any nation had made up its mind to dominate the world by fear of its force, I should feel that it must be resisted. Under such a domination, life for people who believe in liberty would not be worth living; but war is a fearful thing, and we must be very clear before we embark on it that it is really the great issues that are at stake, and that the call to risk everything in their defence, when all the consequences are weighed, is irresistible.'(7)

The next day came the dramatic moment when Neville received the news that Hitler was willing to meet him at Munich and off he went again. When he got back, with his message that 'I believe it is peace for our time', he was deluged with congratulations and thanks from all over the world. Perhaps the most significant of these was one which consisted of two words – 'GOOD MAN'. It was signed 'Roosevelt'.(8)

To Hilda Neville wrote: 'The letters which you and Ida sent me on Friday . . . were what I wanted, for in such moments one's heart goes out instinctively to one's nearest and dearest and the consciousness of their touch gives the strength one needs.' Then he told her of his last few minutes with Hitler:

'I pulled out the declaration, which I had prepared beforehand, and asked if he would sign it. As the interpreter translated the words into German, Hitler frequently ejaculated "*Ja, Ja,*" and at the end he said, "Yes, I will certainly sign it. When shall we do it?" I said "now" and we went at once to the writing-table and put our signatures to the two copies which I had brought with me.(9) Even the descriptions of the papers give no idea of the scenes in the streets as I drove from Heston to the Palace. They were lined from one end to the other with people of every class, shouting themselves hoarse, leaping on the running-board, banging on the windows, and thrusting their hands into the car to be shaken. The scene culminated in Downing Street when I spoke to multitudes below from the same window I believe as that from which Dizzy announced peace with honour sixty years ago.'(10)

22

The End of an Old Adventure

What Neville actually said from the window of No. 10 Downing Street was: 'This is the second time in our history that there has come back from Germany to Downing Street peace with honour. I believe it is peace for our time.' But, in the House of Commons a day or two later, he said, 'I hope hon. members will not be disposed to read into words used in a moment of some emotion, after a long and exhausting day, after I had driven through miles of excited, enthusiastic, cheering people – I hope they will not read into those words more than they were intended to convey. I do indeed believe that we may yet secure peace for our time but I never meant to suggest that we should do that by disarmament, until we can induce others to disarm too . . . I realize that diplomacy cannot be effective unless the consciousness exists, not here alone, but elsewhere, that behind the diplomacy is the strength to give effect to it.'(1)

In spite, however, of this statement and of his undoubted determination to push on with re-armament to the utmost of his ability in the teeth of the opposition of the Socialists, it is probable that, at the beginning of March 1939, he still hoped for and believed in the possibility of peace. 'With a thrush singing in the garden, the sun shining, and the rooks beginning to discuss among themselves the prospects of the coming nesting season, I feel as though spring were getting near. . . . All the information I get seems to point in the direction of peace,' he wrote.(2) In the middle of the month, however, his hopes received a rude shock. On March 14th, Hitler's troops crossed the borders of what remained of Czechoslovakia and, a little later, Hitler entered and occupied Prague.

Neville's first comments on this dastardly and treacherous breach of everything that had been agreed at Munich were not as stern as those which were soon to follow. Speaking in the House of Commons on the afternoon of the day that he got the news he referred to 'internal disruption' which had disintegrated the new state and explained that with this the proposed guarantee had lapsed. 'But,' he added, 'I cannot regard the manner and the method . . . as in accordance with the spirit of the Munich agreement.'

From the mildness of these remarks, some people assumed that he was trying to excuse the German action. There was a storm of protest and denunciation of Hitler from the House of Commons and throughout the country and from the Dominions. Very different was Neville's language when, two days later, on the eve of his seventieth birthday, he addressed a large meeting in Birmingham Town Hall.

Here in the great building which had so often resounded with cheers for his father, the scene of so many of Joseph Chamberlain's greatest triumphs and where he himself had first emerged on to the national stage with his speech to the Trades Union Congress, Neville made his swan song in Birmingham, the last great speech that he would make in that building.

He began with a vigorous defence of the efforts he had made for peace and reminded his audience of the difficulties with which he had had to contend. 'What I had to deal with was no new problem,' he said. 'This was something that had existed ever since the Treaty of Versailles – a problem that ought to have been solved long ago if only the statesmen of the last twenty years had taken broader and more enlightened views of their duty. It had become like a disease which had been long neglected. A surgical operation was necessary to save the life of the patient.' He continued by declaring that after Munich the great majority of people in the country had shared his own hopes of peace. Then he went on: 'Today, I share their disappointment, their indignation [*loud cheers*] that these hopes have been so wantonly shattered. Germany under her present régime has sprung a series of unpleasant shocks upon the world. The Rhineland, the Austrian *anschluss*, the severance of the Sudetenland – all these things shocked and affronted public opinion throughout the world. Yet, however much we might take exception to the methods which were adopted in each of those cases, there was something to be said, whether on account of racial affinity or of just claims too long resisted –

there was something to be said for a change in the existing situation. But the events which have taken place this week in complete disregard of the principles laid down by the German Government itself seem to fall into a different category and they must cause us all to be asking ourselves:

'"Is this the end of an old adventure or is it the beginning of a new? Is this the last attack upon a small state or is it to be followed by others? Is this in fact a step to dominate the world by force?" I shall not attempt to answer these questions to-night. . . . But this I will say. . . . I do not believe there is anyone who will question my sincerity when I say there is hardly anything I would not sacrifice for peace. But there is one thing I must except and that is the liberty that we have enjoyed for hundreds of years, and which we will never surrender [*loud cheers*]. . . . No greater mistake could be made than to suppose that because it believes war to be a senseless and a cruel thing, this nation has so lost its fibre that it will not take part to the utmost of its power in resisting such a challenge if it ever were made. For that declaration I am convinced that I have not merely the support, the sympathy, the confidence of my fellow-countrymen and countrywomen, but I shall have also the approval of the whole British Empire and of all other nations who value peace indeed, but who value freedom even more.'(3)

At the conclusion of this, the last of the great Chamberlain orations in Birmingham Town Hall, Neville received a tremendous ovation. Hard things were being said about him in other places but here he got a demonstration, as his father often had, of the feelings of pride in and loyalty towards him felt by the overwhelming majority of his fellow-citizens. Replying to the vote of thanks he said that 'we need not feel downhearted'. . . . The country was 'united' as never before. As for the Germans, the time would come when they would bitterly regret what their Government had done.(4)

One of the first and most important results of the Prague *coup* was to convince the British Government of the need for Conscription. When, on April 26th, 1939, Neville gave notice in the House of Commons that a Bill providing for compulsory military service would be introduced forthwith he was bitterly assailed by the Socialists. In the ensuing debate, Attlee, the then Leader of the Opposition, said:

'We are opposed to the introduction of Conscription because we believe that so far from strengthening this country it will weaken and divide it. . . . I do not think that the Prime Minister has made out his case. . . . We oppose this proposal because we think it has not been thought out, that it will not add to the strength of the country and that it will not add to our effective fighting forces, but is far more likely to weaken them.'

He continued:

'If a gesture was wanted there is a much more effective gesture which could have been made. The conscription of wealth in a capitalist and class society like our own would have been a most convincing gesture.'(5)

Another violent critic of the Government's proposal was Sir Stafford Cripps, who proclaimed himself to be unequivocally opposed to Conscription but in favour of an agreement with Russia, the democratization of the fighting services and a capital levy.

Hitler's seizure of Czechoslovakia led to a complete re-orientation of British foreign policy. A Treaty was concluded with Poland and it soon became clear, from the intensity of the Nazi propaganda and the demand for the incorporation of Danzig in the Reich, that the guarantee given to that country would have to be implemented in the near future. Apprehensions on these lines proved to be well justified for, on September 1st, 1939, the Nazi hordes, without any declaration of war or even an ultimatum, invaded Poland and German bombs were poured down on Polish cities.

That day, Neville caused a warning to be sent to Germany, but there was no time limit to it and, for more than forty-eight hours there was some uncertainty as to when and even whether Britain was going to declare war on Germany. This led to considerable dissatisfaction in the country and in Parliament. A few days later, Hilda and Ida were given a glimpse of what had been going on behind the scenes; Neville told them that for him the 'final long-drawn-out agonies' of this period had been 'as nearly unendurable as could be'. He had wanted to bring things to a head but there were complications in the form of 'secret communications . . . with Goering and Hitler through a neutral intermediary, the conference proposal of Mussolini, and the French anxiety to postpone the actual declaration as long as possible until they could evacuate their women and children, and mobilize their armies'. Neville felt that he could not for the moment make these matters public and meanwhile 'the House of Commons was out of hand, torn with suspicions, and ready (some of them . . .) to believe the Government guilty of any cowardice and treachery. . . .'(6)

In the evening of September 2nd (Saturday) Neville addressed the House of Commons, which was in an angry mood because of the delay in declaring war. He was received coldly and the coldness increased as his speech continued but failed to throw any light on when war would be declared. He was followed by Arthur Greenwood, a former Labour Minister, who had only been on his feet a few minutes when Amery shouted across the floor of the House 'Speak for England'. After this, as he criticized the Government for the delay, Greenwood was vigorously cheered from the Conservative benches.

That night, Neville and Lord Halifax, Foreign Secretary, dined together at No. 10 Downing Street. Meanwhile an informal meeting of most of the rest of the Cabinet was held in a room in the House of Commons. Sir John Anderson (Lord Privy Seal) was in the chair and beside him was a telephone directly connected with No. 10 Downing Street. Most of the Ministers present felt that war should be declared instantly and some of them said that they would not leave that room until they knew it was going to be. Eventually the message came for them to go across to Downing Street and they did so. It was a very hot night and most of them had had no dinner and were feeling tired out and uncomfortable. When they reached No. 10, they found Lord Halifax with the permanent Under Secretary of the Foreign Office (Cadogan). Both were in evening dress.

Cadogan was talking to M. Bonnet, French Foreign Secretary, who was pleading for further delay in the declaration of war, being convinced that Paris would be bombed immediately. He wanted more time to evacuate women and children. Neville throughout remained calm and collected and when, after he had explained that the French still wanted more time, nearly all the assembled ministers expressed themselves as opposed to further delay, he suddenly exclaimed 'Right, gentlemen, this means war'. Immediately after this there was a violent clap of thunder and the Cabinet room was lit up by a flash of lightning. It was then just after midnight.(7) Shortly afterwards, a message was sent to the British Ambassador in Berlin, instructing him to deliver at the German Embassy at 9 a.m. that morning an ultimatum to expire two hours later calling for the immediate withdrawal of all German troops from Poland.

At 11.15 that same morning, Sunday September 3rd, Neville broadcast a message to the nation in the course of which he said:

'I am speaking to you from the Cabinet room at No. 10 Downing Street. This morning the British Ambassador in Berlin handed the German Government a note stating that, unless we heard from them by eleven o'clock that they were prepared at once to withdraw their troops from Poland, a state of war would exist between us.

I have to tell you now that no such undertaking has been received and that consequently this country is at war with Germany.

You can imagine what a bitter blow it is to me that all my long struggle to win peace has failed. Yet I cannot believe that there is anything more or anything different that I could have done and that would have been more successful. . . . We have a clear conscience, we have done all that any country could do to establish peace, but a situation in which no word given by Germany's ruler could be trusted, and no people or country could feel themselves safe, had become intolerable. . . . Now may God bless you all and may he defend the right for it is evil things that we shall be fighting against – brute force, bad faith, injustice, oppression and persecution. And against them I am certain that the right will prevail.'(8)

And in the House of Commons the same day he said:

'This is a sad day for all of us and for none is it sadder than for me. Everything that I have worked for, everything that I have hoped for, everything that I have believed in during my public life has crashed into ruins. There is only one thing left for me to do: that is to devote what strength and power I have to forwarding the victory of the cause for which we have to sacrifice so much. I cannot tell what part I may be allowed to play myself; I trust I may live to see the day when Hitlerism has been crushed and a liberated Europe has been re-established.'(9)

One of the first things Neville had done after the German invasion had been to invite Churchill to join the Government. This offer was accepted and Churchill became the First Lord of the Admiralty and a signal went out to the Navy – 'Winston is back'. An offer to the leaders of the Labour and Liberal Parties also to join was rejected.

After a short campaign of three weeks, in which the utmost brutality was displayed, the German armies overran Poland, which was then partitioned between Russia and Germany, the two latter countries having made a pact at the end of August. Hitler now opened a Peace Offensive which Lloyd George, alone among British statesmen, considered should be taken seriously. Neville was quite clear that it should be rejected out of hand. 'What we ought to do is just to throw back the peace offers and continue the blockade,' he wrote to his sisters. 'I do not believe that holocausts are required.'(10)

It was to Hilda and Ida that he revealed his thoughts and hopes during the first six months of war. He was on the whole optimistic. He did not think it likely that the Germans would face the wholesale slaughter involved in a direct frontal attack on the Maginot line, nor did he share the view of his military advisers that Hitler would go through Belgium and Holland, because he would be deterred by 'the political reactions of a breach of neutrality so flagrant and unscrupulous. If any doubt remained in the mind of anyone that he was the enemy of the human race surely such an action would remove it.'(11) And he wrote to Ida in November that 'I have a hunch that the war will be over in the spring,' adding, 'It won't be by defeat in the field but by German realization that they *can't* win and that is isn't worth their while to go on getting thinner and poorer when they might have instant relief and perhaps not have to give up anything they really care about. My belief is that a great many Germans are near that position now and that their number, in the absence of any striking military success, will go on growing with increasing rapidity. To my mind it is essential to get rid of Hitler. He must either die or go to St. Helena, or become a real public works architect, preferably in a "home". His entourage must also go, with the possible exception of Goering, who might have some ornamental position in a transitional Government. Having once got rid of the Nazis, I don't think we should find any serious difficulty in Germany over Poland, Czechoslovakia, Jews, disarmament, etc.'(12)

Even such fighting and bloodshed as there were during the first few months of the 'phoney' war filled him with horror and loathing. 'I simply can't bear to think of those gallant fellows who lost their lives last night in the R.A.F. attack [on Kiel] and of their families who have been first called upon to pay the price,' he wrote. 'Indeed I must put such thoughts out of my mind if I am not to be unnerved altogether.'(13) Even of the destruction of the 'U' boats he wrote, 'If they [the German submarines] called in at our ports we should probably say what good fellows the officers and men were. And we have to kill one another just to satisfy that accursed madman. I wish he could burn in hell for as many years as he is costing lives.'(14) Shortly before Christmas he went to France where he visited the B.E.F. and, at the invitation of General Gamelin, French army units as well, and of this experience he wrote: 'It sickened me to see the barbed wire and pill-boxes and guns and anti-tank obstacles, remembering what they meant in the last war. I was glad when it was over.'(15)

Early in April 1940, Neville, addressing the Central Conservative Council, somewhat incautiously remarked that 'Hitler had missed the bus'. Events soon proved otherwise, for, a few days later, the Germans, treacherously but with great determination and skill, invaded Norway and Denmark. Their troops and aircraft pushed rapidly inland and up country and though, as a result of great gallantry by the British armed forces, lodgments were made in various places, these latter soon had to be abandoned mainly because of insufficiency of air cover. At the instigation of the Labour Party a debate on the Norwegian campaign began in the House of Commons on May 7th and lasted two days. It was this debate which brought about the fall of the Government.

When the debate started, Neville had been quite confident. But, as it went on, it became increasingly clear that not only Labour and Liberal but also a considerable body of Conservative opinion was against him. The culminating point was the intervention of Sir Roger Keyes, attired in the uniform of an Admiral of the Fleet, condemning the hesitations and incompetencies of the Norwegian campaign and calling for a National Government. Keyes was not a good speaker but, on this particular occasion, he was all the more effective for that fact. Here was no party hack, no time-serving place hunter, but the hero of Zeebrugge. The combined effect of the man, the uniform and the occasion on the House was electric. Then came the dramatic peroration of Amery who, pointing at Neville, ended his speech with the words of Cromwell to the Long Parliament: 'You have sat here too long for any good you have been doing. Depart, I say, and let us have done with you. In the name of God, go.'(16)

When the Labour Party announced that they would divide the House, Neville, accepting the challenge with some heat, called on 'My friends in the House – and I have friends in the House' – to 'support us in the lobby tonight'. These words provided the opportunity for Neville's old enemy, David Lloyd George, to launch a vicious attack on him on the second day of the debate. This was destined to be the last debate in which either of the two would play a conspicuous part. Lloyd George had been completely taken in by Hitler and was, therefore, hardly in a position to throw stones but this in no way interfered with his determination to be 'in at the kill'. After advising Churchill not to allow himself to be turned into an air raid shelter for the benefit of the rest of the Government he turned towards Neville and said:

'It is not a question of who are the Prime Minister's friends. It is a far bigger issue. He has appealed for sacrifice. The nation is prepared for every sacrifice so long as it has leadership, so long as the Government show clearly what they are aiming at and so long as the nation is confident that those who are leading it are doing their best ... I say solemnly that the Prime Minister should give an example of sacrifice, because there is nothing that can contribute more to victory in this war than that he should sacrifice the seal of office.'(17)

The result of the division was a Government majority of 81. Thirty-three Conservatives had voted with the Opposition and about sixty had abstained. Some of those who had been Neville's greatest admirers voted against the Government on this occasion. One young Conservative member in uniform was seen walking into the Opposition lobby with tears pouring down his cheeks. There was great excitement when the figures were announced and loud cries of 'Resign, Resign' from the Labour benches. One Conservative started to sing 'Rule Brittania'. When it was all over, Neville got up and, looking taut and white in the face, walked slowly out of the Chamber, to the accompaniment of loud cries from the Labour members of – 'Go, in God's name, Go'.

After sitting down in his room for several minutes in silent thought, Neville sent for Winston Churchill. He told him that the debate and the result of the division had made it clear to him that there must now, at all costs, be a National Government. Churchill tried to console him, telling him not to take the debate too much to heart, and pointing out that he still had a good majority with which he could carry on. But Neville refused to be comforted, and evidently made up his mind that if he himself could not form a National Government he would make way for someone else who could. It was after midnight when Churchill left.(18)

On the afternoon of the following day, May 9th, Neville had a conference at Downing Street with Lord Halifax, Churchill and Margesson (Government Chief Whip). Neville was as determined as ever that there must be a National Government but he evidently thought there was still a chance that he might remain Prime Minister, with Liberal and Labour support. The question remained, however, what was to happen if the leaders of the other two Parties refused to serve under him. It is clear from Neville's letters to his sisters that Halifax rather than Churchill was Neville's own preference for Prime Minister if he himself had to go. But, at this interview, Halifax made it clear that, in his view, his position as a member of the House of Lords would make it impossible for him to accept the position.

Later, Attlee and Greenwood arrived to present the views of the Labour Opposition and the discussion continued with them present. Neville renewed the invitation to the two Labour leaders to join his Government. They both made it clear that they did not think there was the slightest chance of this being possible but that the final decision as to Labour's participation in a Coalition would have to be taken by the Labour Party Executive, then in session at Bournemouth, where the Party conference was taking place. Neville asked them to find out from their colleagues whether they would be willing to enter a Coalition under (1) himself, or (2) someone else.

Early on the morning of the following day, May 10th, Hitler invaded Belgium and Holland. Neville's first instinct, on hearing this tremendous news, was to remain Prime Minister at all costs, but Kingsley Wood dissuaded him from this course, pointing out that the invasion made the formation of a National Government more important than ever. Later in the morning, there came a message from the Labour leaders who told him that, after consultation with the Executive, the answer to the first of his questions was in the negative but to the second in the affirmative, i.e. the Labour Party would be willing to enter a Coalition Government but not one of which he was the head. He now felt that there was only one course. He immediately drove to Buckingham Palace and asked the King to accept his resignation.

George VI received him with great kindness and consideration, telling him he thought he had been treated 'grossly unfairly' and that he was 'terribly sorry' about what had happened. They then had an 'informal talk' about the question of a successor and the King's first suggestion was Halifax, but when Neville told him that Halifax was not enthusiastic he himself at once made up his mind that there was only one possibility, namely Churchill, and Neville agreed with this.(19) Shortly after six o'clock that evening, Winston Churchill kissed hands on his appointment as Prime Minister.

In a broadcast to the nation made shortly after his resignation, Neville, after explaining the reasons which had led him to take this course and laying particular emphasis on the need for national unity, said:

'In these circumstances my duty was plain. . . . For the hour has now come when we are to be put to the test as the innocent people of Holland, Belgium and France are being tested already. And you and I must rally behind our new leader, and, with our united strength and with unshakeable courage, fight and work until this wild beast that has sprung out of his lair upon us has been finally disarmed and overthrown.'

One of Churchill's first actions was to write an extremely kind and appreciative letter to Neville, inviting him to join the new Government. 'I must say Winston has been most handsome in his appreciation of my willingness to help and my ability to do so,' he wrote to Ida, adding in the same letter, 'Winston doesn't want me to move from this house (No. 10 Downing Street) for a month or even longer. . . . But Chequers! I shall have to go there some time to collect my things and say good-bye. It will be a bad wrench to part with that place where I have been so happy.'(20) His attachment to Chequers had become stronger with each succeeding month; he had been particularly attracted by its surrounding trees of which he had made a close study.

Neville could have been Chancellor of the Exchequer but his great desire now was to help the new Prime Minister in every way he could and he realized that the Labour dislike of him might make things difficult for Churchill if he (Neville) went to the Treasury, with its continual involvement in the House of Commons. He therefore became Lord President of the Council, in which capacity he felt that he could do good work behind the scenes.

The opportunity for which he longed – to play his part in the war effort – was not, however, to be vouchsafed to him. In June he fell ill, being subjected to acute abdominal pains. An exploratory operation revealed the presence of a malignant, intestinal growth. Until he became Prime Minister, he had been a strong, healthy, happy man and it had undoubtedly been the appalling strain of the last two years that had brought on this horrible illness from which he was to suffer in ever-increasing agony for the few months which now remained to him. 'I frankly envy Austen's peace,' he said once during this terrible part of his life. He bore his suffering with great fortitude and that peace was soon to come to him. In the third week of September, he offered to resign but Churchill at first refused to accept his resignation.

Neville had moved to Hampshire and by the end of the month it was clear that he was a complete invalid, unable to stand the strain of London and with very little longer to live.

It was about this time that he wrote to Lord Halifax:

'Alas I have proved to be a broken reed as doubtless you have heard. If only I were physically fit I could stand that constant "banshee howling" and even the noisy nights. But the conditions were getting worse and worse because this confounded ulcer, from which I suffer and which I suppose will eventually carry me off, developed symptoms which required attention every hour or so and in between gave me sensations which though not painful were so intensely disturbing as to prevent my attending to anything else. . . . Every morning I feel so sick that I can hardly touch anything till lunch.'(21)

At the end of September, Churchill, who was anxious to reconstruct the Government, felt justified in accepting Neville's resignation. Upon this taking effect, Neville wrote to the King and His Majesty replied as follows:

'I was very touched by your letter, and I need hardly tell you how truly sad I am to think that you have been compelled for reasons of health to retire from public life. . . . I know only too well how greatly the loss of your wise and experienced counsel will be felt by your colleagues. . . . As you say, you were my Prime Minister in the early days of my reign and I shall ever be grateful for your help and guidance . . . for me too it will always be a pleasure to recall our many and intimate talks together. I have sympathized with you very much in seeing your hopes shattered by the lust and violence of a single man, and yet, as I told you once before, your efforts to preserve peace were not in vain for they established in the eyes of the civilized world our entire innocence of the crime which Hitler was determined to commit. For this alone, the country owes you a debt of gratitude. . . .'(22)

And, in the middle of October, the King and Queen drove from Windsor to the house in Hampshire (Highfield Park) where Neville was then living and spent about half an hour with him.

He was deeply touched by this and wrote that it was 'a characteristic act of human kindness and sympathy'.

On November 7th, Lord Halifax called to see him. By then it was clearly only a question of a few days. Neville could eat nothing and was getting continually weaker. Describing this visit, Halifax made the following entry in his diary:

'I was taken up to his room before luncheon to find him propped up in bed with a little bed-table on which he had a bowl of blue gentians that someone had sent. I began by saying something about what a rotten time he must have had with his sickness to which he replied that he had been a bit better the last day or two. "Approaching dissolution, I suppose, brings relief," he said with a laugh. Then he spoke of our work together and what it had meant to him in a way that moved me much. And then he was plainly tired, and Anne looked in and I said good-bye. He took my hand in his and held it, and so with no more said but with the full understanding of friends who go to different duties we parted.

It was all quite natural, and no shadow of constraint. He had wondered, he said at one point, how best to satisfy himself that Anne knew how bad he was, but he was happy now that she knew everything, though he feared she would be lonely. I left him with her.'(23)

Two days after this, namely on November 9th, 1940, Neville died and five days afterwards his funeral took place in Westminster Abbey. Like Bonar Law, next to whom his ashes were interred, he had never been a member of the Church which thus took him to her bosom at the last. Indeed, like his father, he called himself a 'reverent agnostic'. And he said to his daughter when he was dying, 'I don't know where I am going or what is going to happen to me.'(24) From Baldwin he had had a number of touching and affectionate letters during the last few months, including one in which the ex-Prime Minister wrote, 'You have passed through the fire since we were talking only a fortnight ago, and you have come out pure gold.' And when Baldwin himself was dying he sent for Neville's daughter and poured out to her his admiration and affection for her father.(25)

With Neville's death, we come to the end of the Chamberlain

story – at least in so far as it relates to the part which the family has played in the shaping of great events upon the national stage, though, in the municipal field, it is satisfactory to know that the fine traditions of 'the clique' are still being carried on though from somewhat divergent points of view by Ald. Stephen Lloyd (son-in-law of Neville), by Councillor A. D. Martineau (nephew of George Kenrick) and by Ald. Mrs. Crosskey (grand-daughter of Arthur senior).(26) Indeed it is one of the peculiarities of the Birmingham City Council as the Lord Mayor of the day remarked recently(27) that both sides claim with equal enthusiasm to be the spiritual descendants of Joseph Chamberlain.

One who would most certainly have carried out those traditions if he had had good health was Neville's son, Frank. In 1937, he had joined the 6th Royal Warwickshire Regiment of the Territorial Army and served overseas in the Second World War in various theatres including Malta. After the war, he went into business in Birmingham, being for a time a director of Hoskins, but he was compelled for reasons of health to retire into the country where he took up farming. Both before and after he left Birmingham, he was intensely and actively interested in social service and welfare work, being particularly keen on the care of the disabled. Like Norman, he had intense sympathy with and compassion for the less fortunate among his fellow human beings and the power to help them without any degreee of patronage. As he himself put it in a broadcast from Australia in 1959, 'The spirit of fellowship depends on our acquiring the ability to listen to other people, to share their joys and sorrows. I think it is really the exchange of ideas and feelings that distinguishes fellowship from patronage and this is a very important distinction.'(28)

For a time he was a vice-president of the Birmingham Federation of Boys' Clubs and chairman of the Birmingham Fellowship of the Handicapped. He was a life governor of Birmingham University. He had an extremely good brain and a wonderful sense of humour.(29) If he had had better health he might well have gone far.

The Chamberlain spirit was also well expressed by Joseph when he said on taking up the position of Lord Rector of Glasgow University: 'I ask you to believe that through all the vicissitudes of things I have constantly sought, it may be with faltering steps and by mistaken roads, the greatness of the Empire and the true welfare of the people at large.' And to a Birmingham audience he once said: 'I was drawn into politics by my interest in social questions and my desire to promote the welfare of the great majority of the population. I saw them condemned by bad laws and by the neglect of their rulers to a life of exacting toil without the advantages and opportunities which education affords and borne down by conditions which I thought to be unfair and unjust. . . . If you cannot revolutionize the world, if you cannot make it perfect all at once, at least be content to leave it a little better than you found it.' And a few months before Joseph's death, a very well-known journalist, the late W. T. Stead, wrote of him, 'From his boyhood up, Joseph Chamberlain has been consumed with a passionate longing to benefit the lot of the common people. Not Burns, nor Keir Hardie is more constantly preoccupied by the necessity for doing something to make the cottage of the labouring man less of a hovel and more of a home.'

But let the last word on the Chamberlains rest with Sir Winston Churchill. No more fitting words with which to take leave of the family as a whole could be found than those which Churchill addressed to the House of Commons on Neville's death:

'. . . History with its flickering lamp stumbles along the trail of the past trying to reconstruct its scenes, to revive its echoes and kindle with pale gleams the passion of former days. What is the worth of all this? The only guide to a man is his conscience; the only shield to his memory is the rectitude and sincerity of his actions. It is very imprudent to walk through life without this shield, because we are so often mocked by the failure of our hopes and the upsetting of our calculations; but, with this shield, however the fates may play, we march always in the rank of honour.

It fell to Neville Chamberlain in one of the supreme crises of the world to be contradicted by events, to be disappointed in his hopes, and to be deceived and cheated by a wicked man. . . . Whatever else history may or may not say about these tremendous, terrible years, we can be sure that Neville Chamberlain acted with perfect sincerity according to his lights and strove to the utmost of his capacity and authority which were powerful to save the world from the awful, devastating struggle in which we are now engaged. . . . After he left the Government, he refused all honours. He would die, like his father, plain Mr. Chamberlain. . . . He was like his father and his brother, Austen, before him, a famous member of the House of Commons, and we here assembled this morning, members of all parties, without a single exception, feel that we do ourselves and our country honour in saluting the memory of one whom Disraeli would have called an "English worthy".'(30)

Notes

1. *The Chamberlains Come to Birmingham*

1. *Notes on the families of Chamberlain and Harben* by Sir Austen Chamberlain (Printed for private circulation)
2. Ibid.
3. Ibid.
4. Ibid.
5. *Praeterita – outlines of scenes and thoughts in my past life*, by John Ruskin
6. *The Right Honourable Joseph Chamberlain – The Man and the Statesman* by N. Murrell Marris (Hutchinson, 1900)
7. Highbury Place, Islington
8. Austen Chamberlain (op. cit.)
9. *The Life of John Bright* by G. M. Trevelyan (Constable, 1925)
10. Marris (op. cit.)
11. *The History of Birmingham* by Conrad Gill and Asa Briggs (Oxford University Press, 1952)
12. *Speeches on questions of public policy by John Bright, M.P.* edited by James and Thorold Rogers, in two volumes, Vol. II (Macmillan, 1869)
13. Ibid.
14. Trevelyan (op. cit.)
15. 'The Educational Policy of the Government from a Nonconformist point of view'. Paper read at the Suffolk Nonconformist conference on April 3rd, 1872, by J. Chamberlain, Esq. (Birmingham, Cornish Bros. 1872, Copy in the British Museum)
16–17. *Victorian Cities* by Asa Briggs (Odhams Press, 1963)

2. *Tragedy*

1. Austen Chamberlain (op. cit.)
2. Ibid.
3. *The Life of Joseph Chamberlain* by J. L. Garvin, Vol. I (Macmillan, 1932)
4. Garvin (op. cit.)
5–6. *The Lloyds of Birmingham* by Sampson Lloyd (Birmingham, Cornish Bros., 1906)
7–11. Garvin (op. cit.)

3. *An Outstanding Mayoralty*

1. C. F. Garvin (op. cit.)
2. Gill and Briggs (op. cit.)

3. Garvin (op. cit.)
4. Garvin (op. cit.)
5. *The Life of R. W. Dale of Birmingham* by his son A. W. W. Dale (Hodder & Stoughton, 1898)
6–8. Dale (op. cit.)
9–12. Gill and Briggs (op. cit.)
13. Marris (op. cit.)
14. Garvin (op. cit.)
15. Garvin (op. cit.)
16. Marris (op. cit.)

4. *The House of Commons and the Caucus*

1. Garvin (op. cit.)
2. *The Life of the Rt. Hon. Sir Charles W. Dilke, Bart, M.P.* begun by Stephen Gwynn, M.P., completed and edited by Gertrude M. Tuckwell (Murray, 1917)
3–5. Garvin (op. cit.)
6. *Reminiscences of a Radical parson* by Rev. W. Tuckwell, M.A. (Cassell, 1905)
7. Gill and Briggs (op. cit.)
8–9. Garvin (op. cit.)
10. *Fifty-one years of Victorian life* by the Dowager Countess of Jersey (Murray, 1923)
11. *Neville Chamberlain* by Iain Macleod (Muller, 1959)
12. Feiling (op. cit.)

5. *Parnell, Ireland and the Peers*

1–4. *Parnell* by St. John Ervine (Ernest Benn, 1925)
5. Garvin (op. cit.)
6. *Lord Randolph Churchill* by Robert Rhodes James (Weidenfeld & Nicholson, 1959)
7. *Joseph Chamberlain, an honest biography* by Alexander Mackintosh (Hodder & Stoughton, 1906)
8–11. *The Letters of Queen Victoria* second series, a selection from Her Majesty's correspondence and journal between the years 1862 and 1885 edited by G. E. Buckle (Vol. II, 1879–1885) (John Murray)
12–15. Garvin (op. cit.)
16. *The Diary of Sir Charles Dilke* – see Gwynn & Tuckwell (op. cit.)
17. *The Life of William Ewart Gladstone* by John Morley, Vol. III (1880–1898) (Macmillan, 1903)
18. *Joseph Chamberlain* (J.C.) to Arthur Chamberlain (8.3.86) (in the collection of Joseph Chamberlain's papers at Birmingham University, hereafter called 'J.C. Papers')
19. J.C. to Morley (4.2.86) (J.C. Papers)

20. Rhodes, James (op. cit.)
21-22. Morley (op. cit.) See also *The Life of Sir William Harcourt* by A. G. Gardiner (Constable, 1923)
23. *Gladstone* a biography by Philip Magnus (Murray, 1954)
24. *James Bryce (Viscount Bryce of Dechmount, O.M.)* by H. A. L. Fisher (Macmillan, 1927)
25. Schnadhorst to J.C. (February 1886) (J.C. Papers)
26. Ibid (11.4.86)
27. J.C. Bunce (11.4.86) (J.C. Papers)
28. Austen Chamberlain (op. cit.)
29. Arthur C. to J.C. (11.4.86) (J.C. Papers)
30. Rhodes James (op. cit.)
31. Arthur C. to J.C. (16.5.86) (J.C. Papers)
32-34. Dale (op. cit.)
35. Garvin (op. cit.)
36. J.C. to Jesse Collings (J.C. Papers)

6. *The Fisheries Commission and its Sequel*

1. *The letters and friendships of Sir Cecil Spring Rice*, a record, edited by Stephen Gwynn (Houghton Mifflin, 1929)
2-3. Ibid.
4. *Grover Cleveland: a study in courage* by Allan Nevins (Dodd, Mead, N.Y. 1944)
5. *With Mr. Chamberlain in the U.S. and Canada (1887-1888)* by Sir Willoughby Maycock, K.G. M.G. (Chatto & Windus, 1914)
6. Nevins (op. cit.)
7. *The Washington Post* (Quoted Maycock op. cit.)
8-10. Maycock (op. cit.)
11. Garvin (op. cit.) Vol. II
12. Spring Rice (op. cit.)
13. *The Washington Post* (Quoted Maycock op. cit.)
14. Nevins (op. cit.)
15. Maycock (op. cit.)
16-17. Garvin (op. cit.)
18. Lord Randolph Churchill to J.C. (J.C. Papers)
19-22. Garvin (op. cit.)

7. *Mary Meets the Clan*

1. Lord Lytton to Lady Dorothy Neville, December 1888 – quoted *Under Five Reigns* by Lady Dorothy Neville (Methuen, 1910)
2-12. The letters of Mrs. Mary Endicott Chamberlain to her mother, Mrs. Endicott, at Birmingham University (M.E.C. papers)
13-15 *Birmingham Daily Post*, January 8th, 1889
16. Marris (op. cit.)

17. Mrs. D. Farmer to the author
18. Mrs. Helen Chamberlain to the author
19. *Under Five Flags* – the story of Kynoch Works, Witton, Birmingham. Commissioned by Imperial Metal Industries (Kynoch) Ltd. to mark the centenary.
20–24. Ibid.
25. *The Life of Neville Chamberlain* by Keith Feiling (Macmillan, 1946)

8. *Sisal*

1. J.C. to H. Lee Warner (J.C. Papers)
2. Ibid. (8.4.79)
3. H. Lee Warner to J.C. (J.C. Papers)
4. Austen Chamberlain (A.C.) to Hilda Chamberlain. The Austen Chamberlain papers at the University of Birmingham (A.C. Papers)
5. Macleod (op. cit.)
6. Feiling (op. cit.)
7. Ibid.
8. *The Life of Joseph Chamberlain* by Julian Amery (Vol. IV, 1901–1903) (continuation of Garvin's Life)
9. Macleod (op. cit.)
10. Feiling (op. cit.)
11. Macleod (op. cit.)
12. Feiling (op. cit.)
13–14. Garvin (op. cit.)

9. *The Cry of Judas and the Downfall of Parnell*

1. By J. L. Garvin (op. cit.)
2. A.C. to Lady C. (A.C. Papers)
3. Alexander Mackintosh (op. cit.)
4. Lady Jersey (op. cit.)
5. The Diary of Sir Edward Hamilton (Quoted Magnus op. cit.)
6. The reminiscences of Lady Dorothy Neville edited by her son Ralph Neville (Edward Arnold, 1906)
7. M.E.C. Papers
8. *The Letters of Queen Victoria*, edited by G. E. Buckel, third series (Murray)
9. Ibid.
10. M.E.C. Papers
11. Garvin (op. cit.)
12. *Bury Times*, October 28th, 1891 (Quoted Garvin, op. cit.)
13. Ibid.
14. J.C. to Morley (30.10.91) (J.C. Papers)
15. J. C. Papers
16–17. *Lord Randolph Churchill* by Winston S. Churchill (Macmillan, 1906)
18–19. Ervine (op. cit.)

20. Dilke's Diary (op. cit.) See also Gardiner (op. cit.)
21. *The Letters of Queen Victoria* (op. cit.) third series, Vol. II
22–26. Garvin (op. cit.)

10. *Cordite, Conservatives and Cleveland*

1. *Under Five Flags* (op. cit.)
2. Ibid.
3. Ibid.
4. *Tempestuous Journey, Lloyd George his Life and Times* by Frank Owen (Hutchinson, 1954)
5. *Selections from the correspondence of Theodore Roosevelt with Henry Cabot Lodge* (Charles Scribner's Sons)
6. Garvin (op. cit.)
7. Senator for Massachussetts. See the author's *Roosevelt and Wilson – a Comparative Study* for an account of his career, and that of Theodore Roosevelt
8. Nevins (op. cit.)
9–10. Ibid.

11. *The Boer War*

1. Garvin (op. cit.) Vol. III
2–3. Ibid.
4. *Under Five Flags* (op. cit.)
5. Feiling (op. cit.)
6. M.E.C. Papers
7. Garvin (op. cit.)
8–11. Owen (op. cit.)
12. *Oldham Evening Chronicle*, September 26th, 1900
13–14. Ibid.
15. *The Times*, September 26th, 1900
16. Garvin (op. cit.)
17–20. Owen (op. cit.)
21. Amery (op. cit.)

12. *Education, Food Taxes and the Liberal Landslide*

1. *The Times*, July 15th, 1902
2. *The Life of Spencer Compton, Duke of Devonshire* by Bernard Holland, C.B. (Longmans, Green, 1911)
3. *The Birmingham Post*, October 10th, 1902.
4–5. *The Life and Letters of the Right Hon. Sir Austen Chamberlain, K.G., P.C., M.P.* by Sir Charles Petrie, Bart (Cassell, 1939)
6–7. Owen (op. cit.)
8. Mrs. Mary Chamberlain to her mother (M.E.C. Papers)

9–10. *The Times*, May 16th, 1903

11. *The Autobiography of Margot Asquith* (Thornton Butterworth, 1922)

12. Owen (op. cit.)

13. J.C. to the Duke of Devonshire, (21.9.03) (Holland, op. cit.)

14. A.C. Papers

15. *Politics from Inside, an Epistolary Chronicle, 1906–1914* by the Rt. Hon. Sir Austen Chamberlain, K.G., P.C., M.P. (Cassell, 1936)

16–18. Owen (op. cit.)

19–22. *The Life of F. E. Smith, First Earl of Birkenhead* ['F.E.'] by his son the second Earl of Birkenhead (Eyre & Spottiswoode, 1960); see also *Salvidge of Liverpool – Behind the scenes 1890–1928* by Stanley Salvidge (Hodder & Stoughton 1934), where a slightly different account is given.

23. *Great Contemporaries* by Winston S. Churchill (Macmillan, 1937)

13. *A Birthday and a Wedding*

1. Gill and Briggs (op. cit.)

2. Speech by Arthur Chamberlain at a meeting of the Birmingham magistrates at the Victoria Courts, Birmingham, in a collection entitled 'Birmingham Institutions', Vol. D.51, at Birmingham Central Reference Library

3. Ibid.

4. Private information

5. *Mr. Chamberlain's Speeches*, edited by Charles W. Boyd with an introduction by the Rt. Hon. Austen Chamberlain, M.P. Vol. II, p.253 (Constable, 1914)

6. *The Chamberlain Tradition* by Sir Charles Petrie, Bart (Lovat, Dickson, 1938)

7. Mrs. Maxwell to the author

8. J.C. to Miss Ivy Dundas (8.5.06) from the collection of Lady Austen Chamberlain's papers at Birmingham University (Lady A.C. Papers)

9. Lady A.C. Papers

10. A.C. to Ivy Chamberlain (1.8.22) and (27.7.23) (A.C. Papers)

11–12. *Birmingham Post*, July 9th, 1906

13. *Birmingham Daily Mail*, July 10th, 1906

14–15. *Birmingham Post*, July 10th, 1906

16–18. Amery (op. cit.)

19. *The Life of Andrew Carnegie* by Burton J. Hendrick (Heinemann, 1933)

20. *The Times*, July 23rd, 1906

21. Spring Rice (op. cit.)

22. Ibid.

23. *Politics from Inside* (op. cit.)

24. Spring Rice (op. cit.)

25.–29. M.E.C. Papers

30. As to Garvin's efforts on Chamberlain's behalf see *Balfour's Burden – Arthur Balfour and Imperial Preference* by Alfred Gollin (Anthony Blond,

1965). This book also deals extensively with Chamberlain's Tariff Reform campaign and with the relations between Balfour and Chamberlain during the years 1902 to 1906

14. *The People's Budget and the House of Lords*

1. *Slings and Arrows*: sayings chosen from the speeches of the Rt. Hon. David Lloyd George, O.M., M.P., edited with introduction by Philip Guedalla
2-4. Ibid.
5. Speeches delivered in the House of Commons and elsewhere 1906–1909 by F. E. Smith, M.P. (Liverpool, Henry Young & Sons, 1910)
6-7. Petrie's *Austen Chamberlain* (op. cit.)
8. *The Times*, September 18th, 1909
9. *The Times*, June 30th, 1909

15. *Death Again Transforms the Scene*

1. Birkenhead (op. cit.)
2. *Politics from Inside* (op. cit.)
3. *War Memoirs of David Lloyd George*, Vol. I, pp. 38 and 39 (Ivor Nicholson & Watson, 1933)
4. Petrie's *Austen Chamberlain* (op. cit.)
5. *The Unknown Prime Minister: The Life and Times of Andrew Bonar Law* 1858–1923 by Robert W. Blake (Eyre & Spottiswoode, 1955)
6. *Lord Derby 'King of Lancashire'*. The official Life of Edward, seventeenth Earl of Derby 1865–1959 by Randolph S. Churchill (Heinemann, 1959)
7. *Politics from Inside* (op. cit.)
8-11. Blake (op. cit.)
12. *Carson: The Life of Sir Edward Carson, Lord Carson of Duncairn* by H. Montgomery Hyde (Heinemann, 1953)
13. M.E.C. Papers
14. Mrs. Enid Chamberlain to the author
15. M.E.C. Papers
16. Mrs. Enid Chamberlain to the author
17. In *The World Crisis* by the Rt. Hon. Sir Winston S. Churchill, C.H. (Thornton Butterworth, 1923)
18. *Down the Years* by the Rt. Hon. Sir Austen Chamberlain KG., P.C., M.P. (Cassell)
19. Ibid.

16. *Arthur junior, Neville and Norman*

1-3. *Under Five Flags* (op. cit.)
4. Mrs. Helen Chamberlain to the author
5-7. Feiling (op. cit.)

Notes

8–9. *Norman Chamberlain* A Memoir, by Neville Chamberlain (printed for private circulation) (Murray, 1923)

10. Sir John Murray, K.C.V.O., D.S.O.

11–12. A.C. to Mrs. Alfred Cole (9.5.05), (29.2.08), (6.4.08) (originals in the possession of Mrs. Enid Chamberlain)

13–17. Neville Chamberlain (op. cit.)

18. *Birmingham Post*, September 5th, 1916

19. A.C. to Hilda and Ida Chamberlain (A.C. Papers)

20–21. *Birmingham Post*, December 20th, 1916

22. N.C. to Norman Chamberlain, May 1917 (original in the possession of Mrs. Enid Chamberlain)

23. A.C. to Ida Chamberlain (16.3.35) (A.C. Papers)

24. Neville Chamberlain (op. cit.) (originals in the possession of Mrs. Enid Chamberlain)

25. Feiling (op. cit.)

26. N.C. to Mrs. Alfred Cole, February 12th, 1918 (original in the possession of Mrs. Enid Chamberlain)

27. Colonel Sir John Hunt, C.B.E., D.S.O., Leader of the Everest expedition and Director of the Duke of Edinburgh's Award Scheme for Youth.

28. Macleod (op. cit.)

29. A.C. to Hilda and Ida Chamberlain (2.11.24) (A.C. Papers)

30. Mrs. Enid Chamberlain to the author

31. The late Frank Chamberlain to the author

32. Mrs. Frank Chamberlain to the author

33. Feiling (op. cit.)

34. Mrs. Enid Chamberlain to the author

35. 'Arthur the Third' to the author

36. Feiling (op. cit.)

37. Mrs. Stephen Lloyd to the author

38. Mrs. Frank Chamberlain to the author

39–40. Feiling (op. cit.)

17. *The Coalition and the Carlton Club Meeting*

1. *The Decline and Fall of Lloyd George* by Lord Beaverbrook (Collins, 1963)
2. Ibid.
3. Blake (op. cit.)
4–5. Montgomery Hyde (op. cit.)
6. Owen (op. cit.)
7. Ibid.
8. For the full text of this letter, see Petrie's *Austen Chamberlain* (op. cit.), Vol. II
9. Blake (op. cit.)
10. *My Political Life* by the Right Hon. L. S. Amery, C.H. Vol. 2 (Hutchinson, 1953)
11. Owen (op. cit.)

Notes

12. *Lord Riddell's Intimate Diary of the Peace Conference and after* (Victor Gollancz, 1933)
13–14. Randolph Churchill (op. cit.)
15–19. Blake (op. cit.)
20. Salvidge (op. cit.)
21. Blake (op. cit.)
22. Petrie (op. cit.)
23. A.C. to Hilda and Ida Chamberlain (A.C. Papers)

18. *The Rise of Baldwin*

1. A.C. to Hilda and Ida (27.5.23) (A.C. Papers)
2. Petrie (op. cit.)
3. N.C. to Hilda and Ida, February 9th, 1924. (Feiling, op. cit.)
4. A.C. to Hilda and Ida (A.C. Papers)
5–6. Ibid. (December, 1924)
7. Royal Archives, Quoted *King George V, his Life and Reign*, by Harold Nicolson (Constable, 1952)
8. A.C. to Lady C. (A.C. Papers)
9–10. *Down the Years* by Austen Chamberlain (op. cit.)
11–12. *Old Men Forget*, the autobiography of Duff Cooper (Viscount Norwich) (Hart Davis, 1957)
13. *The Mist Procession* by Lord Vansittart

19. *Austen's 'Nunc Dimittis': Neville's Ascent*

1. N.C. to Hilda and Ida Chamberlain, March 18th, 1928 (Feiling, op. cit.)
2. Swinburne's 'Ode to England'. Snowden substituted 'Proclaims' for 'acclaims' (*Viscount Snowden, an Autobiography*)
3. Nicolson (op. cit.)
4. A.C. to Hilda and Ida Chamberlain (A.C. Papers)

20. *Hitler and Mussolini*

1. *Parliamentary Debates*, Fifth Series, House of Commons, Official Report, Vol. 276.
2. Ibid.
3. Ibid. (Vol. 304)
4. A.C. to Hilda and Ida C. (7.5.33) (A.C. Papers)
5. *The London Star*, October 23rd, 1933
6–7. Macleod (op. cit.)
8. N.C. to Hilda and Ida, December 9th, 1934 (Feiling, op. cit.)
9. At Hastings, October 1st, 1933
10. *Parliamentary Debates*, Fifth Series, (op. cit.) Vol. 292
11. *Parliamentary Debates*, Fifth Series (op. cit.) Vol. 302
12–13. Macleod (op. cit.)

14. *Parliamentary Debates* (op. cit.) Vol. 301
15. A.C. to Hilda and Ida Chamberlain (A.C. Papers)
16. Ibid.
17. *The Eden Memoirs*: 'Facing the Dictators', by the Rt. Hon. The Earl of Avon, K.G., P.C., M.C. (Cassell)
18–19. A.C. to Hilda and Ida Chamberlain (A.C. Papers)
20. Feiling (op. cit.)
21. A.C. to Hilda and Ida Chamberlain (A.C. Papers)
22. Chastenet, J.: *Histoire de le troisième République* 7 Vols. Vol. 6 (Librairie Hachette, 1963)
23. Feiling (op. cit.)
24–25. *The Times*, March 12th, 1936
26. *The Times*, March 16th, 1936
27–29. A.C. to Hilda and Ida Chamberlain, February and March 1936 (A.C. Papers 698–701)
30. *Parliamentary Debates*, 5th series, House of Commons (Official Report) Vol. 310
31. *The Times*, December 3rd, 1936
32–33. *The Times*, July 9th, 1936
34–35. Feiling (op. cit.)
36. A.C. to Lady Chamberlain (A.C. Papers)
37. Lady C. to A.C. (12.7.07) (Lady C. Papers)
38. A.C. to Hilda and Ida, October 1925 (A.C. Papers)
39. At Eastleigh, Hants., March 15th, 1937
40. Mrs. Frank Chamberlain to the author
41. Francis Chamberlain (Frank) in a letter to the *Daily Telegraph*, dated December 29th, 1962

21. *Two Ladies in Hampshire*

1. Mrs. Carnegie, formerly Mrs. Joseph Chamberlain
2. Ida to N.C. (18.8.17) (Macleod, op. cit.)
3. Hilda C. to N.C. (24.8.17) (Macleod, op. cit.)
4. N.C. to Hilda C. (27.8.17) (Macleod, op. cit.)
5. A.C. to Lady C. (7.5.33) (A.C. Papers)
6. N.C. to Ida C. (19.9.39) (Quoted Feiling, op. cit.)
7. *The Times*, September 28th, 1938
8. The President's message was sent by telegraph to Ambassador Kennedy at the American Embassy in London in the following form: 'Personal for Prime Minister Chamberlain (quote) Good man signed Roosevelt (unquote). *FDR his personal letters*. Vol. II (Darll Sloan & Pearce)
9. N.C. to Hilda, (2.10.38) (Quoted Feiling, op. cit.)

22. *The End of an Old Adventure*

1. *Parliamentary Debates*, 5th series, House of Commons (op. cit.) Vol. 346.
2. N.C. to Hilda and Ida (19.2.39) (Quoted Feiling, op. cit.)
3. *The Times*, March 18th, 1939

Notes

4. Ibid.
5. *Parliamentary Debates*, 5th series, House of Commons (Official Report) Vol. 346
6. Feiling (op. cit.)
7. Sir Reginal Dorman Smith in the *Sunday Times*, September 6th, 1964
8. *The Times*, September 4th, 1939
9. *Parliamentary Debates*, 5th Series (op. cit.) Vol. 351
10–15. Feiling (op. cit.)
16–17. *Parliamentary Debates*, 5th Series (op. cit.) Vol. 360
18. 'History of the Second World War', Vol. I, *The Gathering Storm* by Winston S. Churchill (Cassell, 1948)
19. *King George VI, His Life and Reign* by John W. Wheeler-Bennett. (Macmillan, 1958)
20. Feiling (op. cit.)
21. *Halifax: The Life of Lord Halifax* by the Earl of Birkenhead. (Hamish Hamilton, 1965)
22. Wheeler-Bennett (op. cit.)
23. Birkenhead's *Halifax* (op. cit.)
24–25. Mrs. Stephen Lloyd to the author
26. Mrs. Evelyn Margaret Crosskey, Labour member of Birmingham City Council since 1945 has served on the Public Works, Housing Management and Museum and Art Gallery Committees since then and was elected an Alderman in April 1963
27. In the course of the luncheon following the official opening of 'The Norman Chamberlain Playing-fields' at which the author was present, the Lord Mayor being Ald. Corbett Barrow
28–29. Mrs. Frank Chamberlain to the author
30. *Parliamentary Debates*, 5th series, House of Commons (Official Report) Vol. 365

Bibliography

BOOKS NOT REFERRED TO IN THE NOTES

BIOGRAPHIES AND AUTOBIOGRAPHIES

BALDWIN, A. W., *My Father the True Story* (Allen & Unwin 1955)

BULLOCK, Alan, *A Study in Tyranny* (Odhams 1952)

CHURCHILL, Winston S., *My Early Life* (Thornton Butterworth 1930)

    Liberalism and the Social Problem: Speeches 1906–1909 (Hodder & Stoughton 1909)

    Step by Step: Speeches 1936–1939 (Thornton Butterworth 1939)

CLARKE, Rt. Hon. Sir E., *The Story of My Life* (Murray 1923)

COLLINGS, Jessie, and GREEN, John, *Jesse Collings* (Longmans Green 1920)

CREWE, Marquess of, *Lord Rosebery* (Murray 1931)

Dictionary of American Biography

Dictionary of National Biography

DOUGLAS OF KIRTLESIDE, *Years of Command,* Vol II of the Autobiography (Collins 1966).

DUGDALE, Blanche, *Life of Arthur Balfour*, 2 vols. (Hutchinson)

GARVIN, Katharine, *J. L. Garvin: A Memoir* (Heinemann 1948)

GREY, Viscount, *Twenty-five Years, 1892–1916* (Hodder & Stoughton 1928)

HENDERSON, Sir Nevile, *Failure of a Mission* (Hodder & Stoughton 1940)

HOARE, Sir Samuel (Viscount Templewood), *Nine Troubled Years* (Collins 1954)

JENKINS, Roy, *Asquith* (Collins 1965)

JENKINS, Roy, *Sir Charles Dilke: A Victorian Tragedy* (Collins 1963)

LANG, Diana Whitehall, *Mistress of Herself* (Barro Massachusetts 1965)

Bibliography

LEE, Sir Sydney, *Edward VII* (Macmillan 1925)

LONGFORD, Lady, *Victoria R.I.* (Weidenfeld & Nicolson 1964)

MAGNUS, Sir Philip, *Edward VII* (Murray 1965)

MORLEY, Viscount, *Recollections* (Macmillan 1917)

NEWTON, Lord, *Life of Lord Lansdowne* (1929)

SCHMIDT, Paul, *Hitler's Interpreter* (Heinemann 1951)

SIMON, Viscount (Sir John Simon), *Retrospect* (Hutchinson 1952)

SPENDER, H. and ASQUITH, C. *Asquith, Life of Earl of Oxford and,* 2 vols. (Hutchinson 1932)

ST. HELIER, Lady, *Memories of Fifty Years* (Edward Arnold 1909)

WHALEN, Richard J., *Joseph P. Kennedy, The Founding Father* (Hutchinson 1965)

YOUNG, K., *Life of Arthur Balfour* (Bell 1963)

HISTORY OF BIRMINGHAM

BUNCE, J. T. *The History of Birmingham*

History of the County of Warwick, Vol. VII, *The City of Birmingham* (Oxford University Press 1964)

DENT, Robert, *The Old Birmingham and the New; a History of the Town and its people* (Birmingham, Houghton & Hammond 1884)

ENGLAND

BEAVERBROOK, Lord, *Politicians and the War* 2 Vols.
  Vol. 1 (Thornton Butterworth 1928)
  Vol. 2 (Lane Publications 1932)

ENSOR, R. C. K., *Oxford History of England* Vol. 14 (1870–1914) (Clarendon Press 1936)

MARRIOTT, J. A. R., *England since Waterloo,* 9th Ed. (Methuen 1929)

JENKINS, Roy, *Mr. Balfour's Poodle* (Heinemann 1954)

TAYLOR, A. J. P., *Oxford History of England* Vol. 15 (1914–1945) (Clarendon Press 1965)

TREVELYAN, G. M., *Modern England 1885–1945* (Methuen 1945)

Bibliography

TREVELYAN, G. M., *British History in the Nineteenth Century and After* (Longmans Green 1941)

WEBB, Sidney and Beatrice, *English Local Government from the Revolution to the Municipal Corporations Act* (Longmans Green 1908)

BOOKS REFERRED TO IN THE NOTES

Subject	Author, Description or Title	Chapter	Note
Amery, L. S.	'My political Life'	17	10
Asquith, Margot	*Autobiography*	12	11
Birkenhead, 1st Earl of	Birkenhead 2nd Earl	12	19–20
Birmingham	*History* by Gill & Briggs	1	11
	Victorian Cities by Briggs	1	16 & 17
Bonar Law – See Law			
Bright	Trevelyan	1	9
Bright (speeches)	Thorold Rogers	1	12
Bryce	Fisher	5	24
Carnegie	Hendrick	13	19
Carson	Hyde	15	12
Chamberlain, Austen	Petrie	12	4 & 5
	Down the Years	15	17–19
	Politics from Inside	12	15
Chamberlain, Joseph	Amery	7	8
	Boyd	12	5
	Garvin	2	3
	Mackintosh	5	7
	Marris	1	6
	Maycock	6	5

307

Bibliography

Subject	Author, Description or Title	Chapter	Note
Kynochs	*Under Five Flags*	7	17
Law, A. Bonar	Blake	15	5
Lloyd George	Beaverbrook	17	1
	War Memoirs	15	3
	Owen	10	4
Lloyd George (Speeches)		14	1
Lloyds of Birmingham		2	6
Lodge		10	7
Neville, Lady Dorothy	*Remininscences*	9	6
Norwich, Lord	*Old Men Forget*	18	11 & 12
Parnell	Ervine	5	1–4
Riddell, Lord	*Diary of Peace Conference and After*	17	12
Roosevelt, F. D.	*Letters*, etc.	20	8
Roosevelt, Theodore	Correspondence with Lodge	10	5
Ruskin	*Praeterita*	1	5
Salvidge, Sir A.	Salvidge	12	19–20
Smith, F. E. (and see Birkenhead)	Speeches	14	5
Snowden, Viscount	*Autobiography*	19	2
Spring Rice	*Letters and Friendships*	6	1
Tuckwell	*Reminiscences*	4	6
Vansittart	*Mist Procession*	18	13
Victoria, Queen	*Letters*, etc.	5	8–11
		9	8 & 21
World War I	Churchill	15	17
World War II	Churchill	22	18

Index

Index

Index

Index

Ribot, M., 96
Rhineland, The, 261–5
Riciotti, M., 36
Riddell, Lord, 233
Ripon, 1st Marquess of, 125
Ritchie, Rt. Hon. C. T. (later Lord), 138, 142, 144, 145
Roberts, Field Marshal Earl, 129, 130, 179
Roosevelt, Edith Carow (wife of Theodore), 168
Roosevelt, Franklin Delano (President of U.S.), 268, 274
Roosevelt, Theodore (President of U.S.), 120, 168, 179
Rosebery, Earl of, 116, 119
Rothschild, Lord, 175
Ruskin, John, 3
Russell, Sir Charles (Lord Russell of Killowen), 111

Sackville West, Sir Lionel (later Lord Sackville), 69, 70, 72, 83
Sackville West, the Misses, 72
St. Helier, Lady, 104, 151
St. Helier, Lord, 104
Salisbury, 3rd Marquess of, 51, 53, 57, 66, 67, 78, 79, 106, 110, 113, 119, 121–3, 137, 138
Salisbury, 4th Marquess of, 233
Salvidge, Sir A., 150, 151, 185, 236
Samuel, Rt. Hon. Sir Herbert (Lord Samuel), 250
Sarraut, M., 262
Schacht, Dr., 262
Schnadhorst, Francis, 41, 42, 60, 61, 62, 66, 80
Sclater Booth, Rt. Hon. G. (later Lord Basing), 32
Scott, Sir Leslie, 97
Shea, Sir Ambrose, 99
Simon, Rt. Hon. Sir John (later Viscount), 258
Smith, F. E. See Birkenhead
Snowden, Rt. Hon. Philip (later Viscount), 250, 251
Spring-Rice, Sir Cecil, 69, 167, 168

Stamfordham, Lord (Sir Arthur Bigge), 183, 244
Stead, W. T., 291
Stevenson, Miss Frances (later Countess Lloyd George), 226, 227
Stresemann, Dr. Gustav, 245, 246
Sturge, Charles, 24
Sturge, Joseph, 24
Swinburne, Algernon Charles, 250

Taft, William Howard (President of U.S.), 179
Trevelyan, Sir George Otto, 59
Tube Investments Ltd., 93, 265
Tupper, Sir Charles, 70

University of Birmingham, 164–6

Vansittart, Sir Robert (Lord Vansittart), 246
Victoria, Queen of England, 53, 79, 105, 127, 137, 204
Vincent, Sir Edgar. See D'Abernon, Lord

Warner, H. Lee, 95, 96
Washington, George (President of U.S.), 75
West, Sir Lionel. See Sackville
West, The Misses Sackville, 72
Westminster, Duke of, 173
William II, German Emperor, 167, 179
Williams, Colonel, 89
Williams, Lilian. See Cole
Wilson, Field Marshal Sir Henry, 232
Wilson, Rt. Hon. Sir Leslie, 232, 234
Wilson, Thomas Woodrow (President of U.S.), 244
Wood, Mrs. Benjamin, 47, 49, 112
Wood, Katherine. See O'Shea
Wood, Rev. Sir John Page, 46
Wood, Rt. Hon. Kingsley, 286

Younger, Sir George (1st Viscount Younger of Leckie), 230, 231, 234

318